THE RISE OF WORDS
AND THEIR MEANINGS

THE RISE OF WORDS
AND THEIR MEANINGS

BY
SAMUEL REISS

PHILOSOPHICAL LIBRARY
NEW YORK

PRINTED IN THE UNITED STATES OF AMERICA

To

MILDRED REISS

CONTENTS

THE RISE OF WORDS
AND THEIR MEANINGS

CHAPTER ONE

INTRODUCTION

THE PURPOSE OF this book is to introduce a certain new viewpoint into the closely associated sciences of linguistics and semantics. This viewpoint relates to the subjects of word and language kinship, the sounds and meanings of words, and the basic character itself, or origin, of words. Fundamentally the new viewpoint rests on a single concept, namely, that of a linkage, the precise nature of which forms the subject of our study, between the sounds of words and their meanings. The twin sciences of phonetics and semantics, which are generally treated apart from, and even in contrast to each other, are here fused into what might appropriately be called a new science of "phoneto-semantics".

It will be of interest in this introduction to state how the author arrived at his viewpoint, summarize briefly the prevailing views on word and language kinship, and point out some of the difficulties and unsolved problems in connection with these views.

The reader may be familiar with the fact that most of the languages of Europe, including the "Germanic" languages such as English, German, Swedish, the "romance" languages such as French, Spanish, Italian, the "Slavic" languages such as Russian, Polish, Czech, the

"Baltic" languages such as Lithuanian and Latvian, as well as Greek, Gaelic, Welsh and even Albanian are all classified within the single large "Indo-European" family of languages, a family which moreover includes a good many Asiatic languages as well. A relatively small number of European languages however, among which are Hungarian, Finnish, Esthonian, Turkish, Basque, have managed to "escape" the Indo-European family and are thus conceived as bearing no relation at all for example to English. The first three named above are members of the "Finno-Ugric" subfamily of languages while Turkish is a member of a widely spread "Turkic" subfamily, both subfamilies being included within a broader "Ural-Altaic" family of languages. It is thus implied by such classification that Hungarian bears some kinship with Turkish. It should be remarked however that the inclusion of Hungarian and Turkish under one large "Ural-Altaic" family is not at the present time considered to rest on the same basis of certainty as the inclusion of the various Indo-European subfamilies within the parallel Indo-European family. That is to say, there is no unanimous agreement among philologists that Hungarian is in fact related to Turkish. As for the Basque language mentioned above, it stands by itself, unclassified and unincluded within any larger language group.

It is of course implicit under any such classification of languages into families or language stocks that any two languages belonging to different families bear absolutely no relation to each other except insofar as there may have occurred mutual borrowings or other influences arising from historical factors. Each family of languages is in theory derived from a single parent language, the words of such primitive parent languages undergoing in the course of history various changes in

2

sound and meaning and thereby giving rise to the variety of languages within that family. Thus, all the Indo-European languages are assumed to have sprung from a primitive Indo-European language which, though no longer in existence, is stated to be capable of being hypothetically reconstructed on scientific philological principles.

Now, although languages may thus at any given time be classified within certain families it does not mean that philologists make no further attempts to link together different language families as being possibly related to each other, or to prove that a language under a given classification should perhaps come under a different classification. For it is often observed that a language exhibits certain features of vocabulary and grammar such as to cast some element of doubt on its existing classification. The Hungarian language for example, though not at present considered Indo-European, might thus conceivably, through further investigation, turn out to be Indo-European.

The present author, intrigued by the many resemblances he had observed between Hungarian and Indo-European languages such as Latin, English or German, had attempted to establish if possible a kinship between the Finno-Ugric and Indo-European languages in the usual genetic sense in which the term "kinship" is used, since such kinship had moreover at various times been surmised by investigators. The surmise is based not merely on the presence in Hungarian of such Indo-European roots as might presumably be borrowings reblances he had observed between Hungarian and Indo-European speaking German or Iranian tribes but, as stated by a known authority J. Szinnyei in his "Finnisch-Ugrische Sprachwissenschaft", on the presence of (pre-

3

sumably) Indo-European roots of a kind which can not readily be explained as borrowings. There are, in addition, grammatical affinities which would appear to point to the Indo-European origin of Hungarian. The evidence which however had thus far been presented has generally not been deemed as sufficient to establish beyond question such suspected kinship.

Now it is of interest that precisely the same difficulty that arises in the case of Hungarian, namely, the difficulty of accounting for the presence of roots which stand for common every-day concepts and can not readily be explained as borrowings, is encountered by investigators in other cases. Thus, in his book "A Manual of the Malay Language" William E. Maxwell presents a sketch of the Sanskrit element in Malay. (Sanskrit is an ancient Indo-European language stated to possess features most nearly approaching those of the primitive, no longer existing, Indo-European parent language, while Malay is a modern member of a distinct "Austronesian" family of languages). A fairly large list of words is cited which includes not merely such words as could presumably have been borrowed from a Sanskrit speaking people (or a people speaking a language closely related to Sanskrit) because associated with religion, commerce, etc. but words which, to quote Maxwell himself, "are so necessary to every-day life that it is difficult to conceive the poverty of a dialect which contained no words to express them".

The perplexing difficulty mentioned above is by no means however confined to the case of the Hungarian and Malay languages. As a matter of fact it is encountered in every attempt that has been made to establish, or at least render likely, the kinship of languages provisionally belonging to different stocks. For any such attempt, aside from grammatical and possibly other con-

4

siderations, consists in setting up parallel word lists in which the words are compared in sound and meaning. From such lists, aided by other considerations, conclusions are drawn as to the certain or probable kinship, in the sense of the possession of a common parent language, of the languages compared. Numerous parallel word lists of this type have been constructed at various times by investigators attempting to prove or at least discuss certain suspected kinships, since the method appears to be most natural and basic.[1]

The present author, in his attempt to establish a connection between Hungarian and Indo-European languages proceeded in the usual manner to set up a list of Hungarian words with their equivalents or near-equivalents in Indo-European languages like ancient Greek and Latin and modern German, English, Lithuanian and others. In setting up such list it was necessary of course to take into account simultaneously the sounds and meanings of the words compared. Some resemblances might be too obvious and if such they might be interpreted, subject to the difficulty mentioned above, as borrowings. For example, Hungarian *név* - 'name' might

1. For purely illustrative purposes it is not necessary to mention more than a few such word lists here selected at random from the large literature on comparative linguistics.

An extensive list comparing ancient Egyptian roots, the Egyptian of the hieroglyphics, with Semitic roots, indicating a possible kinship between that language and Hebrew for example is given by Franz Calice, "Grundlagen der ägyptisch-semitischen Wortvergleichung". A possible kinship of ancient Sumerian and the "Oceanic" languages is indicated by Rivet in his "Sumerien et Oceanien". The Japanese language occupies a somewhat isolated position but is stated to be distantly related to Korean and perhaps to the Ural-Altaic languages (which, as we mentioned above, includes the Hungarian and Turkish languages). A discussion of the possible relation between Japanese and the Oceanic languages, which are included in the "Austronesian" family mentioned above, is given by Matsumoto in his "On the Relation between Japanese and Oceanic Languages", based on word parallels. The Ainu language, spoken by the Ainu people of Japan, is another example of an isolated language. Its possible relation with others is discussed by Gjerdman in his "Word Parallels between Ainu and other Languages".

conceivably be a borrowing from a Germanic source (compare it further with Danish *navn*) and similarly *ház* - 'house'. To be significant the resemblance must therefore not be too obvious. The author was then confronted with the practical problem, namely, in the absence of any other information, for example, available historical documents, *within what limits of word sound and word meaning was it necessary for him to remain before deciding whether the words in question were or were not related.*

It was soon realized however that this problem was fundamental not only for the particular case in question of the possible kinship of the Hungarian and Indo-European languages but for the entire question of word and language kinship in general. The author was thus led to give some thought to the general problem of *the possible scope of the phonetic changes* that might be exhibited by words together with *the possible scope of meaning* that could be associated with a word.

Now although the author did succeed in setting up quite a sizable list of Hungarian words with corresponding closely resembling Indo-European (particularly English!) words (an extract from that list is given in Appendix 2) it was clear to him upon reflection that the genetic kinship of languages compared (that is, their traceability to a common parent language) could not thereby be conclusively shown. For if such were the case then Malay, the "Austronesian" language mentioned above, Chinese, Hebrew, Tamil, a member of the distinct "Dravidian" family spoken mainly in southern India, and Swahili, a language of the African "Bantu" family, would also bear a kinship with Indo-European! Such surprising conclusion would follow from the fact that the author succeeded, as in the case of Hungarian, in setting up sizable

6

lists embracing the greater part of the basic vocabularies of these languages where it was always possible to find Indo-European (and again specifically English!) words of closely resembling sound and meaning to the words of these languages. (See Ch. X and Appendix 2).

Why it was possible to set up word parallels between Hungarian and Indo-European languages, between Malay and Sanskrit, between ancient Egyptian and Semitic languages, between ancient Hittite and Indo-European languages, between ancient Sumerian and Oceanic languages, etc. was now readily understood. In fact, it became quite evident that, provided the "sound preferences" of the languages are comparable, that is, provided the languages are comparably rich and varied in their sounds and sound combinations, it should be possible to set up parallel word lists exhibiting an apparent genetic kinship between *any* two languages at all, for example between any language and English!

It turned out then, as may be gathered from the above remarks, that the question of genetic kinship became secondary to more fundamental considerations and concepts. These relate namely to the full scope of operation of phonetic and semantic phenomena in words, to a new concept of the meaning of the term "kinship" as applied to words, not only in comparing words of different languages but in comparing words *within a given language itself*. Moreover these considerations led to a simple concept of the basic character itself of all words of all languages. These results are all a consequence of our new "phoneto-semantic" approach already referred to and which we shall discuss in the following chapters.

A word may be said with regard to the arrangement of the material and the division into chapters. The nature of the concepts presented is such that the significance of any one of them can not be fully grasped before the significance of the others is fully grasped. This arises from the fact that they are not mutually independent but are intimately interlinked any one of them implying the others. Thus, the concept of the "scope of meaning of words" discussed in Ch. II is not independent of that of the "vocabulary building mechanism" discussed in Ch. VII nor is the concept of "word variable" discussed in Ch. VI independent of that of the "striking character of words" discussed in Ch. VIII and IX. That is, all of the chapters possess a single organic unity which must be grasped as a whole. The individual chapters may thus to some extent be likened to the words of a sentence whose full meaning hangs in suspense as it were until all of its words have been spoken. Since practical considerations demand however, as in the case of the words of a sentence, some definite sequence, a chapter sequence has been chosen which it is hoped, bearing the above remarks in mind, will permit the simplest development of the ideas presented.

It should be remarked, finally, that, since in our viewpoint toward words and their meanings we are "starting from scratch", we need assume no more on the part of the reader than a genuinely lively curiosity about words and an ability to follow a rather simple, and as will appear in many cases, an almost obvious line of reasoning based on the linguistic data presented.

CHAPTER TWO

THE SCOPE OF MEANING OF WORDS

A PRELIMINARY INDICATION of the meaning intended to be conveyed by the term "phoneto-semantic" can be given by considering the two English words *hole* and *hollow,* stated to be akin to each other. These are evidently related in sound and associated in meaning. In fact their sound resemblance would have no significance or interest if the words were not associated in meaning, if the word *hole,* for example, had its usual meaning while the word *hollow* meant "the color green". We may thus say that the words are "phoneto-semantically related" (Greek *phōnē* - sound, *sēmainein* - to signify). Other phoneto-semantic pairs, stated in etymological dictionaries to be related in the "ordinary sense" are *grate-scratch, stripe-streak, deaf-dumb.*

From the above brief indication of what we wish to convey by the term "phoneto-semantic" it would appear that there is really nothing that is new or novel in our viewpoint. For after all, is this not precisely what is done in existing etymologies, which are all based on the historical approach, namely, that a comparison is made between words of associated sound and meaning? This is indeed true and the fact that all "conventional" etymologies are in essence phoneto-semantic in character is

9

in itself a fact of prime significance for our viewpoint. The novelty of the new viewpoint however, one which justifies the introduction of the term "phoneto-semantic", lies in carrying out this idea of phoneto-semantically linked words *to its fullest, which simultaneously is its logical, possibilities.*

Since we shall speak of "phoneto-semantically linked words" we wish first of all to present some considerations relative to the meanings associated with words. In this connection we shall emphasize our concept of *the full actual and potential scope of meaning that may be associated with a word.*

Normally if one were asked to define a simple English word one would answer by giving one or more "synonyms". Similarly a highly abbreviated "vest pocket dictionary" limits itself to one or two synonyms and might define the word *hole* above, for example, as "an aperture, a perforation". A larger dictionary will cite more meanings while an "unabridged" may devote a half page or more to "tracking down" and recording different meanings and shades of meanings that are now or have in the past been associated with the word.

Now in order that he may appreciate the underlying nature of the phoneto-semantic approach it is essential that the reader grasp the concept of the scope or range of meaning that may be associated with any simple word. For this reason we shall cite the following definitions (among others) given in Webster's New International Dictionary, 2nd edition, of the word *hole*:

1. An opening into or through anything; an aperture of any sort, whether a natural orifice or an artificial perforation.
2. a. A hollow place; a cavity in a solid body or area,

10

spec. a: An abrupt hollow in the ground; an excavation; pit; cave.

b. A hollow in the firm ground filled with soft material, as a boghole; also in streams a place where the water is comparatively deep, c. a shaft, a mine.

3. a. An underground habitation or lurking place; a den or burrow; any mean or dark place of lodging, hiding, etc. b. Dial. E. A house, also, a recess; nook. c. slang. place - used in contempt.

4. A defect of character or the like; a flaw, esp. when viewed as blameworthy; as to pick holes in one's friends, that is, to find faults in them.

5. Obs. a. A place where unlawful business is secretly carried on, as unlicensed printing. b. A prison; a prison cell.

6. An embarrassing position; a fix. Colloq.

7. Local U.S. a. A small bay; a cove. b. A narrow waterway. c. A level grassy mountain valley.

8. Naut. The hold of a ship.

Evidently the simple word *hole* is associated with a variety of meanings ranging from those which may be said to differ by a "shade", like 'recess-nook', to those which differ by considerably more than a shade, like 'defect (of character)- house'.

Similarly the word *hollow* is found associated with a range of meanings which includes that of 'empty', 'depressed', 'concave', 'sunken', 'deep, muffled, as a hollow roar', colloquial 'complete, thorough'.

Now the pair *hole-hollow*, as mentioned above, is a phoneto-semantically linked pair of words which are stated in conventional etymologies to be akin to each other. Such linkage or kinship appears obvious enough if the words are considered in their "overlapping" sense of "a hollow place". Suppose however we fix our attention on the meaning of *hole* as 'a house, a nook, a recess' and on the meaning of *hollow* as 'complete, thorough'. With these meanings in mind the semantic divergence of *hole-hollow* is so great that in spite of the phonetic resemblance we may say that the words are not phoneto-semantically linked, although from the conventional viewpoint the words are still "related".

Our challenging reader may now be expected to raise the following objection. The author's procedure in selecting one of the meanings associated with each word of the pair *hole-hollow* and then comparing them on the basis of these meanings alone is arbitrary and devoid of any true significance. For, the essential or primary meanings of these words are respectively 'an opening' and ' a hollow place' both of which meanings can readily be linked in thought, while the other meanings given in the dictionary are derived meanings which in a natural way have become associated with these primary meanings.

It will be observed that in the reader's reasoning assumed above the meanings given after a word in an "unabridged" dictionary are divided into two categories, namely, the "basic", "essential" or "primary" meaning which presumably is also the more "primitive" meaning of the word and the "secondary" or "derived" meanings which have been acquired by the word in the course of its historical development and are "natural extensions" of the primary meaning. Included among such secondary meanings are the "figurative" use of the word, that is, "transferred in sense from the plain or literal" (Webster's definition) as contrasted with the "concrete", "plain" or "literal" use, the latter again being assumed as belonging to the first category.

In answer to our challenging reader we reply as follows: He is right in saying that the definitions given after a word are not really independent of each other but are associated in a natural way. He is wrong however in his implied assumption that one particular meaning can be taken as "basic" relative to which the others are "derived". The viewpoint adopted in our phoneto-semantic approach is in fact based on the concept, whose justification will appear more and more obvious as we proceed, that no meaning given after a word is to be singled out as primary although it may at any time be the more predominant meaning. Further, the degree of association of meanings, and therefore the actual and potential range of definitions that could be given after a word is far greater than is commonly realized, so great in fact as to make an "unabridged dictionary" of English or of any other language not only a practically but a theoretically "nonexistent entity".

The reason for the above two admittedly broad and sweeping statements will become quite clear after we discover, in our later chapters, what sort of entities words are and what is the essential nature of the linkage by which words are associated with their meanings. But we should like, in further preparation for that "discovery", to proceed along "conservative" grounds in emphasizing the two ideas contained in the above statements, namely, the idea of a widely and vaguely delimited scope of definition associated with words and the idea of "relativity of meaning", that is, the absence of an absolute, basic, or "reference" meaning associated with a word.

We shall do this by asking the reader to reflect on the nature of the definitions, cited from Webster's, of a few further simple English words.

The word *bite* in addition to its meaning 1. 'to seize with the teeth so that they enter, nip or grip the thing seized; to lacerate, crush or wound with the teeth' has among others, the following further meanings:

2. to cut, gash or pierce - of an edged weapon or the person wielding it.
3. to eat, obs. (transitive) and dial. (intransitive)
4. to cause sharp pain or smarting to; to hurt
5. to take hold of; to hold fast, as the jaws of vises are cut to bite the work
6. to corrode; to eat into
7. to seize; impress; affect profoundly
8. to slander; criticise spitefully, obs.
9. to cheat, trick or take in
10. to cause a smarting, be pungent
11. to produce an impression

The word is "traced" in accordance with the historical approach to the Sanskrit root *bhid* meaning 'to cleave', Sanskrit being one of the most ancient of Indo-European languages and presumably most nearly akin to the primitive Indo-European mother tongue whence sprang the entire extensive Indo-European family. The word is also "traced" to the rather less ancient Latin root *find,* of *findere-* 'to cleave' (note the phonetic divergence between *bite-find;* we shall say more on the subject of range of phonetic variation in our next chapter). Thus it is apparently intended to imply that the basic idea behind the word *bite* is that of 'cleaving' so that relative to the Sanskrit root *bhid* the "primary" meaning of English *bite,* that of "biting with the teeth", is secondary or derived.

Note now that as a transitive verb the word *bite* had the obsolete meaning 'to eat' while it has the dialectal meaning 'to eat' as an intransitive verb. Let us therefore take this particular meaning of *bite,* that is, 'to eat' and

14

compare the definitions given after *eat* with those given after *bite*.

The word *eat* is traced to Sanskrit *ad,* Greek *ed,* and Hittite (a very ancient language which is stated to "bear some relationship, not yet determined", to the Indo-European family) *ad,* all meaning 'to eat'. Besides being traced to these ancient languages however the word is stated to bear kinship with the English word *etch* whose meaning resembles one of the meanings of *eat,* namely, 'to form by a wearing or corrosive action'. If now we consider the pair *eat-etch* simultaneously as being, in this case, relatively slight phonetic modifications of each other, which meaning shall we say is "basic" to both of them? Is it 'to partake of food' or 'to corrode' or some other associated meaning? Is the word *etch* which does *not* have the meaning 'to partake of food' actually derived from Sanskrit *ad* - 'to eat', so that the sense of 'to partake of food' is the primitive idea behind *etch,* the sense of 'to corrode' growing out of the sense of 'to partake of food'?

It will be evident from the examples given above that the historical approach, in tracing any word to a primitive language, selects from the range of meanings which appear after a word one which overlaps with one of the meanings of the ancient word but somewhat arbitrarily leaves out of account the other associated meanings, of the possible scope of which we have already received some indication. We shall gain still further insight into such scope of meaning by considering the range of meanings associated with a few more simple English words.

One of the meanings associated with *bite* is, as we have seen, 'to cut, gash or pierce'. Let us now compare the meanings of *bite* with those of *cut.* But right here we run into a practical difficulty, for Webster's cites three full fine-print columns of definitions of *cut* and it hardly seems fair to fill the next ten pages or so in quoting the definitions of *cut,* however instructive it may be to do so. We shall therefore content ourselves with citing just a few of these definitions:

1. to penetrate or divide; gash, slash
2. to fell; to hew; to mow; to reap
3. to carve; to shape
4. to intersect; to cross
5. to shorten
6. to strike sharply as in cutting, as with a whip; to wound the sensibilities of
7. to cause to be less viscous, tenacious or the like; to dissolve
8. to refuse to recognize (an acquaintance), colloquial
9. to absent oneself from, colloquial
10. to perform, as to cut a caper, colloquial
11. to interfere, as a horse
12. to cut out, cease from doing, slang
13. to strike (a ball) in such a way as to deflect it
14. to proceed by passing, especially with speed or dexterity or to save time
15. to speak; to utter, old thieves' slang

It should be remarked, in connection with *cut,* that unlike *bite, eat* and *etch* above, the word is traced no further than to Middle English *cutt, kitt, kett* and is stated to be "of unknown origin". The classification "unknown", or "obscure" or "uncertain origin" is incidentally applied, as the reader will see by consulting the dictionary, to a considerable number of some of the commonest words in the language, such as 'boy', 'girl', 'tag', 'hit', 'slash' and particularly to a large number of dialect words.

Since the word *cut* is of "unknown origin" it would

appear to be a little more difficult than in the case of *eat* to state which of its manifold meanings is the basic and which the derived. If the reader reflect however on the surprisingly wide range of meanings associated with *cut* it is not unlikely that he may doubt whether the word possesses any basic meaning at all *beyond a vaguely delimited striking action of some sort, which, depending on the context in which the word is used, acquires a more specific "shade of meaning"*.

It will be noted that the words *bite, eat, etch* above similarly appear to involve, if not explicitly then implicitly, a striking action of some kind. In fact, from the viewpoint which we have adopted, we do not regard the distinction in classification of *eat* and *cut* as being respectively of "known" and of "unknown origin" as a particularly significant one. That is, in spite of the fact that the word *eat* has apparently been traced to Sanskrit *ad,* Greek *ed,* German *ess,* etc. we regard the word *eat* to be essentially of the same character as the word *cut* in that the phrase "of unknown origin", if it applies to *cut,* applies with equal justification to *eat.* This statement will be amplified and seen in its true significance as we proceed with our discussion.

It is interesting to note that included among the meanings of *cut* is that of 'to speak, to utter' in which meaning it was employed in "old thieves' slang". Now it is our "fixed policy" not to exclude from consideration any meaning at all that is or ever has been associated with any word whether such meaning has been "stigmatized" as slang or whether not so stigmatized as a dialectal, local or colloquial meaning. As we shall see later, there is no essential difference in character between certain types of slang meanings of words and the "respectable" meanings, both types being products of fundamentally the same process by which words become associated with their meanings. As a further illustration of our "impartial attitude" indicated in the above statement, we do not distinguish as less basic the slang meaning of the word *knob* as 'the head' as compared with its "respectable meaning" 'a round protuberance or mass; a bunch; bump; lump'.

To return to our word *cut* in its slang meaning 'to speak, to utter'. The word *cut* also means, as we have seen, 'to strike sharply as in cutting', 'to strike (a ball) in such a way as to deflect it'. Is the slang meaning 'to speak' in any way related to the sense of 'to strike'? Let us cite a few more words associated with the sense of speaking. The word *chatter* means 'to talk idly; to prate'; it also means 'to make a noise by rapid collisions'; the word *patter* means 'to chatter', also, 'to strike with a quick succession of pats or slight sounds'; the word *clatter* means 'to chatter', also, 'to make a rattling sound by striking hard bodies together', the word *clack* means 'to prattle', also, 'the sharp noise of bodies striking together'; the word *crack*, as a Scottish dialect word, means 'to talk, chat', also, 'to strike with a sharp noise'; the word *hack*, as a dialect word, means 'to chatter', also, 'to cut or mangle', the word *chop* means 'to utter in a short or abrupt way', also, 'to cut by striking', the word *rap* means 'to smite or strike with a quick smart blow', also, 'to utter suddenly and forcibly'.

Is there any surprise then that one of the meanings associated with *cut* should be an old slang meaning of 'to speak, to utter'? Evidently, the idea of 'strike' is in some way associated with the idea involved in 'talk' or 'speak'. Is it possible then that the word *prat*, an obsolete word occurring in Shakespeare with the meaning of 'spank, beat' is simply a slightly modified form of *prate*

18

meaning 'to prattle' and is therefore "related" to *prate*? What do we really mean by "related"? If the sense of 'striking in some manner or other' is involved in the meanings of *eat, bite, cut, prate* is it possible that the same idea is involved in a good many other simple common words, perhaps in all words, so that the "striking idea" is after all the "basic idea" common to all words?

We shall return to the above questions in our fuller discussions given in later chapters. It is hoped however that through citing the above examples the fact of the occurrence of an unsuspectedly wide variety and divergence of meaning associated with simple words has been sufficiently well brought out. Evidently, the meanings, however divergent, must be linked in thought, that is, must possess a conceptual element in common. Thus the different meanings linked with any word are the products of the associative, and imaginative, activity of the human mind which constantly finds a connection of one idea with a "related" one. Such activity, as we shall presently see, is intimately connected with the fundamental character itself of all simple words.

Not only however are ideas linked so as to produce a vaguely delimited multiplicity of meanings associated with any simple word but words themselves are linked so as to produce a multiplicity of "related" phonetic variants. To this subject, that is, the scope of sound variation of words, we turn in the following chapters; first discussing however, in the chapter immediately following, the concept of sound kinship.

CHAPTER THREE

THE CONCEPT OF SOUND KINSHIP

THAT THE SOUNDS associated with words are not rigidly and invariably fixed is a well-known, rather common sense observation. Now it will clarify our discussion if at the outset we distinguish two classes of changes, namely, those which involve the time factor and those which do not. For not only do sounds of words undergo changes *in the course of time* but *at any given time* words *within the same language* may not be spoken exactly alike by various groups of people within some given region.

A good illustration of these two classes is provided by the "romance" languages, that is, French, Spanish, Italian, Portuguese, Rumanian, and a few others all derived from Latin. These languages developed through a historical process from ancient Latin so that the relation between any of them and Latin is a "parent-offspring" relation. On the other hand, each of these languages did *not* develop from any of the others but constitutes rather one of several *contemporary dialects* developed from Latin. (In fact, these languages may be regarded as contemporary dialects *of* the spoken or "vulgar" Latin of the time). It is important to emphasize this distinction of "parent-offspring" relation and "cousin" relation because it is the latter relation which, from our viewpoint, is the more significant as throwing light on the essential character of words (as well as on the essential nature of the parent-offspring relation itself).

On comparing corresponding words of two languages, whether in the "parent-offspring" or in the "cousin" relation, the sound differences may vary to a degree such that the word kinship may not be immediately apparent. Thus it is not immediately apparent that the Spanish word *hermoso* - 'beautiful, handsome' is "no other" than the Latin *formosus* - 'of beautiful form', so that the word *hermoso* is akin to our English *form*. We observe here a correspondence between the sound of initial Latin *f* and initial Spanish *h*, which in modern Spanish is silent. Other examples evidencing the same *f-h* correspondence between Spanish and Latin are *hierro-ferrum* (iron), *horno-furnus* (oven), *humo-fumus* (smoke, vapor). Evidently such a shift of sound implies a certain *kinship* between the sound *f* and the sound *h*, whether the latter is aspirated or is silent. What we now wish to develop in the present chapter is precisely this concept of the kinship of sounds.

It is possible to proceed to elucidate the concept we wish to develop of the kinship of sounds by citing from an entire mass of phonetic data derived from many diverse and "outlandish" languages. We might say, for example, relative to the kinship mentioned above in connection with the *f* and *h* sounds as observed in Latin *formosus*-Spanish *hermoso*, that Japanese *h* before *u* is ordinarily represented in transliteration by *f* (though in the later "Romaji" system it is still transliterated by *h*) and is then given a sound which is described as "intermediate between *h* and *f*". Or again, that an intimate connection between *h* and *f* is found in Hausa, a native

African language (the term is also applied to the people), a northern Hausa using an *h* where a southern Hausa will use an *f*. So as not to distract the reader with what may appear, at this stage of our discussion, as too wide an excursion into unfamiliar territory, we shall confine our illustrations to more familiar languages.

Depending on their quality or on the organs of speech that are emphasized in their production, sounds are described by such terms as guttural, palatal, labial, dental, cerebral or retroflex, fricative, aspirate, sibilant, liquid, semi-vowel, mute or hard, sonant or soft, nasal, continuant, stop, and others. In terms of processes we speak of "palatalizing", "nasalizing", "dentalizing", "aspirating", etc. a consonant sound, thereby implying that the sound and its modification are *related* sounds.

Since this is not a textbook on phonetics it is not necessary that we go into any detailed description of what each of these terms or processes means. Such descriptions will be found in connection with the grammar dealing with any particular language. For example, the nature of cerebral or retroflex *t* or *d*, as distinguished from dental *t* or *d*, is dealt with in any Sanskrit grammar (though the sounds occur also in English). What particularly concerns us however is the fact that while the nature and kinship of particular sounds has been amply discussed in numerous books and grammars dealing with particular languages or language families, no discussion of the concept itself of sound kinship in general has, so far as is known to the author, appeared anywhere. To what extent then may two sounds be regarded as *related* and what is the real significance of the term as applied to sounds?

If we cite such simple pair as *t-d* it seems that the significance of the concept of relatedness is obvious; for it may be said that *d* is simply "voiced" *t* and conversely, *t* is unvoiced *d*. Theoretically it should be possible to voice or unvoice any consonant sound. Thus the voiced "mate" of English *ch* is *j*, of *k* is *g*, of *p* is *b*, of *f* is *v*, of *s* is *z*. English *l* is voiced. What is unvoiced English *l*? Such sound is not recognized as occurring in English; it is however represented by a separate letter of the alphabet in Welsh. The sound *ch* in Scottish *loch* or German *ach* is unvoiced. What is voiced *ch*? The sound does not occur in English but does occur in modern Greek. That is, each language selects from the theoretically available sounds only such as are congenial to the "genius of the language". We shall have more to say on the subject of "sound preferences" in a later chapter.

Instead of voicing *s* to give *z* we may "lisp" it, that is pronounce *s* as *th* in *thin* and similarly *z* as *th* in *them*. Though lisping is a "speech defect" if English *say* is pronounced *thay*, it is no defect if "in the course of history" Anglo-Saxon *se* comes to be pronounced *the*, the modern definite article. Is the same phonetic phenomenon evidenced in the modern pair *swack-thwack*, both meaning 'to strike', that is, do we here have the "same word" with *s* unlisped and lisped respectively?

Since *th* as in *think, this,* is obviously akin in sound to *t* and *d* (compare *think*-German *denk, this*-German *dies*), while *th* is "lisped" *s* or *z*, the sounds *s-z-t-d-th* may all be said to be akin, though the kinship between *s-t* is not as immediately obvious as that between *t-d*. (Those familiar with Spanish will at once recall in this connection the sound of Spanish *c* before *e* and *i* in "Castilian" as *th* but in South American Spanish as *s*). Such kinship is exhibited in comparing English words with the closely related German words, for example, English *white, what* - German *weiss, was*. Is it also exhibited *within*

23

English itself in for example the words *sing* with its meaning 'to be filled with a humming or buzzing; to ring' - *ting* (to sound with or make a ting) - *zing* (a shrill humming noise) - *ding* (to sound as a bell; to ring)?

Not only may we thus construe *s* as related to *t*; we may construe *s* as related for example to the guttural *k*, a kinship which offhand is not at all evident. This may be seen from the following line of reasoning, which however is merely illustrative and not necessarily the only line of reasoning by which the concept of the kinship of *s-k* can be justified.

If we return for a moment to Spanish we shall find that Spanish *c* is pronounced, as already mentioned, as *s* or *th* before the front or "soft" vowels *e, i* while the same letter before the back or "hard" vowels *a, o* is pronounced like *k*. In Italian, a related "romance language" the letter *c* before the corresponding vowels has respectively the sounds *ch* and *k*. Thus Latin *c*, whose precise sound before *e* and *i* we do not actually know, is represented in Spanish and Italian words derived from Latin by the sounds *s, th, ch, k*. In French, which is another romance language, the *c* is pronounced *s* before the front vowels while before the back vowel *a* the Latin *k* is often represented by the sound *sh*, for example, Latin *cantio*-French *chanson*.

We may thus say that the sounds *k, ch, sh, s, t, th* are all related sounds, though the relation *k-s* may strike us as of a less obvious kind than that of *k-ch*. If we take a "dynamic" point of view and regard a sound as obtained from another *through a process* we may explicitly express the relation of *k-ch* by saying that *ch* is palatalized *k*, or conversely that *k* is "unpalatalized *ch*". We might similarly express the *k-s* relation more explicitly by saying that *s* is "sibilized *k*" or conversely that *k* is "gutturalized *s*".

Another point should here be noted. From the fact that *c* is palatalized or "sibilized" before the vowels *e, i,* which are sometimes referred to as "palatal vowels" and "gutturalized" before the vowels *a, o, u,* which are sometimes referred to as "guttural vowels" it follows that the letter *c,* when isolated, has, strictly speaking, no independent sound of its own but rather *a potential range of "related sounds",* any precise value of which depends on the "environment" of the letter.[1]

The interchange between *k-s,* it may be remarked, is one of the distinguishing characteristics of the two divisions, namely, the "satem" and the "centum" (from the corresponding word for hundred in Latin and Avestan) into which the Indo-European language family is divided. Thus, the Greek (a "centum" language) word for heart is *kardia* corresponding to Lithuanian (a "satem" language) *širdis.* Note however that the Latin word *centum* itself is in French, a "centum" language, at present pronounced as though the word were spelled "sent". Is the interchange *k-s* also exhibited *within English itself* in the pair *clap-slap* or the interchange *g-s* in the pair *glide-slide*?

1. It is significant to point out in this connection the relationship between the concept of sound kinship and that of "phonemic variants" of sounds. A "phoneme" is defined as "a group of variants of a speech sound, usually all spelled with the same or equivalent letter and commonly defined as the same sound but varying somewhat with the same speaker according to different phonetic conditions (neighboring sounds, stress, length, intonation, etc.)." The concept of a phoneme thus constitutes a partial recognition of the fact that a letter of the alphabet represents not a unique sound but rather a range of sounds. What is apparently not realized is that such range is of far greater scope than the "somewhat varying sounds" associated with a "phoneme". Our concept of sound kinship as discussed above is thus a logical extension of the concept of a phoneme, the sounds *k* and *th* (or *s*) for example of the Spanish letter *c* before the "back" and "front" vowels respectively constituting "phonemic variants" of a rather less "anemic" type.

We have spoken of *ch* as a palatalized or "softened" *k*. In the word *pitch,* for example, which is stated to be related to the word *pick* the *ck* has been palatalized to *tch*. But we may regard *ch* as palatalized *t* as well as palatalized *k*. For example, there is in English an obsolete word *fet* which means "to fetch" while Anglo-Saxon had both *fecc*an and *feti*an meaning 'to fetch'. From such examples as above it appears convenient to assign to the sound *ch* the role of "intermediary" between the "stops" *k* and *t* so that we may regard these two sounds likewise as related. The kinship of *k-t* may also be justified on the principle that "sounds related to the same or related sounds are related to each other". For we have already discussed the kinship of the pairs *k-s* and *s-t*. Is the same phenomenon exhibited in Anglo-Saxon *fecc*an-*feti*an and modern *fetch* exhibited *within modern English itself* in *tick* (touch, tap) - *touch-tat* (dial. tap, touch)?

We have seen above how, by taking the "dynamic" viewpoint, sounds can be conceived as related to others by having them subjected to the processes of voicing, lisping, palatalizing, gutturalizing, and sibilizing. We naturally have not exhausted all possible methods of "converting sounds into other sounds". Thus we may "aspirate" the mute stops *p, t, k* by pronouncing them respectively *f, th, kh* (the latter intended to represent the sound *ch* of German *ach*). English *ship,* for example, corresponds to German *Schiff,* English *book* to German *Buch*. The sound *kh* is however not far removed from the simple aspirate *h* and we need not therefore be very much surprised to find that in Middle English the word *hollow* was variously spelled as *holow, holgh, holh*. Thus a kinship of sounds is implied between the guttural *g* (and its obviously related *k*) and the "bilabial" *w*, which

26

in turn is more obviously akin to the "fricatives" *v, f* and labials *p, m*. As a further illustration the word *rough,* pronounced, and as a dialect word also spelled, *ruff* was in Middle English spelled *rough, row, ruw, rugh, ruh* and is stated to be related to German *rauh* and *rauch*. Is this same kinship exhibited *within English itself,* in the pair *rough-raw* or in *rough-rag* (to cut or dress roughly, as a grindstone) or in *rag* (obsolete, to become tattered)-*rip* (to become torn apart) and to our previous triplet *tick-touch-tat* may we add as further relatives *tag* (touch or hit)-*tap?*

We have thus extended the concept of sound kinship to include the stops *k, p, t* and their more obvious modifications *g, kh, f, v, w, m, b, th, ch,* etc. The above examples illustrated the interchanges as observed at the end of words. From the concept of the kinship of these sounds such interchanges should also be observed at the beginning of words. As a matter of fact they are noted in isolated cases in conventional etymologies and in accordance with the historical viewpoint or "bias" are interpreted as exhibiting a slow gradual development of the operation of a phonetic law between two languages or language groups. Thus the English word *heart* is traced to the Greek *kardia,* the interchange Greek *k*-English *h* illustrating the operation of "Grimm's law of consonant shifts". In accordance with this law certain regular changes have been undergone by the stops *k, p, t* of the "primitive" Indo-European consonant system (which is stated to have been established comparatively by Sanskrit and Lithuanian, Greek, Latin, etc.) in the Teutonic languages, that is, English, German, Swedish, etc. These changes or shifts are supposed to have taken place independently and at different times. (We have already remarked on a similar assumed shift between the

27

two large divisions, the "satem" and the "centum" of the Indo-European family and given as an illustration English *heart* - Lithuanian *širdis*). It should be remarked in this connection that many "apparent exceptions" have been observed in the operation of Grimm's law, exceptions which necessitate the discovery of new "ammendatory laws" such as Grassmann's law and Verner's law.

We now anticipate our later results and state here that Grimm's law, like the law of consonant shifts between the "satem" and "centum" languages, while perhaps of nominal, is of *no essential significance* as indicative of a genetic shift of "primitive Indo-European consonants", the idea of such primitive consonants being illusory. Regular consonant shifts are indeed observed between such obvious parent-offspring languages as Latin-Italian or between "cousin" languages as German-Dutch. Where however the "jump" is as great as between Sanskrit (or Greek) and English the application of the Latin-to-Italian analogy is misleading. Moreover the changes undergone by any language as it develops into its offspring languages are "irreversible", that is, where the parent language no longer exists we can not reliably reconstruct it by tracing backward. In fact, were Latin not preserved in the literature, we should have only the vaguest idea of its sounds, syntax and inflections.

To the reader who has grasped the concept of sound kinship we have presented above these statements should appear rather "reasonable". For in accordance with this concept a consonant is not a very stable entity at all but must be construed as essentially fluid. We should, furthermore, on the basis of such "dynamic" concept, expect such shifts as are stated to have taken place between languages to occur "in reverse" between the languages considered, as well as in either direction *within a given language*. As a matter of fact a random illustration of the Grimm shift Greek *k*-English *h* occurring "in reverse" (that is, Greek *h*-English *k*) is provided by Greek *herp*ein-English *creep*; Sanskrit *hrid*-English *heart* shows no shift, while within English itself such pairs as *cuddle-huddle*, *cot* (a small house; a cottage or hut)-*hut* appear to indicate an "intralingual reversible shift". Further insight into the underlying nature of these shifts will be gained when we come to our later chapters.

We have so far confined our discussion to the kinship of consonants. We now turn to a consideration of the vowels. It should first of all be pointed out that the distinction between consonants and vowels is by no means as clear-cut as one would at first glance be led to believe. This fact is explicitly recognized when we term such sound as *y* as being a "semi-vowel", that is, a sound that is "a vowel yet not a vowel".

Now it is evident that the semi-vowel *y*, as in *young*, is akin to the vowel sound *i* in *machine*. The semi-vowel *y*, however, through a relatively slight modification, converts to the palatal sound *j*, as is illustrated for example by the statement that English *joke* is related to Latin *jocus* (pronounced *yocus*). In fact the letter *j* is itself merely a modification of the letter *i*. The vowel *i* is thus akin to the palatal sound *j* (the vowel is sometimes called a "palatal vowel") and therefore also to *ch* which is "unvoiced" *j*. We may in fact regard *y* as a certain intermediate gradation between *i* and *j*. Since *j* is on the other hand a "palatalized *g*", just as *ch* is palatalized *k*, the semi-vowel *y* and vowel *i* are akin to "guttural" *g*. Such kinship is exhibited for example in German *tag*-English *day* or in Anglo-Saxon *geong* or *gung*-English

29

young. The kinship between *g-j-y* is further illustrated within English itself in such words as *gabble-jabble* (to jabber)-*yabble* (Scottish, gabble).

Consider now the vowel *u* as in "lune". Evidently this vowel is akin to the sound of *w* ("double *u*"), which in English represents a vowel in diphthongs, as in the word *how*, pronounced as though it were spelled "hau". We may thus regard *w* as a "semi-vowel" corresponding to the vowel *u*. Since *v* is a more emphatically pronounced *w*, *v* too may be taken akin to *u*; and so may *f*, *b* and *m*, in fact, all labials. Thus we can see that such Middle English variants as *ruh-ruw* should correspond to modern English *rough* pronounced (and also spelled dialectally) *ruff*, for the *f* of *ruff* may be construed as a more definitely labialized *u* with friction. (It may be of interest in this connection to remark that Welsh *w* is used to represent both the consonant sound *w* and the vowel sound *oo*).

By analogous discussion it may be shown that just as *i* bears close kinship with the palatals and *u* with the labials, the vowel *a* as in "father" bears close kinship with the gutturals and is in fact sometimes referred to as a "guttural" vowel.

Not only the consonants *y*, *w* but the sounds *l*, *m*, *n*, *r* may be construed as semi-vowels since they more evidently partake of a vowel character. We wish in particular to discuss the consonants *l*, *r* sometimes termed "liquids", that is, "flowing or vowel-like consonants". It is of interest to note that these, together with the *y* and *w* sounds, were by ancient Sanskrit grammarians classified as "semi-vowels". Moreover, the Sanskrit alphabet possessed two letters, *ri* and *li*, classed with the vowels. In modern Czech the letters *l*, *r* similarly serve as both vowels and consonants. Because of the vowel-like character of *r, l* they may be expected to interchange with each other as well as to "crop up" for example at the middle or end of a word. Thus we may describe the difference between Anglo-Saxon *spec*an, *sprecc*an, both meaning 'to speak' as due to an internal vowel difference, the form *spec* differing from the form *sprec* in that the latter is pronounced with the "*r* vowel".[2]

We hope in the above paragraphs to have sufficiently brought out the fact that the idea of related sounds, an idea whose meaning appears so obvious if we consider such pairs as *t-d, t-th, w-v,* involves a far broader concept than is immediately apparent. For if we take the "dynamic" viewpoint, any sound, by being subjected to some phonetic process, may be "modified" to a corresponding different sound which, in view of the modification, may still be construed as "related" to the "initial" sound. The existence, though not the scope or significance of such modifications, and therefore the implied kinship, is recognized in the conventional etymologies based on the historical approach. The latter approach stresses these modifications as they occur between words of different languages (the words compared often being

2. It is instructive in connection with our discussion of the vowels to point out that our letters for the vowels *a, e, i, o, u,* were derived via Latin and Greek from the ancient Phoenician alphabet. Now the latter, which is the same as the ancient Hebrew alphabet, in accordance with the general view, is said to have consisted of "pure" consonants and therefore to have possessed no vowels, the vowels having been obtained through a suitable modification or adaptation of the Phoenician consonants. Now such a view, while it appears true when superficially considered, is certainly not true if considered from the more fundamental viewpoint stated above. That is, the Phoenician, and therefore also the Hebrew, alphabet contains both consonants and vowels, such letters as Hebrew aleph, vau, he, yod, serving, because of their semi-vocalic nature, both as vowels and consonants. The clear-cut distinction of vowels from consonants is an abstraction which for certain purposes may be useful. Such an abstraction tends however to overlook the fact that a vowel may be construed as a "softened consonant" just as a consonant may be construed as a "hardened vowel", a construction which is of significance if the basic phonetic character of words is to be grasped.

31

cited, as we shall see, with a considerable degree of arbittrariness). The "phoneto-semantic" approach however, as indicated above, taking the essential fluidity or "instability" of sounds as a fundamental notion, lays stress on the occurrence of these sound kinships, or phonetic changes in general, *as they appear within one language, for example English itself.* In our later chapters this idea will be further amplified.

CHAPTER FOUR

HISTORICAL WORD LINKING

OUR PHONETO-SEMANTIC VIEWPOINT requires of us that we consider not only the full scope of actual and potential meanings that may possibly be associated with a word but that we at the same time take into account the full range of the possible variations in the sounds of words which may be associated in meaning. We have already, in Chapter II, dealt, to a degree possible in our first stage of presentation, with the answer to the question, namely, given a word, what is the full scope of meaning with which it is or may be associated. We next have to deal, again to a degree consistent with our first stage of presentation, with the correlative question, namely, *given a meaning, what are the different words associated with this meaning which possess what may be regarded as "related sounds"*? This will lead directly to the concept we wish to develop in succeeding chapters of the "phoneto-semantic kinship" of words. In the present chapter this question will be considered in the light of the prevailing conventional or historical approach.

It should first of all be remarked that the question above, in the precise manner in which it has been posed, has never, to the author's knowledge, hitherto been raised. This is natural since, from the historical view-

33

point or attitude toward words, which for all practical purposes is the one which dominates present-day thinking on the subject, the question, implying as it does some other than predominantly historical approach to the answer, is not quite a "proper" one to ask. The question however, like that relating to the full scope of meaning which is to be associated with a word, is an entirely legitimate one and, as we shall see, the complete answer to it provides us with the very key to the understanding of the basic character of all words.

Before presenting our own "phoneto-semantic" procedure in dealing with the question raised above let us see what the conventional historical approach has to offer by way of an answer. We shall see that this approach gives us a partial, and we may add, *essentially arbitrary,* answer to this question. That is, while it does provide us with a number of phonetic variants associated in meaning with a given word, both the number and choice of these variants is quite arbitrary. Moreover, while in general the words cited may be said to bear kinship with the given word, *the underlying character of such kinship is not clearly grasped.* The meaning of this latter statement will be understood after we have discussed the essential character of all simple words of all languages.

For the present however, in order to bring out sharply the difference between the approach we shall describe in the following chapter and the conventional historical approach we shall seek to answer our question posed above, namely, to find phonetic variants corresponding to a given word, by calling upon the latter approach. For this purpose it will be necessary for us, at the risk of imparting to our discussion a somewhat "learned" character, to cite several examples of the etymologies of words as given in a standard work based on the historical approach. Our examples will be cited from Webster's Unabridged Dictionary, although it should be clearly understood that this is done as a matter of convenience only and any other "standard" etymological work such as the Oxford dictionary could equally serve our purposes of illustration.

Let us return to our familiar example of *hole-hollow* already discussed in Chapter II. It is stated in Webster's etymology that these words are related, in the ordinary genetic sense of course, to such words as Greek *koilos*-hollow, Dutch *hol*-hold (of ship), hole, dialectal English *howk*-to hollow out by digging, Middle English *holk*en-to hollow out, Swedish *hålk*a-to gouge, scoop, Middle English *holow, holgh, holh*-hollow. These words are further stated to bear genetic kinship to the word *hold* (of a ship), "probably" to the word *hulk*-a ship; obsolete, the hull of a ship, to the Latin *caul*is-a stalk, stem, and "perhaps" to the Latin *cavus*-hollow, as well as to other words.

It will be seen from the above etymology that we are confronted with a variety of words exhibiting sound and meaning resemblances to *hole* and *hollow* some of which appear to be sufficiently obvious while others are less obvious. Among the more obvious for example are the resemblances between English *hole*-Dutch *hol*-Middle English *holow-holgh-holh*. Less obvious is the resemblance between *hole-howk*. Note however how, by inserting the "intermediary" ME *holk*en-to howk, thus: *hole-holk-howk* the resemblance is rendered more obvious, the medial *l* of *holk* being as it were dissolved into the vowel *ow* of *howk* (confer the discussion of the liquids and semi-vowels in the preceding chapter).

Let us dwell a little longer on a few of the other

35

words cited in the above etymology. Latin *cavus*-'hollow' is stated to be "probably" akin to *hole* (or *hollow*) and indeed the sound resemblance between the "roots" *hole-cav* is not likely to strike the ordinary reader as too obvious although the meaning resemblance is obvious enough. In the case of the Latin *caul*is-'stalk', however, which is stated to be related to *hole* without any factor of probability, the sound resemblance between the roots *caul-hole,* particularly if further compared with the Greek root *koil*-'hollow', may be taken as "reasonable" but the meaning resemblance between *hole-stalk* may possibly elude the reader. Of course it is not unlikely that the reader may at this point think of a meaning association not between *hole-stalk* but between *hollow-stalk,* an association which, since many stalks are hollow, seems less "stretched". This however raises the question, already mentioned in our Introduction, namely, how far we may go, when we compare words, in "recognizing" a meaning resemblance or association. To what extent, that is, may the meanings of words diverge and yet be recognized as having a conceptual element in common? We have already given some consideration to this question in our chapter on the scope of meaning of words and shall further consider it in our succeeding chapters.

The phonetic variants of *hole* cited above were obtained by stressing the concept of the genetic kinship of languages and therefore the history of the word and its interrelations with words of ancient languages. The assumption, implicit in such etymology as given above, is that the phonetic changes in question, from the ancient to the modern language are the results of a historical process. Thus the "roots"of our English *hollow* apparently extend back to the Greek word *koilos* of the same

36

meaning, the initial Greek *k* having "evolved" through such historical process to the initial *h* of the corresponding English word.

We shall presently see that the above concept of a historical process by which Greek *koilos* gave rise to English *hollow* is open to considerable suspicion. And the same holds true whenever a simple English word is apparently traced to a Greek, Latin or Sanskrit word. Now the concept itself appears so natural and even attractive that the above statement may strike some readers particularly those who have been thoroughly imbued with the "historical bias" as, to say the least, highly presumptive. For if our assertion is true then it would appear that the author is not merely rejecting the essential significance of a method and viewpoint which has the weight of leading authorities behind it and has in the past achieved considerable success, but is rather arbitrarily and "high-handedly" discarding well-established historical data painstakingly gathered in the past 150 years or so. To the above assumed objection the author's reply is the following: The author is not rejecting the historical method but is merely assigning it a secondary place of significance. As for the historical linguistic data, far from discarding them, he fully utilizes these very data, such as the etymologies given after an English word, to demonstrate the essentially arbitrary character of the kinships adduced and the failure of the historical approach to throw any true light on the word in question.

Let us bring out the meaning of the last statement above by dwelling somewhat further on the conventional etymology of the word *hole*. It will be observed in connection with that etymology that while the word *hulk* meaning obsoletely 'the hull of a ship' is stated to be

37

"probably" related to *hole,* in its sense of 'hold of a ship', nothing is stated about the possible kinship to the word *hull* itself which has the meaning 'hulk of a ship' and which certainly resembles *hole* in sound even more than does the word *hulk.*

Note however some further facts about *hull* and *hulk.* The dictionary lists "several hulks". There is a *hulk,* obsolete except in its dialectal use, which means 'to disembowel'. This *hulk* is identified with Middle English *holk*en, already mentioned above, meaning 'to howk' and is thus stated to be akin to *hole.* There is however "still another hulk", not stated to bear any kinship with *hole,* which has the meaning 'a hut; a hovel', also, 'a husk or hull, as of grain'. Is this actually a "different hulk" from the one meaning 'a hull or ship'? But the "same hull" with its meaning of 'hulk of a ship' is given with an additional dialectal meaning as 'a hut, hovel or shed'. Why then are the two meanings of *hulk* assigned to different hulks while the corresponding meanings of *hull* are assigned to the same hull? This question is moreover of pertinence when it is recalled that, in our chapter on the full scope of meanings associated with words, we found that the word *hole* is associated with the dialect meaning of 'a house', a meaning which is also associated with *hull* and with the *hulk* meaning 'a hut'.

It should be clear upon some reflection that the failure to mention *hull* as possibly akin to *hole* or the assigning of different meanings to "different hulks" but to the "same hull" is purely arbitrary.

Now such phoneto-semantic pairs as *hole-hollow, hole-hulk, hold-holk, hulk-howk* are illustrative merely of a few types of phonetic variants which are observed in connection with conventional etymologies. Different types of phonetic variants will be encountered in the etymologies of different words. For example, if we consult the conventional etymology of the word *wheel* we find among the variants given the following: Anglo-Saxon *hwēol, hweogul, hweowol,* Dutch *wiel,* Old Norse *hvēl, hjōl,* Greek *kyklos,* Sanskrit *cakra* (pronounced chukra), Old Slavic *kolo,* all of which mean 'wheel'. Further variants are provided by stating that English *wheel* is also related to Latin *colere* - to be busy, cultivate, dwell, to Greek *polos* - axis, *pelomai* - I go, move, am, *telos* - end, *teleos* - complete, *tēle* - far, *palai* - long ago, *palaios* - ancient, Sanskrit *carati* - he moves, goes. Disregarding for the moment the question whether the words are actually related in the sense alleged and fixing our attention on the phonetic variants, we may exhibit them, for readier comparison, as follows: *wheel* - *hwēol* - *hweogul* - *hweowol* - *wiel* - *hvēl* - *hjōl* - *kyklos* - *cakra* - *kolo* - *pol*os - *col*ere - *pel*omai - *tel*os - *pal*aios - *car*ati.

As the reader will note, there is quite a range of variation here providing new types of phonetic variants of a word. Thus *hwēol* - *hweogul* differ by the "excrescence" of a medial guttural *g,* and *hwēol* - *hweowol* similarly by the excrescence of a medial labial *w; wheel-kolo* differ by the interchange of an aspirated labial *wh* with a guttural *k, wheel* - *tel*os by an analogous interchange with a dental *t,* and so on.

As our last example illustrating how phoneto-semantic variants of a given word are obtained from the point of view of the historical approach, we consider the word *beast.* This word is stated to be related to Latin *bestia* of the same meaning. It is further stated to bear kinship with the following words: Greek *theos* - God, Lithuanian *dvase* - spirit, soul, ghost, breath, Anglo-Saxon *dwaescan* - to extinguish, Middle High German *getwas* -

39

ghost, Latin *feralis* - relating to the dead, Old Slavic *duchu* - breath, Gaulish *dusios* - unclean spirit, demon, incubus, Latin *fumus* - smoke, and English *deer*. Disregarding again for the moment the question of the genetic kinship of *beast* with the above words we therefore have the following range of phonetic variation: *beast* - *theos* - *dvase* - *dwaesc*an - *getwas* - *fer*alis - *duchu* - *dus*ios - *fum*us - *deer*.

It will be noted in the above example as in the examples of *wheel* and *hole,* that a considerable latitude in phonetic resemblance is permitted in the historical tracing of words. Not only that but a considerable latitude of semantic resemblance is similarly permitted. Thus the pair *beast -theos* do not appear to bear much resemblance either in sound or meaning. Such latitude of difference in sound and meaning resemblance of words stated to bear genetic kinship to each other is quite commonly found in conventional etymologies. It is of course assumed that in spite of the considerable divergence in sound and meaning the kinship is established through interrelations with other words with which the given pair is associated. It is nevertheless open to some question whether, and if so with what frequency, an arbitrary element does not enter into these conventional etymologies of words. *As a matter of fact such arbitrary element does enter and is to be expected from the very nature of the historical approach, an approach which fails to take into account either the full logical scope of meaning or the full logical scope of phonetic variation of words.*

CHAPTER FIVE

PHONETO-SEMANTIC WORD LINKING

IN OUR CHAPTER on sound kinship we suggested the linkage of such a word pair as *tick* (touch, tap) - *tap* (with which we also linked *touch-tag* (touch or hit) - *tat* (dial. tap, touch)). These words are not stated to be related in the conventional sense. On the other hand, the pair *stripe-streak,* evidencing the similar phonetic phenomenon of interchange of the final stops *k* - *p* is stated to be a related pair. What we propose to do in the present chapter is to remove the arbitrary element that is characteristic of the historical approach by formulating the following principle which is suggested by the concept of the full actual and potential scope of meaning associated with a word and that of the essential fluidity of sounds: *A type of phonetic change that is observed in connection with a word pair within one language must not be construed as restricted in its application to the particular word pair in question or perhaps to a few other similar word pairs but must be thought of as applying in its full logical scope to the entire native vocabulary of the language.*

We have already seen that the pair *hole-hulk* (a ship) was cited by a conventional etymology based on the historical approach as being "probably" related.

Now from our approach, to be developed in the present chapter, we do not concern ourselves primarily with such question as to whether the words are "probably" related or not. What concerns us primarily is *the fact that there exist in English native words which, like hole-hulk, are associated in meaning and evidence a particular type of phonetic difference,* in the case cited, the excrescence of a final *k* of *hulk* as compared with *hole*. In accordance with our enunciated principle above we inquire *how many other word pairs are there in English of associated meaning and exhibiting the same type of phonetic difference?* When we find such words we merely link them as constituting "phoneto-semantic pairs".

We are now ready to answer the question raised in the preceding chapter, namely, given a simple English word, to find the words associated with it in meaning and possessing what may be regarded as "related" sounds. Instead of seeking to establish a linear sequence of development in time of the word in question we focus our attention on exhibiting the *simultaneous occurrence* of phonetic variants of the word *within the same language*. Thus we do not primarily "look backward" but "look sideways and about us". Or we may also say that instead of tracking down word ancestors we round up "word cousins" of all degrees of kinship in our immediate neighborhood. By such a procedure, by which the sound and meaning resemblances of word pairs is brought into sharp relief, our attention becomes focussed on *the mutual interrelationships of the sounds and meanings of words as they are observed within any language*. We shall see presently what significance such viewpoint has in revealing to us the very nature of all words, that is, *the fundamental character of the link by which a word is associated with its meanings.*

We proceed now with a systematic discussion of the different types of phonetic variation that a word pair may exhibit. Logically considered, a word may exhibit changes in each of two distinct ways (disregarding vowel changes for the present as being of a secondary character), namely, 1. consonants may be substituted for others, and 2. consonants may be added or dropped. (It should be clearly understood that we limit our discussion throughout to words or "roots" which are not decomposable into two or more words; that is, we do not consider compound words like *transfer,* derived from the Latin *trans* - across, *and fer*re - to carry, though we would consider words or roots like *trans* and *fer*). Since every root has a beginning, middle, and end, these changes may occur initially, medially, or finally. Furthermore, any of these changes may in theory occur singly or in combination with others.

The first type of phonetic variant we shall discuss is that in which the initial consonants of words are interchanged. We have already encountered such interchange in our example of *hollow* where it was found "admissible" to interchange initial *h* with initial *k* of Greek *koil*os (under the implied assumption that *k* in *koil*os, and similarly in the case of other corresponding words such as in Greek *kardia* - English *heart,* developed by a historical process into English *h*). Similarly *wh* in *wheel* was found to interchange with *k, p, t* respectively in the Greek words *kykl*os, *pal*ai, *tel*eos.

Recalling now the concept developed in Chapter III of the kinship or "fluidity" of sounds, in particular, of the stops *k, p, t,* and looking "about us" rather than "backward" we do not hesitate to associate, as exhibiting the *wh-k* interchange, not merely English *wheel* - Old Slavic *kolo* but English *wheel* - English *coil,* one of whose meanings is 'a ring'. Recalling what was said on the vowel character and close nature of the kinship between the liquids *l-r* we associate further, as exhibiting the *wh-t* interchange, not merely *wheel* - Greek *tele*os (complete) but *wheel - tire* (a hoop or band of a wheel) and *wheel - tour* (a round, a circuit).

Before proceeding to find other phoneto-semantic relatives of *wheel* we wish to add a further remark on the kinship of *wheel* - Greek *tele*os (complete). Note that the meaning resemblance between this pair is less evident than that between *wheel-tire* or *wheel-tour.* Though less evident the linkage in meaning between *wheel-complete* can nevertheless be effected by considering for example that the word *round,* taken as a noun, includes as one of its meanings 'a ring', a meaning possessed by *wheel,* while taken as an adjective, it includes among its meanings that of 'complete'. It thus seems natural enough to link the concept of 'rounded' with that of 'complete'. As a matter of fact it is not here implied that the Greek word *teleos* is not in some way akin to the English word *wheel.* The kinship is not however necessarily genetic, that is, the word *wheel* is not necessarily derived from *teleos* by the historical conversion of *teleos* into *wheel.* The nature of the kinship between the two words will become clear after we discuss the underlying character of *all words of all languages.* Meanwhile it may be remarked that if it is not too far-fetched to link as akin English *wheel* with Greek *tele*os (complete) then it is certainly not too far-fetched to link English *wheel* with English *whole,* one of whose meanings is 'complete' and which certainly resembles *wheel* phonetically more than does Greek *tel*eos.

With the word *tour* above which means as a dialect verb 'to turn one's steps; to go' (note that *wheel,* in the conventional etymology, was related to Sanskrit *car*ati - he moves, goes) we link the obsolete word *chare* - 'to turn, a turn', the *ch* of *chare* being the palatalized *t* of *tour* (note that Sanskrit *c* in *car* has the palatal *ch* sound) and the word *sheer* - 'to turn aside, swerve'. The word *tour* is of course readily recognized as being akin to English *turn* itself, from which it differs phonetically by the relative addition of final liquid *n,* a type of phonetic variant we shall consider later on.

We thus find that our common English *wheel* which, as a verb, has the meaning 'to turn, revolve' is in fact a "phoneto-semantic cousin" of the word *turn* itself. This fact, which may appear rather surprising, will appear considerably less so after we discover, in a later chapter, what really "lies behind" such a word as *wheel* or *turn* or even a Sanskrit root such as *car* of *car*ati - 'he moves, goes'. Meanwhile however, applying our "phoneto-semantoscope" let us see if we can not "round up" a few more unsuspected cousins of *wheel.*

The *t-p* interchange that is exhibited in Greek *telē* (far)-Greek *palai* (long ago) is exhibited no less in English *tour - wire* (to coil about or encircle, to wind about) - *veer* (to change direction, to turn) - *whir* (to move, fly or revolve) - *burr* (a ring, corona, halo).

We have thus found *within English itself* a family of words all of which *overlap in meaning* and exhibit the phonetic phenomenon assumed to hold for the Greek words *kykl*os - *pal*ai - *tel*eos, namely, an interchange of the initial consonants *k, t, p* or any of their more obvious

45

modifications. Thus we have linked *wheel - whir - veer - wire - tour - sheer - chare - tire - coil.* Other examples of this type of phonetic variant will be found in the Appendix.

Suppose now we consider another type of phonetic variant likewise exhibited at the beginning of a root but this time illustrating the change effected in the root through the adding or dropping (the terms are relative and for briefness we shall henceforth use the phrase "relative excrescence") of an initial consonant. Consider the words *grate - scratch.* These words are stated in the conventional etymologies to be akin. Again we are less concerned with whether the words are related or not in the conventional sense than with the mere *fact of the existence within English itself* of pairs of words which are associated in meaning and which exhibit the type of phonetic change illustrated by *grate - scratch*, namely, the "relative excrescence" of initial *s* (the word *scratch* exhibits in addition the "palatalization" of *t* of *grate* to *tch* of *scratch*; there is however a Scottish dialectal word *scrat* meaning 'scratch' which shows no such palatalization).

In accordance with our point of view therefore we link, as phoneto-semantic variants of the type *grate- scratch,* the pair *wheel - sweel,* a Scottish word meaning 'to swirl'. Recalling the remarks in Chapter III on the nature of the kinship between the 'sibilant' *s* and 'dental' *t,* we further link *wire* (to coil about, to encircle) - *twire* (obsolete, to curl or twist), also *tour - steer* (to take a direction or course).

If we now compare *tour - twire*, both of which through different types of phonetic variants we linked with *wheel*, we see that this pair exhibits another type of phonetic variation, this time appearing in the middle

46

of a root, namely the relative excrescence of medial *w*. Another rather obvious example of such relative excrescence of medial *w* is given by *tirl* (chiefly Scottish, 'to twirl, whirl, turn rapidly) -- *twirl*.

The consonant *w* may be construed as a "semivowel" and thus is akin to the liquid *r*, which, as already discussed, similarly partakes of a vowel character. (Thus a child may pronounce *crush* as "cwush" and in fact our viewpoint explicitly recognizes the linkage in *crush - quash*, meaning 'to crush"; as already mentioned in Chapter III *r* is treated as a vowel in for example Czech and Sanskrit). We may therefore expect to observe the medial excrescence of *r* as well as *w*. As a matter of fact such pairs of words of associated meaning exhibiting the phonetic difference in question are not at all confined to such isolated cases as are observed in English *speak* - German *sprech*en or Anglo-Saxon *spec*an-*sprecc*-an, noted in the conventional etymologies, but occur with a frequency, which, until the underlying character of all words is grasped, appears surprising.

The relative excrescence of medial *r* is thus exhibited in *sweel - swirl, coil - curl, wheel - whirl, wheel - hurl* (obsolete, to turn or twist), *purl* (to whirl, wheel)- *whorl* (a coil), *ton* (obs. except dial. to turn) - *turn*, while the excrescence of medial *w* is observed in *ton- twine* (to wind, bend, turn). Further, the same linkage that is observed in *crush - quash* applies to *tirl* or *trill* (obs. to turn, twirl or roll) - *twill* (to quill or flute, dial. a spool) and to *curl - quill* (to wind on a quill; a spindle).

Observe now how our "wheel family" has grown. We have now linked as phoneto-semantic variants *wheel- whir - wire - veer - burr - purl - hurl - whirl - swirl - sweel - twill - twirl - twire - turn - ton - twine - tirl -*

47

trill - tour - sheer - steer - chare - coil - quill - curl -whorl.
Our familiar *wheel* is anything but a lonely member
whose relatives must be sought in the distant past. On
the contrary, it is tied by phonetic and semantic bonds
to existing relatives within its own immediate family, to
enumerate all of whose members would, as will be realized presently, be entirely impractical.

Since the liquids *l* and *r* are closely akin and interchangeable the relative excrescence of medial *l* should
be expected to occur with about the same frequency as
medial *r* and not only in isolated cases as in *sputter-
splutter.* A recognition of this fact helps us to understand why a word like *plat* should have the (obsolete)
meaning 'to strike, to slap' or the word *prat* should
mean (obsoletely) 'to spank, to beat' provided we know
why *pat* should mean 'to strike, to tap'; that is, *pat - plat-
prat* are phoneto-semantic variants exhibiting the relative excrescence of medial liquid *l, r,* as is also exhibited
by *cuff* (to buffet) - *cluff* (Scot. cuff, slap), or *cop* (dial.
a blow, to strike*) - *clap,* or *cob* (same as cop) - *club.*
(From the point of view of the vowel character of *r, l*
the word *prat* or *plat* may be construed as differing
from *pat* by the interchange of the medial vowel *a* of *pat*
by the "*r* vowel" or "*l* vowel", *ra, la* of *prat* or *plat*).
For other examples consult Appendix.

The consonants *m* and *n,* as discussed in our chapter
on sound kinship, are linked with *l, r* with which they
are sometimes classed as liquids, all partaking of a vowel
character. Thus we may take *pink* (to stab, to pierce as
with a sword), for example, as exhibiting the relative
excrescence of medial *n* as compared with *pick,* in the
same way that *prick* exhibits the relative excrescence of
medial *r* as compared with *pick.* It is more instructive
however, instead of viewing the *n* in such word as *pink*

as an isolated consonant, to consider *n* as imparting a "nasalization" to *k*, that is, to consider the *k* (or *ck*) in *pick* as replaced by *nk* in *pink*. Similarly, the *tt* in *butt* is replaced by "nasalized *t*", i.e. *nt*, in *bunt* (to butt) or the *t* in *put* (obs. exc. dial. to push, thrust, dial. to butt) by *nt* in *punt*.

In general the stops *k, p, t* are found to interchange with their nasalized counterparts *nk, mp, nt*. (The labial *p* is nasalized by the corresponding "labial nasal" *m*; similarly the *n* of *nk* is a "guttural *n*", the *n* of *nt* a "dental *n*" and the *n* of *nch* a "palatal *n*". The different n's are in Sanskrit distinguished by different letters of the alphabet; such distinction is of course not observed in English and would moreover, as is also true in Sanskrit, be a superfluous one since the particular shade of sound assumed by *n*, as indeed by any other consonant, automatically adjusts itself to its "environment", that is, its juxtaposition to other consonants).

Further examples exhibiting nasalization are *tack* (dial. to slap, clap) - *tank* (dial. knock, hit, bang) - *touch* (to hit or strike lightly) - *dunch* (Scot. and dial. to strike or shove with a short solid blow) - *tat* (dial. to tap, touch) - *dunt* (chiefly Scot. to strike, knock, etc. with a dull-sounding blow). (Note that the palatal *ch* in *touch* "mediates" between *tat* - *touch* - *tack* and similarly in *tank* - *dunch* - *dunt* since the *ch* may be regarded alike as palatalized *k* or palatalized *t*). "Nasalization" of *p* is exhibited in *tap* - *thump, club* - *clump*. Additional examples are given in the Appendix.

It has already been stated that not only initial *s* but initial *t* may be construed in certain word pairs as relatively excrescent initial consonants. This follows from the kinship of *s-t*. Since however all of the stops *k, p, t,* as has already been discussed in our chapter on sound

49

kinship and illustrated in our first type of phoneto-semantic variants at the beginning of this chapter, may be construed as akin to each other, a similar relative excrescence should be observed with respect to guttural *k* and labial *p*. Thus the word *quirl* (pronounced 'kwirl') meaning 'to bend, coil, twist' may be construed either as linked to *twirl* by the *k-t* kinship or as relatively excrescent to *whirl*.

We present below additional examples of the relative excrescence of initial *k*, *p*, *t* (and their more obvious modifications):

lump - clump
lop - clip
rumble - grumble
look - gleek (an enticing look)
roll - curl - crull (obs. curly)
widdle (dial. wriggle) - *twiddle* (twirl, wriggle)
rattle - prattle
rim - brim
rundle -trundle
lag (dial. slacken) - *flag*
lab (dial. blab) - *blab*
lap (a loose part) - *flap*

Further examples will be found in the Appendix.

Let us now consider still another type of phonetic variation that may be exhibited at the beginning of a word. The English *shriek* is stated to be akin to English *screak* and *screech*. We have here an example of the interchange of a single consonant sound, like *sh*, by a "composite consonant" *sk*. Now it is a characteristic of English (as it is also of the closely related German, Swedish and Dutch) that such combinations as *sk*, *st*, *sp*, that is, of a stop with a sibilant, is of relatively frequent occurrence. It is convenient, from our phoneto-semantic viewpoint, instead of regarding such combinations as composite consonants, to regard them as "unit sounds" representing the "sibilized" variants of the corresponding stops, in the same way that the combinations *nk*, *nt*, *mp* have been construed as "nasalized stops". Such interchange as *sh - sk* as in *shriek - screek* or *s - sk* as in *sklent* (obs. to slant) - *slant, sklander* (obs. slander) - *slander,* thus represents the interchange of one unit sound by another. (It is of significance in this connection to note that such "sibilized stop" need not always be represented by a "digraph", but may, like the ancient Greek letter zeta (ζ), which it is stated may have had the sound of *zd,* be represented by a single letter of the alphabet).

The "sibilization" of *k, p, t* need not always precede the consonant but may follow it, thereby giving rise to the unit sounds *ks, ps, ts.* (Note again that the sounds *ks, ps* as unit sounds are represented in the Greek alphabet by the single letters xi [ξ] and psi [ψ], while *ks* is represented in the Latin and English alphabets by the single letter *x*). As unit sounds these may interchange with the corresponding *sk, sp, st* as well as with the unsibilized *k, p, t.* We thus have such phoneto-semantic variants as *sklenter* (Scot. splinter) - *splinter* or *scatter - spatter* (to scatter by splashing). In connection with our discussion of *wheel* and its relatives we have already linked *steer - chare* (to turn) - *sheer.* This illustrates the particularly common interchange of *st* (and *sk*) with the palatal *ch* (and the voiced palatal *j*) and the sibilant *sh.* Further illustrations are offered by the pairs *stab - jab, stump - chump,* and others will be found in the Appendix.

So far we have discussed the interchange of the stops

k, p, t and their corresponding sibilized sounds *sk, sp, ts, ps*, etc. as occurring at the beginning of any word. It is quite evident however from the very nature of the concept underlying these interchanges, namely, the kinship or "fluidity" of sounds, that the same interchanges will likewise be observed at the end of words. Thus the word triplet *flip - flick - flit* or the triplet *slap - slug - slat* (a resounding blow, a slap) are two of dozens of illustrations of such interchange given in the Appendix. Again, the interchange of the final sibilized stops *sk, sp, st* with each other, with the unsibilized stops and with the palatals *ch, j* and sibilant *sh* or spirant *th* is illustrated by such examples as *box* (a receptacle) - *buck* (a basket) - *bowk* (dial. a kind of iron bucket or pail); *basket - bucket; grab - grasp; cop* (slang and dial. to catch, capture) - *cops* (obs. to fasten or shut in) - *cosp* (Anglo-Saxon a fetter); *hap* (obs. seize, snatch) - *haps* (dial. a hasp) - *hasp; husk* (an outer covering) - *hutch* (a hut or hovel) - *hud* (dial. a husk or hull) - *hut-house; tusk - tush* (a long pointed tooth, a tusk) - *tooth; bask - bathe.* (Note that *hap-cop, haps-cops* illustrate the initial interchange *k-h*). A particularly interesting example of this type of phoneto-semantic variant is furnished by *god - ghost.*

The concept of unit sounds associated with such "digraphs" as *sk, sp, nt, mp, ps*, etc. is also applicable to such combinations as *kr, kl, pr, pl, shr, sl* (the combination *sr* does not occur in English; it does of course occur in other languages as in Sanskrit), that is, to a stop or sibilant combined with one of the liquids *r, l*. Thus, instead of construing the phonetic variation illustrated by *pick-prick* or *pick-pluck* as a "relative excrescence" of medial *r, l* or as an interchange of the vowel *i* of *pick* by the "*r* or *l* vowel" we may regard the pair as exhibiting an interchange of the "rhotacized" or "lingualized" *pr, pl* for the simple stop *p*.[1]

Before proceeding with a discussion of further types of phoneto-semantic variants it is well to summarize the types we have already discussed. We may list them conveniently as follows:

1. phoneto-semantic variants illustrating the interchange of initial or final stops *k, p, t* (and their obvious variants), typified by *slap-slug-slat* or *flick-flip-flit*.
2. phoneto-semantic variants illustrating the relative excrescence of initial sibilant *s*, typified by *scratch-grate*.
3. phoneto-semantic variants illustrating the relative excrescence of initial stops *k, p, t,* (and their obvious variants) typified by *lump-clump, lunge-plunge, rundle-trundle*.
4. phoneto-semantic variants illustrating the interchange of initial or final unit sounds *st, sp, sk, ts, ps, ks* with each other and with simple sounds, typified by *stab-jab, steer-chare-sheer, grab-grasp, hut-hutch-husk*.
5. phoneto-semantic variants illustrating the relative excrescence of medial "semi-vowel" *w* and liquids *l, r, n, m,* typified by *titter-twitter, sputter-splutter, prick-pick, pick-pink, club-clump*.

We proceed to discuss several additional types.

We have found, in connection with the word *wheel* that the Anglo-Saxon possessed the variants *whēol, hweogul, hweowol*. This example thus illustrates the relative excrescence of a guttural *g* or labial *w* before a final

1. It may be remarked, as providing further insight into the significance of the construing of such "digraphs" as *pr, tr, pl, tl* etc. as unit sounds, that in some American Indian languages, as for example in Eskimo, Nahuatl and Navaho, the characteristic sound combination *dl* or *tl* is generally recognized as a unit sound sometimes represented by a single letter. See our further discussion below on the type of phoneto-semantic variant illustrated by *nill* (a dialectal variant of needle) - *needle*.

53

liquid *l*. A similar excrescence of a dental *d* before final *l* is illustrated by the pair *nill* (dial. Eng. variant of needle) - *needle*. Thus, in addition to the relative excrescence of medial *l*, *r*, *w*, *m*, *n*, as discussed above, we here encounter the relative excrescence of any of the medial stops *k*, *p*, *t* (and their more obvious modifications). Again, in accordance with our fundamental principle, namely, that any phonetic variant, noted in any particular case, can not, on the basis of the "fluidity" concept, be construed as isolated but must have a wide scope of application, we can seek and find further word pairs illustrating this type of variant. By doing so we obtain a greater insight into the nature of the words that are paired. Thus we find the phoneto-semantic linkages: *ball-bubble, flare-flicker-flutter, trill-trickle-dribble, bowl-bottle, glare-glitter-glimmer, sneer-snicker, pool-puddle*. The additional examples given in the Appendix emphasize the frequency of occurrence and significance of this type of phoneto-semantic variant.

The above type of phoneto-semantic variant now leads us to consider two other types. For it seems sufficiently obvious that the word *bottle,* for example, is akin, as stated in the dictionary, to the word *butt* meaning ' a cask'. Therefore the word *bowl,* which we linked with *bottle,* is likewise a phoneto-semantic variant of *butt*. We are thus led first to consider the type of phoneto-semantic variant in which a final *t* interchanges with an *l*, or in general, a final stop *k*, *p*, *t* interchanges with a liquid *l* or *r*, and secondly, the type of phoneto-semantic variant in which the words compared differ by the relative excrescence of final *l* or, more generally, of any consonant.

In our chapter on sound kinship we did not, in order

not to confuse the reader with too extended a discussion, consider the nature of the kinship of the stops *k, p, t* with the liquids *l, r*. We must now consider this question briefly.

It will at first glance probably appear as rather odd to the reader that such sound as *d* is in any sense akin to the sound *l* for example. Consider however the fact, namely, that the Old Latin form for *lingua* - 'tongue' was *dingua*. Evidently there has been an interchange of *d-l*, which implies an affinity or kinship between the two sounds. Now in saying that *d* is akin to *l* it is proper to ask "which d" is meant? For, as a matter of fact, there is more than one variety of *d* just as there is more than one variety of *r*. For it has already been emphasized, in the chapter on sound kinship, that, properly speaking, an isolated letter of the alphabet has no unique sound of its own, but possesses rather a range of sounds, any particular one of which depends on the "environment" in which the letter occurs, that is, the sounds to which it is juxtaposed or in the neighborhood of which it occurs.

Now we have for example referred to the letters *t, d* as "dental". This however is not, strictly speaking, an accurate characterization for not all t's and d's are dental. In fact, initial English *t, d* might generally more aptly be described as "gingival" (from the Latin *gingiva*- 'gum') since they are more nearly pronounced with the tongue near the gums than near the teeth, as they are pronounced in Italian. It will be recalled now that, in our chapter on sound kinship, certain consonants were characterized as "cerebral" or "retroflex". Thus, the Sanskrit alphabet, to which we have already had occasion to refer several times, possesses, as distinct letters of the alphabet, the so-called cerebral *t* and *d*, which are

55

distinguished from "ordinary" or "dental" *t* and *d*. The cerebral (or retroflex) letters are pronounced by turning the tongue as far back as possible and touching the palate. Other letters besides *t* and *d* may of course be "retroflexed" by being pronounced far back in the mouth. Thus Sanskrit further distinguishes by separate letters of the alphabet "ordinary" or dental *s* and cerebral *s* which tends to be pronounced like *sh* (there is also a "palatal" *s*). Now the fact that the varieties of *t, d* are, as in Sanskrit, distinguished by separate letters of the alphabet does not mean of course that in a language where such alphabetic distinction is not made such varieties do not exist. In fact, "cerebral" *t, d* exists in English as well as in Sanskrit. For when the consonant *t* or *d* is in the neighborhood of other sounds, whether vowels or consonants, which have a cerebral character, the *t* or *d* must "adjust itself to its environment" by assuming a similar character. Thus *t* and *d* in such English words as *butter, ladder* are cerebral. It will be observed now that in a "somewhat careless" pronounciation these words are hardly distinguishable in sound from "burrer", "larrer". That is, the *t* and *d* in the cerebral or retroflex position are very closely akin to the sound of *r* pronounced back in the mouth, that is, "cerebral" *r*. Since the "ordinary" sounds and the cerebral sounds are modifications of each other we may thus say in general that the sounds *t, d, r, l* can be construed as being akin to each other. Thus such pairs as *roe - doe, ring - ding, rap - tap, lug - tug, lag - tag* are phoneto-semantic variants illustrating the interchange of the dentals *t, d* with the liquids *l, r* at the beginning of words. The pairs *knot* (any swelling or protuberance in the tissues of a plant) - *knur* (a hard excrescence, as in a tree trunk) or *knot* (Scot. a knob-shaped hill) - *knoll* (a little round hill, a mound) illustrate the corresponding interchange at the end of words.[2]

We come now to the second of the two types of phoneto-semantic variants we are led to consider from our example of the pair *bowl-bottle,* namely, that which is illustrated by *butt-bottle,* or in general, the type where the two words differ by the relative excrescence of a final consonant. The final consonant may be any of the liquids *r, l, m, n,* the stops *k, p, t* or any of the modifications of the latter.

In our earlier chapters we have already mentioned as a commonly recognized example of this type of phoneto-semantic variant the pair *hole-hollow* and further compared *hollow-holgh* (Middle English hollow) and *hole-hulk, hole-hold* (of a ship) all considered as akin from the conventional historical viewpoint. Again applying our fundamental principle we remove the arbitrary restriction that this type of phoneto-semantic variant is observed only in isolated cases. We therefore link as further examples exhibiting the same type of phonetic variation such pairs as *bore - burrow, shin - shank, tell - talk, well* (obs. to boil) - *wallop* (dial. to boil), *wire* (to wind about) - *warp* (swerve, turn or bend), *stir - start, bud - button, ball - bulb - bulge, peck - pecket* (to peck repeatedly). Like the other types of phoneto-semantic variants their frequency is of far greater scope than is suggested by the above illustrations. Other examples are given in the Appendix.

2. It will add to our further insight into the nature of this interchange of dentals with liquids if illustrations are given from other languages. Thus in Gujarati, an "Indo-Aryan" language spoken in the Gujarat province of India, the common people are said to confuse constantly the three consonants *d, l, r.* In Swahili, a native African language, the *d* is felt to be so distinctly related to *r* that after the prefix *n,* placed before many nouns and adjectives, every *r,* which the Swahilis have difficulty in distinguishing from *l,* becomes a *d,* thus, *refu - ndefu* (long), similarly *limu - ndimu* (lime).

It is convenient at this point to illustrate the application of the phoneto-semantic viewpoint to gain better insight into the true nature of "diminutive" endings such as *en* of *kitten* or into the true nature of the "frequentative" ending *le* of *waggle* (as contrasted with *wag*).

In comparing the Middle English *holgh* with Middle English *holow* or with modern *hollow* it will be noted that the latter has a short vowel before its final consonant as compared with the absence of such vowel before the final consonant of the former. A similar difference is observed in comparing for example Swedish *huvud* (head) with German *Haupt* (head). Now we shall find it of significance from our viewpoint to construe such vowel as the second *o* in *hollow* or the second *u* in *huvud* as a "neutral link vowel", that is, one which merely serves the purpose of facilitating the phonetic linkage of the final consonant to the preceding one. From this point of view the words *hollow* or *huvud* are, like *holgh* and *Haupt,* construed as *essentially one-syllable words.*

Now in such a word pair as *pack-packet,* the *et* of *packet* is generally interpreted as an independent syllable possessing a diminutive significance. A similar significance is assigned in English to the ending *ock,* viewed as an independent syllable, as in *hill - hillock,* also to *en* as in *cat - kitten.* (In German the syllable *el* and in Latin the syllable *ul* are similarly assigned diminutive meanings, as in *Maid - Mädel,* Latin *catulus* (young animal, esp. dog or cat)). In the pairs *peck - peckle* (to peck lightly and repeatedly) and *pat - patter* the syllables *le* and *er* are similarly assigned a "frequentative" meaning. In accordance with our viewpoint however the interpretation of such final syllables as *et, en, ock, le, er* as possessing in themselves a diminutive or frequentative significance is, so to speak, an "afterthought". Such pairs as *cat-kitten, peck-peckle, pat-patter* essentially exhibit the relative excrescence of final consonants to which a diminutive, frequentative, or other interpretation *is conveniently assigned,* in accordance with the "vocabulary building mechanism" to be described in a later chapter.

We may therefore expect that any diminutive or other interpretation of the final syllable is not clear-cut and need not be felt at all. As a matter of fact there is no distinction in meaning between *peckle* and *pecket* (to peck repeatedly) or between *jiggle* and *jigget* (colloq. to move in a jigging or jerky way), there being no more justification for construing the final *le* of these words as an inherently frequentative ending than there is for construing the final *et* as a frequentative ending. Similarly there is no essential distinction between *wag-waggle, kit - kitten, tump* (a hillock) - *tummock* (a hillock) or between *hill,* in the sense of 'a heap or mound', and *hillock.*

Our viewpoint on the nature of the final syllable will be further clarified if we compare, as phoneto-semantic variants of the same type as "hole-hollow", the pair *well* (to seethe) - *wallop* (dial. to boil with a continued boiling noise). The final *ock* of *hillock, et* and *le* of *pecket* and *peckle, er* of *patter* and *en* of *kitten* are construed as being essentially of the same "relatively excrescent character" as the *op* of *wallop* as compared with *well,* where the syllable *op* is not associated with any particular significance. The endings *et, en, le* (equivalent to *el*), *er, ock* are therefore not construed as independent suffix syllables but simply as final consonants joined to the preceding consonants by a neutral linking vowel, the entire word, like the words *huvud* (Swedish 'head') and *hollow* above, being construed as an *essentially one-syllable word*.

We can gain further insight into the significance of the remarks made above if we consider the final consonants or syllables from still another viewpoint. In connection with our discussion of the sibilized stops, *sk, sp, st, ks, ps, ts,* we noted that these may interchange with one another giving such phoneto-semantic variants as *hasp - haps* (dial. English variant of hasp) or *wips* (obs. wisp) *-wisp*. These examples illustrate the relative inversion of the final two consonants *s, p*. A similar inversion should be observed between any two final consonants, in particular, between two final consonants one of which is any of the liquids *l, r, n*. Construing the *e* of *er* in for example the word *patter* as a neutral linking vowel, we therefore associate the pair *patter* (to chatter; talk glibly) - *prate* as illustrative of a type of phoneto-semantic variant in which the position of the final two consonants is relatively reversed.

In order to bring out more clearly the frequency of occurrence of this type of phoneto-semantic variant and its significance in relation to the above remarks on the diminutive, frequentative and other interpretations of final syllables we give below some additional examples illustrating this variant type.

flitter (dial. flutter, flicker) - *flirt* (to move jerkily, obs. to flick)

sputter - spurt (to spout forth; obs. to sprout, shoot up) - *sprout*

spatter (to scatter by splashing; to sprinkle around) - *spread*

batter - prat (obs. to spank, beat) - *patter* (to strike with a quick succession of sounds)

60

paddle (to beat or stir with a paddle) - *plat* (obs. to strike, slap) - *pelt*

peckle (to peck slightly or repeatedly) - *plug* (slang, to strike with the fist; punch)

plum (obs. to fall like a plumb; dial. to plump) - *pummel* (to thump)

waggle - *walk* (obs. to toss to and fro)

wabble - *wallop* (to move in a rolling cumbersome fashion; waddle)

waddle - *waltz* (German *walz*en - to roll)

chatter - *clat* (dial. chatter)

cackle - *clack*

babble - *blab*

dagger - *dirk*

jigger (colloq. to jerk) - *jerk* - *jiggle*

fickle (not fixed or firm) - *flick* - *wiggle* - *waggle*

smicker - *smirk*

daggle (to draggle) - *drag*

fimble (dial. to feel with the fingers moving lightly over anything) - *palp* (to touch, feel)

bubble - *bleb* (a bubble)

pebble - *blob* (dial. a bubble or pustule; a pimple; a small lump of something viscid or thick) - *pimple*

cobble - *club* - *clump*

coggle (a cobblestone) - *clog* (Scot. a short thick piece of wood); *cudgel* (German *Kugel* - a ball)

wattle (to plat) - *plat*

guggle (dial. the windpipe) - *gorge*

kittle (to kitten, bring forth young) - *child* (obs. to produce young)

kitten - *kind* (obs. to beget, German *Kind* - child)

It should of course be clear that the linking of a word pair as illustrating a particular type of phoneto-semantic variant is quite independent of any linking of the same words to others as illustrating a different type of phoneto-semantic variant. Thus the linkage *waggle - walk* is independent of the linkages *wag - waggle,* or *wag* (obs. to wander from place to place; coll. to go, depart) - *walk,* illustrating other types of phoneto-semantic variants already discussed.

We shall close this chapter by considering one more type of phoneto-semantic variant. The type just discussed illustrates the relative inversion of part of a root, that is, of the last two consonants. Now the simple example of *pat - tap* illustrates the inversion of the consonants of a word as a whole. We therefore inquire, as in the case of the other types considered, is this example a more or less isolated one and if not with what frequency does this phenomenon of the relative inversion of roots occur within English for example?

In answer to this question we find as a result of our quest for such "inverse" word pairs, that is, pairs of words which have associated meanings and exhibit the sounds in reverse, that the frequency of their occurrence is much greater than one would at first suppose. In fact, the phenomenon of "relative inversion" occurs with as great a frequency as the most frequent types of variants discussed above. This statement may strike us as surprising since it seems to be indicative of a certain degree of "unconcern" as to which "direction" a word is pronounced. Once we realize however just what sort of entity a word actually is, the statement will acquire an entirely "reasonable" character. (We therefore expressly avoid the term "metathesis" which is applied to certain observed isolated cases as misleading in its implication of a "mispronunciation").

For the present however let us, on a purely classificatory basis, that is, without seeking the reason why it should be so, take note of the fact that the phoneto-semantic variants of the inverse type do occur, in English for example, with considerable frequency.

The pair *pat - tap* illustrates a particularly simple type of inversion, namely, that of words consisting of an initial and final consonant sound with an intervening vowel. Let us see now how we may augment this pair by applying the principles of sound kinship already discussed in Chapter III. Since *b, d* are simply voiced *p, t,* we may augment the above pair as follows: *pat - tap - bat* (to beat) - *dab* (to strike or hit with a sudden motion; to peck) - *beat*. Further, since *ch, j* are palatalized *t, d,* while *sh* is akin to *ch,* we can add *bash* (dial. beat, smash) - *jab - tup* (to butt, as a ram) - *put* (dial. to thrust, push) - *butt - push* (dial. to butt) - *shove*. But, as already discussed in the chapter on sound kinship, not only may *ch, j,* be construed as palatalized *t, d;* they may also be construed as palatalized *k, g,* the palatals serving to mediate between the dentals *t, d* and gutturals *k, g.* Further, the kinship of *h-wh-w-f-v-m* is of a more evident type. We may thus augment our initial *pat-tap* to form the following "pat family":

pat - tap - bat - dab - beat - bash - jab - tup - put - butt - push - shove - cop (dial. to strike) - *puck* (dial. to strike, butt) - *cob* (dial. to strike, beat) - *buck* (colloq. to butt) - *cuff - whack - hack - paik* (Scot. to strike, beat) - *chop* (to make a quick stroke) - *peck* (strike with the beak, colloq. to eat) - *potch* (dial. slap, strike) - *chap* (obs. exc. dial. chop, pound, mash) - *peg - butch* (dial. to hack) - *chip* (to cut small pieces from) - *bite - cham* (obs. exc. dial. to chew, bite, champ) - *chew - champ - tew* (obs. exc. dial. beat).

Each of the above words is associated in meaning

63

with a striking action which may take the form of a 'butting', 'jabbing', 'shoving', 'pecking', 'hacking'. Note the *interplay of meanings*. The inclusion of such words as *bite* and *chew* in the "pat family" will then be understood. The meanings of these words involve the idea of striking that is expressed in a more explicit form in *pat-tap*. A further discussion of "striking words" and their significance will be given in later chapters.

In addition to the *pat-tap* type, inversions are observed of pairs of words consisting of more than two consonant sounds. Illustrations are offered by *club - block, knob - bunch, whisk - scuff* (brush aside, wipe off). If we now recall what was said on the "r and l vowels", on the "nasalized consonants" *nk, mp, nt* and on the "sibilized" unit sounds *sk, sp, st, ts,* etc. it will be seen that this type is not essentially different in character from the *pat-tap* type, that is, it exhibits the inversion of words that consist of initial and final "unit sounds" with a medial vowel. The *club - block* pair may be augmented to form the wider group: *club - block - clump - group - flock - crew,* and similarly for the others.

In connection with our inverse type of phonetosemantic variants we have thus given a "family" of words grouped about some given word. The members of a family have of course associated meanings whose "shades of difference" exhibit various degrees. It is natural, in thus linking words of associated sound and meaning, that the attention is thereby focussed on the *interplay* of the definitions recorded by the dictionary of the different words. This in turn leads to a consideration of what actually "lies behind" a word's meaning, that is, precisely what is the nature of the link which associates the word sound with the word sense. One outstanding fact should now be clearly evident to the reader. A word, if it is desired to obtain any true insight into its nature, is not to be treated either as an isolated member of the native vocabulary or as a member of a relatively small group of words of different related languages. Instead of thinking about words we must think of word families *within the same language.* This viewpoint will be further elaborated in the following two chapters.

CHAPTER SIX

WORD VARIABLES

WE HAVE AT THE END of the preceding chapter given illustrations of "word families" clustering about a given word within a given language. In this connection we wish in the present chapter to introduce the concept of a "word variable".

This concept is simply a logical extension of the concept of phoneto-semantic linkage of word pairs, as discussed in the preceding chapter. The concept is particularly useful as we shall see in focussing the attention on *the interplay of sound and meaning* of words within a given language and provides us with added insight into the nature of the phoneto-semantic linkages.

The term "variable" is familiar in connection with its use in mathematics to denote a quantity that may assume a succession of values. The variable itself is therefore not a value and is not represented by a particular value but may be represented by a succession of values or by a "form" which may assume any particular value or a sequence of values.[1]

1. The concept of variable is used in connection with symbolic logic in such terms as a "propositional function", that is, a "blank form" proposition which becomes a specific proposition when the blanks are filled by specific subjects and predicates. Our concept of word variable as discussed below is not to be confused with such logical terms as these since we are not here directly concerned with questions of logic. Naturally however since we *are* concerned with *meaning* our phoneto-semantic viewpoint necessarily does have a bearing on those problems that come within the province of logic. Such bearing will briefly be touched upon in the final chapter.

Let us see now how the concept of "variable" can be introduced in connection with words and how such concept helps us to gain a better insight into the nature of the link that associates the sound of a word with its meaning.

It should be remembered that there are two correlated ideas standing in reciprocal relation to each other which underlie the phoneto-semantic approach, namely,

1. to each simple word there corresponds a range of meanings which diverge to various degrees from each other

2. to any meaning that may be assigned there corresponds a range of words of associated meanings that exhibit "related" sounds. By considering these two ideas simultaneously we arrive at the idea of a "word variable". The concept will best be brought out in connection with a specific illustration.

Consider therefore the simple "native" English word *knot*. The meaning that is immediately associated with this word is that given by the first definition in a standard dictionary (as is our practice we shall always, in giving a word's meaning, refer to Webster's but it should be clearly understood that any other standard dictionary would equally serve our purpose of illustration), namely, 1. An interlacement of the parts of one or more slender and flexible bodies, as cordage, forming a lump or knob'. By principle 1. above we must give due weight to all the definitions given of the word. We need therefore to know that *knot* is associated with (among others) the following further definitions:

2. Figuratively a. something not easily solved, b. the main point of a problem; the point of a story

3. An ornament tied in a knot, a bow

4. A knob, lump or protuberance, as in a muscle or gland

5. A cluster of persons or of things; collection; group; band; clique

6. A carved or hammered knob or boss; a stud

7. A knob-shaped hill; a moderately high rocky summit or peak. Scot. and N. of Eng.

8. a. Any swelling or protuberance in the tissues of a plant, as the node of grass; hence any unusual excrescence, esp. the hard irregular lump formed at the point of insertion of a branch in a tree trunk. b. a bud.

Now it is well for the reader to reflect on these definitions. They are evidently not independent but are obtained from each other by dwelling on and emphasizing a particular aspect of the idea that is associated with *knot*. In accordance with the prevailing notions the "primary" idea of *knot* is that given by its first definition. In accordance with the viewpoint here presented however, as already stated in Chapter II on the scope of definition of words, there is no definition which is "inherently primary" although at any given time some definition may be more predominant than others. The full significance of this statement will be grasped when we discuss the basic character of all words. It will however also be seen to be justified on the basis of the concept of a "word variable" which we now present.

We note then that one of the meanings associated with *knot* is 'a knob, lump or protuberance'. We therefore link phoneto-semantically *knot* and *knob*, (which means 'a rounded protuberance', etc.). Noting further

that *knot* has the meaning 'any swelling or protuberance in the tissues of a plant as the node of grass' we
further link *knot* and *knag* one of whose meanings is 'a
knot in wood'. We thus have the linkage *knot - knob -
knag* which are phoneto-semantic variants of the type
exhibiting interchange in the final stop, *k, p, t* (or any
of their more obvious modifications).

Now once we are aware of the fact that a "word
triplet" like *knot - knob - knag* exists which evidences
an association of meaning and a certain clearly defined
phonetic difference it is only natural that we should seek
to extend such group by "hunting" *within the native
vocabulary* for additional words that could be included
within the "knot family", that is, whose meanings are
associated with *knot* and whose final consonants may be
regarded as more or less obvious modifications of the
stops *k, p, t.* We thus find that we can extend our group
by adding the word *knop*, which means 'a knob; a bud;
a button, Scot. and dial. a projection up or out, as a
hill', *knap*, meaning 'a top or crest (of a hill); a summit,
hill; knoll', *knock*, a Scottish word meaning 'a hill; hillock'. (Compare these definitions with the definition of
knot as a 'knob-shaped hill; a moderately high rocky
summit or peak'). Further we can add the word *knitch*,
a dialect word meaning 'a bundle or fagot' (compare
with the meaning of *knot* as 'a cluster of persons or
things'). In addition we can add *knub*, a dialect word
meaning 'lump; knob' and *knuck*, a colloquial word
stated to be 'short for knuckle'. The word "knuckle" includes among its meanings the obsolete one of 'a joint
of a plant; a node' (compare with the definition of *knag*
and of *knot* - 'a node of grass'). Recalling what was said
in the chapter on the kinship of the labials *p, b, w, m, v,*

69

f and the vowels we link *knob - know* (Scot. and N. of Engl. a hill or mound). Further, recalling the semi-vowel character and therefore the interchangeability with each other of *w, r, l,* we link *know - knoll* (a little round hill, a mound) - *knur* (a hard excrescence, a gnarl) - *knar* (a knot or burr in wood). (Recall also discussion of preceding chapter). Further, recalling the interchange of the "unit sounds" *sk, sp, st, ks, ps, ts,* with each other and with the corresponding unsibilized sounds, we add *knosp,* meaning 'a knob; a boss'.

We have thus expanded our *knot-knob-knag* triplet into the variant group: *knot - knitch - knock - knag - knuck - knop - knob - knap - knosp - knub - know - knoll - knar - knur.* All these words have associated meanings, which in some cases may coincide or overlap, and exhibit the common feature of a difference in the final consonant.

Now a word group such as the above suggests that we formulate the following concept with respect to words. In place of a "static" view it appears more significant to take a "dynamic" view of words. That is, we regard both the sounds of words and the meanings associated with them essentially fluid in character. By this we mean simply that instead of regarding *knot* and its meanings, *knob* and its meanings, etc. in isolation and essentially independently of each other, we regard, borrowing the language of mathematics, such group of words as *knot-knob-knag-know-knoll,* etc. as representing different "values" of one "word variable". The particular type of phonetic change exhibited represents the result of the operation of a "phonetic operator" or "function". In the last analysis, the action of such "phonetic operator" is intimately associated with the very mechanism of speech production, the underlying concept being the essential fluidity and therefore interchangeability of sounds.

From the viewpoint here developed therefore, in considering the sound and definition of any simple common word, we must always be aware of the existence *within the same language* of other words of sounds and meanings associated with the given word, that is, of other "values" of the "word variable" of which the given word represents but one "value". With this in mind *a deeper insight is gained into the scope of meaning associated with the given word.*

Let us bring out the significance of the last statement by dwelling somewhat further on the values of the "knot variable". Once a word exhibits a modification in sound, the language avails itself of the multiplicity of words thereby produced to associate with each a more or less circumscribed meaning. That is, the words acquire different "shades of meaning" making them, in some instances at least, not interchangeable. *In this manner different words spring into being within a language.* Thus, the particular value of the "knot variable" *knag,* like the word *knot* means 'a knot in wood', but while it may be possible in some cases to use *knot* and *knag* interchangeably in this sense, the word *knag,* in view of the range of definition at present associated with it, can not interchange with *knot* in the sense of 'a cluster; a group'. Note however that both 'a knot in wood' and 'a cluster' *can be linked in thought* as "varieties of a lump".

To continue with our illustration, the word *knot* has as one of its meanings "a lump, a protuberance". Now a "bud" is a small lump of a sort while a "hill" or "hillock" may be viewed as a large lump, and as a matter of fact, as already pointed out, the word *knot* has both the meanings of 'bud' and 'hillock'. The Scottish word *knock,* however, which in accordance with our concept is a value of the word variable associated with the "knot complex", is "reserved" for the meaning of 'hillock' and can not therefore interchange with *knot* in the sense of 'a bud' for example. Associated with the idea of 'a lump or protuberance' is also that of 'a cluster or group', a meaning which, as we have seen, is likewise possessed by *knot.* The value *knitch,* however, of the word variable associated with the "knot complex" is "reserved" to designate 'a fagot, a bundle'.

The "shades of meaning" that distinguish the different values of the word variable may differ in "thickness" and may become thick enough so that the linkage in meaning may not at once be apparent. The linkage however can nevertheless be effected. This fact is a consequence of *the psychological thought process itself that is characteristic of the human mode of thought by which concepts are linked, one idea leading to another "related" idea.* We shall give further illustrations of the operation of this process in our next chapter on the "vocabulary building mechanism".

The "word variable", then, focusses the attention on the variable or dynamic aspect of words and actually exhibits *the utilization of the fluidity of sounds for the production of new words.* Once however the full significance of this idea is fully grasped, it will be seen to be natural, given certain words, to expect in advance the occurrence of other words, associated in sound and meaning with the given words. *We are thus in some measure able to predict the occurrence of certain words and meanings within a language.* This is a very striking result whose significance can best be brought out with the aid of illustrations.

It will be noted in our "knot variable" that it includes among its values words of a generally unfamiliar kind. Thus it includes the word *know*, a Scottish word with the meaning of 'a knoll or mound'. Now the author could hardly be expected to be on terms of intimate acquaintance with regional, dialectal, obsolete, colloquial, slang, and in general less well known words, and therefore "to know" that there is "another know" in the Scottish dialect with the meaning given. As a matter of fact, the author was quite unaware of the existence of such a word. What he did was simply to "guess" that such word as *know* with the meaning of 'knoll' or similar associated meaning *could occur in English*, possibly as a dialect word, an obsolete word, or some other "unusual" word, and such guess was confirmed by looking for and actually finding the word recorded in an "unabridged" dictionary. The existence of *know* meaning 'a knoll or mound' could be predicted as plausible from the consideration of the interchange of the "semi-vowels" *w* with *l* in *knoll-know,* as is exhibited in such further example as *poll* (the head) - *pow* (dialectal variant of poll)[2] The possible existence of *know* with the meaning 'knoll' could also be predicted from the concept that the labial *w* of *know* is akin to the labial *b* of *knob* (a lump; a rounded hill) or from the kinship of *w* with the *g* of *knag* (or the *ck* of *knock*) as illustrated by *drag-draw.*

In connection with such prediction through the con-

2. The interchange of "semi-vowel *l*" with full vowel *ow* is merely an instance in English of the regularly observed interchange of final *l* of Latin words to final *eau* (*o*) of French as observed in *bel-beau,* etc. As usual, instead of interesting ourselves in any particular "consonant shift" between languages we focus our attention on the underlying significance and general applicability of the type of "shift" illustrated.

cept of word variable of the existence of words, it is of significance to consider the following. While we have in our discussion above confined our attention to the operation of the word variable idea *within a given language,* specifically English, it is evident that it would not take us too far afield if we included in our consideration words from such languages as German, Dutch or Swedish, languages which have an obviously close kinship with English. These languages may in fact be construed as constituting together with English a group of more or less divergent dialects *of a single language.* We may therefore extend the "variable field" of an English word variable so as to include "values" obtained from these languages. In doing so we gain added insight both into the significance of the word variable concept and the concept of "kinship" between two such languages as English and German for example.

Let us illustrate this by returning to our familiar "knot variable". We saw that we could extend our values by predicting the occurrence of such value as *know.* Similarly, since *f* is a "more emphatic w", we might guess for example that some such English word like "knuff", whether dialectal, obsolete, etc. might occur in English with a meaning associated with that of *knob* or *know.* Search in the dictionary does in fact reveal the existence of a "knuff", which is stated to be an obsolete variant of *gnof,* the latter meaning however, as an obsolete word, 'a churl; lout'. There is also found a word *kneaf,* a dialectal English variant of *nieve,* which, as an archaic and dialectal word, means 'the fist; the hand'. Neither of these words apparently has any association with any of the meanings of *knot* or *knob* so that we do not (for the present at least) include these words as

74

values of our "knot variable". We find however, by extending our "field of variables" into German, the value *Knauf,* meaning 'a button, knob', while the word *Knopf,* in which the final *p* and *f* seem to be "in competition", means 'button, button-like thing, knot, knob, bud, dumpling', also colloquially, 'fellow'.

Again, knowing the existence of *knosp,* we might guess, in view of what we already know of the interchangeability of final *sp, sk, st, ps, ts, ks,* some such word in English like "knost", "knist", etc. Search in the English dictionary fails to reveal (at least in Webster's) the existence of such a "word value" in English. There is however a German *Knast* which means 'knot (in wood), log of oak; stiff person', while Dutch *knoest* means 'knot, gnarl' and Dutch *knots* means 'club, cudgel'.

Thus if we extend our "field of variables" so as to include such obviously related languages as German, Dutch, Swedish, we may fill in, at least in some cases, the "gaps" that occur in the English values.

In connection with these "gaps" it is now of significance to make the following observations. We saw above that we were apparently unsuccessful in predicting the existence of some such word as "knuff" with a meaning more or less associated with that of *knob* or *knot.* We did indeed verify the existence of a "knuff" with the meaning however 'obs. a churl; a lout', and also found a "kneaf", a dialectal English variant of the archaic and dialectal word "nieve" meaning 'the fist; the hand', both sets of meanings having at first glance no association with those associated with *knot* or *knob.* But are we sure that such is in fact the case?

Let us utilize our extended field of variables made

available by the inclusion of languages closely related to English to show that the words *knuff* and *kneaf* are in fact values of the "knot variable".

It will have been remarked that the German word *Knopf*, in addition to its meaning of 'button, knob, bud' has the colloquial meaning 'a fellow'. In connection with the "knob-fellow" meaning association note further the meanings associated with the German word pair: *Knoten* - 'a knot, knob', *Knote* - 'a boor'. Similarly compare German *Knopf* with German *Knabe* - 'boy, lad' and *Knappe* - 'boy, youth' and compare these with English *knave* meaning 'a tricky, deceitful fellow' and archaically 'a boy servant'. Note further the 'knob or lump' - 'boy or fellow' semantic linkage in the definitions given of the following English words:

knar—'a knot or burr in wood', also, 'obs, a tough thickset man'

chump—'a short thick heavy piece of wood; a block', also, 'colloq. a blockhead'

chunk—'dial. a log, stump or stick, colloq. a short thick fragment', also, 'colloq. a short thickset person'

club—'a knob or bunch', also, 'obs. an awkward fellow, a yokel'

lump—'a piece or mass of indefinite shape, a protuberance', also, 'colloq. a sluggish or dull person; a heavy-set or sturdy person'

Evidently the idea of 'a block or lump of some kind' as associated with *knob* and *knot* is also linked with the idea of 'a boy, a lad, a fellow, a chump'. It is clear then that our word *knuff* meaning 'a churl; a lout' as well as the more familiar *knave* constitute values of the "knot variable". Indeed it will be evident on a little reflection that the word *chunk* itself is the word *knag* or *knock* with *k* palatalized to *ch* just as the word *chump* is the word *knob* or *knop* with *k* palatalized to *ch* and with the natural replacement of *n* by *m* immediately before the labial.

Similarly our word *kneaf* meaning 'the fist; the hand' turns out to be a value of the "knot variable" if we note for example that Dutch *knuist* means 'fist', Dutch *knok* means 'knuckle' (compare with *knuck,* 'short for knuckle') and that English *knuckle* as a noun means 'a sharply flexed part or loop' while as a verb it means 'to bend the fingers as in clenching the fist'. If we note further that the word *knuckle* means also 'the knee or hock joint of a quadruped' and 'obs. a joint of a plant; a node' and that the word *knee* has such meanings as ' a joint or articulation, as in certain grasses; a rounded or spurlike process arising from the roots of certain swamp-growing trees' it is evident that we can add the word *knee* itself to our "knot variable".

It is possible, by construing the *na* in for example *knag* as a "nasalized vowel" or as an *"n* vowel" and construing the medial *lo* in for example *clod* as an *"l* vowel", to extend our range of word values further by such values as *cob* - 'a lump or piece of anything', *club, clump, clod, clog* - 'a block or lump'; Scot. 'a log', and so forth. It is of course not practical to cite all the definitions given after a word in the dictionary so as to exhibit the full interplay of corresponding meanings.

By thus viewing a given word not as a more or less isolated static entity but as merely one of a dynamic series of values of a word variable some of the "mystery" that is associated with any particular value, that is, with a given simple word, is dissolved. We are therefore to some extent able to answer the simple and fundamental question, namely, why do words mean what they do?

77

Thus we may say that we know to some extent why Scottish *know* should mean 'a knoll or mound' if we view it as one of the members of the series: *knop - knob - know - knoll - knar,* etc. in which it is "imbedded". We shall find the mystery of "why know means know", or indeed why any simple word should mean what it does, dissolved still further as we proceed with our discussion.

CHAPTER SEVEN

THE VOCABULARY BUILDING MECHANISM

THE CONCEPT OF "word variable" presented in the preceding chapter calls our attention sharply, as already remarked, to the *interplay* of the meanings that are associated with words. Though the "shade of meaning" may become "thick" enough so that the linkage in meaning may not at once be apparent, such linkage, through a consideration of the full interplay of the meanings of the "values" of the word variable, can nevertheless be effected. And as already observed, this fact is a consequence of the psychological process itself that is characteristic of the human mode of thought by which common conceptual elements are constantly recognized, one idea being linked to another "related" idea.

In the present chapter we wish to exhibit, more fully than we did in the previous chapter, the mode of operation of this process in giving rise to the native vocabulary of a language. We shall refer to this process as "the vocabulary building mechanism" for it actually *exhibits* the manner by which, through "differentiation" and "specialization" the different words constituting the basic vocabulary of a language come into being. This "mechanism" is itself merely an expression of the full force of application of the phoneto-semantic principle

79

which lies at the basis of our work. Striking as the results may appear, they are all a consequence of the operation of this essentially simple principle to its fullest, which is at the same time its logical, extent.

In the illustrations of the "vocabulary building mechanism" which we now give we shall apply the full range of the phoneto-semantic variant types which we discussed in Chapter V and further examples of which are found in the Appendix.

We start with the simple English word *blot*. Its definition is given (in Webster's) as 'a spot or a stain, as of ink'. (Not all of the meanings given after a word can of course at any time be quoted in their entirety. It will be instructive for the reader to consult and compare the additional meanings given after each word as well as its conventional, that is, its historical approach etymology). With this word we readily link, as a more evident type of phoneto-semantic variant exhibiting the palatalization of dental *t*, the word *blotch* - 'a blot or spot'. Through the "intermediary" of *blotch* we now link *blot* with English *fleck* - 'a spot, a streak, a speckle', *ch* (or *tch*) being palatalized *k* as well as palatalized *t*. (The linkage may be made still more apparent if we extend our "field of variables" to include Dutch "values". Thus *blotch* is linked with Dutch *plek* meaning 'a spot, a place, a stain' and with Dutch *vlek* - 'a blot, spot, stain').

Referring now to the phoneto-semantic variant of the type "grate-scratch" we next link *blotch* with *splotch* or *splodge* meaning 'a spot, stain, blot, blotch'. Now referring to the phoneto-semantic variant of the type "sputter-splutter" we link *splotch* with *spot*. With *spot* we further link, as exhibiting the interchange of the labials *p, m,* the Scottish word *smot* meaning 'a stain' and the rather obvious additional "values" *smut, smutch, smudge.*

All the phoneto-semantic variants associated with blot above emphasized the meaning of *blot* as 'a stain'. The word means however also 'a black or dark patch', a meaning which is "naturally" linked, by the thought process which we remarked on at the beginning, to the meaning of the word as 'a stain'. We now link, as illustrative of the "sputter-splutter" type of phoneto-semantic variant *blotch* or *plotch* (obs. a blotch) with *patch* (a large spot or blotch). And referring to the "knot-knag" type of variant, we further link *spot-speck*.

Note now the meaning of *spot* as 'a stain', also, 'a small extent of space; a place; any particular place or area'. These meanings, as in other cases, are not independent of course but illustrate the associative thought process already referred to. The meaning of *spot* as an extended space is obtained for example by dwelling on the "expansive" aspect of a spot as "a space" rather than on its "contractive" aspect as a "mere speck". (It will be recalled that a similar thought linkage was noted in connection with the meanings of knot as both 'a bud' and 'a hill'). We thus link *spot* with English *space* (which may *but need not necessarily* be identified with Latin *spati*um - 'space'). Similarly we link *blot* with *plot* - 'a small area of ground' and with *place* (as well as with the German "value" *Platz* - 'a place, spot, room, space' and the Norwegian "value" *plett* - 'a spot').

Now linked with the concept of 'a place' are the concepts of "broadness", "flatness". In fact, the word *plot* cited above, besides meaning 'a small area of ground' means 'a plat' while the word *plat* has the present meaning of 'a small plot of ground' and the obsolete meaning 'a flat thing'. We therefore link, as values of a word variable, *plot - plat - flat - blade* (dial. a broad flat leaf) - *plate* (a flat sheet of material) - *plaque* (any flat thin piece of metal, clay, etc.) - *board - broad* (and, extending the field of variables to German) - *Blatt* (a leaf, blade, sheet) - *Brett* (a board, plank, table).

Our starting word *blot,* by using intermediate phoneto-semantic variants as a "bridge" can thus be linked in meaning as well as in sound to such a word as *board* and the adjective *broad.* Compare also *plaque - plank* (a heavy thick board) - *planch* (dial. a plank, board or slab) in which the *k* of *plaque* is nasalized to the *nk* of *plank* and in addition palatalized in *planch.*

We have in our discussion above made use of the definition of *blot* as a noun, that is, as the "name" of a thing, an idea or an action. Taking the word now in its "verbal aspect" as denoting "an action", we note that it means 'to spot, stain or bespatter'. Noting that the word *splash* in its "nominal aspect" means 'a spot of a different color from the main color appearing as if splashed on; a blotch' and in its verbal aspect 'to strike and dash about (water, mud, etc.)' we link *splotch,* and therefore also *blot,* with *splash,* while as phoneto-semantic variants of the "grate-scratch" type we link *splash - plash* (to strike and break the surface [of water, dust, etc.] with a spattering noise; to splash) and with *plash* we further link *plout* (Scot. to splash; to fall heavily, a dash, plash, splash) and *platch* (Scot. to splash). We also link, as of the "bat-batter" type, *splash - splatter* (to spatter, splash) - *splutter,* and as of the "sputter-splutter" type, *spatter - splatter - sputter.* . Finally, with *splash* or *splotch* we link *splat* (to spread or flatten out; obs. to flatten on impact) - *spread* (to scatter, strew or disperse; to extend in length and breadth or in breadth only; to flatten out).

We could continue in this manner to extend the "blot family" so as to include a surprisingly large number of further members. A sufficient number however has been cited to give an idea of the operation of the "vocabulary building mechanism". It is seen that *words arise through phonetic modification with associated semantic modification, the different meanings, however divergent, still possessing a conceptual element in common.*

We note further that included in the "blot idea-complex" are phoneto-semantic variants such as *splash, platch, splat,* which involve the idea of striking in some manner or making a striking noise of some kind or other. We shall return to consider the significance of this observation later.

To the reader who has not grasped the full force of the phoneto-semantic principle the above discussion of *blot* and its "relatives" though "apparently reasonable" may still perhaps appear as somewhat elusive and a little confusing. While he may follow through the word comparisons, it is not improbable that he may see some "fortuitous element" in the process. This is not entirely to be unexpected in view of the strongly entrenched historical viewpoint in accordance with which the only "legitimate" way of regarding a word is through its "ancestry" As we have stated however in a previous chapter, the phoneto-semantic viewpoint looks "about us" as well as "backward" (and in so doing incidentally reveals the significance and true interpretation of the "backward" or historical view). The process of the "vocabulary building mechanism" may be compared, in its "differentiation" and "specialization" to the analogous process of the cells of a body which, while of the same "protoplasmic stuff" differentiate to form specialized units. (We shall consider in the following chapters the nature of the "common stuff" that words are fashioned of).

Additional illustration of the vocabulary building mechanism will provide us with further insight into the character of the process, where we start out with some simple "basic" word and "build the vocabulary around it".

Speaking of "around" let us now start out with the word *ring*. Included among the meanings given after this word are "any circular band of metal, wood, etc.', also, 'the rim or border of a disk or wheel'. "Emphasizing" the latter definition we link *ring - rim* (the border, edge or margin of a thing, usually of something circular or curving; a ring or narrow strip at the edge or border), the *ng* of *ring* being construed as nasalized *m* of *rim*. Recalling the semi-vowel character and interchangeability of the liquids *r, l,* we link *rim - limb* (a border or edge, as the graduated margin of an arc or circle) - *lime* (obs. variant of limb). Further, on the basis of our phoneto-semantic approach we have no hesitation in linking *limb - lip* (any edge, rim or margin). Emphasizing the "roundness aspect" we further link these words with *loop* (a ring or fold forming a catch) and in fact further link as phoneto-semantic variants of the type "knot-knag", *ring - round* (anything round, as a circle, a globe, a ring) - *rink* (Scot. and dial. E. a ring, a circle) - *link* (a single ring of a chain; a loop) - *rung*. Coming back to the "edge - around" emphasis, we further "link" *ring* (the rim or border of a disk or wheel) - *rand* (obs. exc. dial. a border, edge or margin) and emphasizing the "encircling aspect" we link *ring - rind* (the crust or outer layer of anything).

Let us "round up" some more members of our

"ring". Again returning to the "edge-around" idea we link, as phoneto-semantic variants of the "rattle-prattle" type, *rim - brim* (archaic, the edge or margin of anything; the brink, border) and *rink - brink* (a verge; a border or border line, archaic and dial. the brim of a hat). (The phonetic relation of *brim - brink* is that of *rim - rink*). We further associate *brink - fringe* (a border, edging, margin, an external rib or rim) - *flange* (a part that spreads out like a rim) - *flanch* (rare, a flange) - *frounce* (a curl or frizz, obs. a flounce) - *flounce*. (Observe that in *frounce, flounce* the emphasis is shifted on the "curliness" associated with "around"). Construing the *ng* as simply "nasalized *g*" we link *fringe - verge* (a border, limit or boundary; a circumference, range; an enclosing or encircling boundary, as a circle or ring) - *marge* (a margin) - *march* (a territorial border or frontier) - *mark* (archaic and historical, boundary, limit, border, march).

From the "edge-around" idea we shift our emphasis on the "aroundness", "curvedness" or "crookedness" aspect of the "ring idea-complex". We then link, as phoneto-semantic variants of the "lump-clump" type, *ring - crink* (dial. Eng. a bend or twist) - *crank* (something crooked; obs. any bend, turn or winding). Construing *nk* as "nasalized *k*" we further associate *crink - crook* (a bend, turn or curve), and, as phoneto-semantic variants of the "knot-knag-knob" type, *crook - curve - curb - gird* (obs. a girdle, girth or strap) - *girth*. As phoneto-semantic variants of the type "wag-waggle" we associate *crink - crinkle* (a winding or turn; wrinkle), as of the "whirl-curl" type, *crinkle - wrinkle* (obs. a winding; a twisting or sinuous formation), *crink - wrink* (obs. Scot. a turning; a trick) - *wrench* (obs. a sharp turn) - *wring* (act of wringing, obs. sharp pain; writhing), and as of the "sputter-splutter" type, *wrench - winch* (a crank with a handle) - *wince* (dial. variant of winch).

All of the above words were taken in their nominal aspects. Let us now emphasize the verbal aspect. In so doing we find that to the notion of "round" or "around" there comes to be associated the idea of an "action", for example, "a motion around" so that we have the conceptual linkage of "motion" and "around". Thus the word *round*, construed as a verb, has the meanings 'to go round, to turn round, wheel about'. Similarly the word *ring*, construed as a verb, has as one of its meanings 'to move in a ring or rings', while the verb *wring* means 'to twist round forcibly; to wind or wreathe in coils or revolutions'. Hence, construing *ch* as palatalized *t* or *d* we link *winch - wind* (to twist, twine, coil, wreathe). As phoneto-semantic variants of the "wag-waggle" type we link *round* (to turn in or as if in a circle) - *rundle* (something which rotates about an axis, as a wheel) and *wind - windle* (Scot. and Dial. E. to wind yarn; to whirl around). (Note that we can also link *wind - round, windle - rundle* as phoneto-semantic variants illustrating the interchange of the "semi-vowels" *w - r*). As phoneto-semantic variants of the type "whirl - twirl" we now link *rundle - trundle* (a rolling motion or the sound due to it; to go or roll by revolving, as a hoop, also, to twirl) - *trindle* (obs. exc. Scot. and dial. to roll, trundle, bowl along), *wind - twind* (obs. to twist; twine). Further, we link, as illustrating the palatalization of *d* to *j*, *twind - twinge* (tweak; twitch), and as of the "wag-waggle" type, *twinge - twingle* (Scot. and dial. to turn; wind). Again, construing *nj* as nasalized *j*, we link *twinge - twitch - tweak*, and construing *st* as a "unit sound" we link *twitch - twist*. Now, as phoneto-semantic variants of the type "win (dial. wind) - wind" or "roun (Scot. variant of round) - round" we further link *twind* (obs. to twist; twine) - *twine* (obs. exc. Scot. and dial. to twist, turn; to turn around; to revolve; to warp; to bend out of shape). As phoneto-semantic variants of the type "sump - swamp" we next link *twine - ton* (obs. exc. dial. variant of turn), and, as of the "pick-prick" type, *ton - turn*. (Note that the linkage *twine - turn*, like that of *round* or *rind - wind*, could be effected through the interchange of the "semi-vowels" *r, w*). With the word *turn* we link the words *tour* (to turn one's step, go) - *chare* (obs. to turn, a turn) - *sheer* (to turn aside, swerve) - *tire* (a hoop) - *twire* (obs. curl or twist) - *wire* (to coil about) - *veer* (to change direction, to turn) - *whir* (to move, fly or revolve) - *wheel - whirl - curl - purl* (to whirl, wheel) - *twirl -swirl - sweel* (Scot. to swirl) and the other words already discussed in connection with *wheel* in Chapter V, Phoneto-Semantic Word Linking.

We have seen that taking the verbal aspect of *ring* we link to the idea of "round" that of "action round" so that we have the concept of "moving around in some manner". Let us follow this "shade of meaning" somewhat further. The word *wring* which has the meaning 'to wind or wreathe in coils or convolutions' also, 'obs. to wriggle oneself by insinuation or wheedling" has already been linked to *ring*. We further link, as of the "wag-waggle" type, *wring - wringle* (obs. to writhe), and as before, construing *ng* as nasalized *g*, we link *wringle - wriggle* (to move by twisting and turning; to writhe). We also link *wring - wrink* (obs. Scot. a turning trick) - *wrench - wrong* (dial. twisted, wry, crooked). Further, as of the "wag-waggle" type, we link *wriggle - wrig* (obs. exc. dial. to wriggle), as of the "knot-knag" type, *wrig -*

writhe (to move, go, fly, flow, etc. with twists or turns) - *wreathe* (twist), and as of the "knot-knob" type, *wreathe* (to encircle with or as with a wreath) - *wrap* (to wind, coil or twine so as to encircle or cover something) - *warp* (to turn or twist out of shape; to wind [yarns] on a warp beam). We now link, as of the "pick-prick" type, *wriggle* - *wiggle* (to waggle, wriggle) - *waggle* (to reel, sway or move from side to side; to wag). It will be recalled, in connection with our discussion of *wheel* in Chapter V, that we took note of the Anglo-Saxon forms corresponding to *wheel*, namely, *hwēol, hweogul, hweowol*. Taking account of the fact that one of the meanings of wheel, in its verbal aspect, is "to reel" (the pair *wheel* - *reel* again illustrate the interchange of the "semi-vowels" *w-r)* we are able to see more clearly the linkage *wheel* - *hweogul* - *waggle* - *wiggle* and *wheel* - *hweowol* - *wobble* - *whiffle* (to shift, turn or veer about, said of the wind; to change from one opinion or course to another). Similarly we link *wheel* - *waddle* (to walk with short steps swaying from one side to the other). We have already in Chapter V linked *wabble* (or *wobble*) - *wallop* (to move in a rolling cumbersome fashion; to waddle), *waggle* - *walk* (obs. to toss to and fro), *waddle* - *waltz* (German *walzen* - to roll).

We thus find our starting word *ring* to be linked, through the *phoneto-semantic bridging process,* with such words as *wheel, turn, walk,* as well as with an unexpectedly large number of other words all included within the "ring idea-complex" just as we have already in a similar manner found the word *blot* to be but one member of an extensive word family associated with the "blot idea-complex". The bridging in both cases is effected by simply making use of what we have already learned of the scope of meaning of words and of the existence of

88

the different types of phoneto-semantic variants which we have discussed in Chapter V.

Our results will very likely, particularly at their first presentation, appear to be very striking, if not somewhat puzzling, in character. It would almost seem as though we were engaged in a word game of a sort to see how many words, via an association of sound and meaning, could be linked up with a given word. The element of surprise is accounted for however by the failure to realize the full implications of the concepts introduced in the previous chapters. Just as a body of "remarkable" geometrical propositions are "implicitly contained" in a number of rather "innocent appearing" axioms so our results are implied in, that is, they are logical consequences or extensions of the very simple idea which underlies the phoneto-semantic linkage of words. Such linkage of a word pair which differ by "a shade of sound" and by "a shade of meaning" is of course a quite familiar one to etymologists; in fact, it forms the very basis of the conventional or historical approach etymologies as given for example in standard dictionaries. For, after all, the conclusions of the latter approach are based on the comparison of word pairs in which certain sound and meaning deviations are noted. In its zeal however for tracing a word to its "ancestry" the historical approach has lost sight of the more fundamental aspect of the problem, namely, the basic concept itself which underlies any such word comparisons. Such concept, as we have seen, necessarily involves on the one hand the "limits of definition" of any particular word and on the other hand, "the limits of sound variation" of words of the same, associated, or overlapping meanings.

It will thus be seen, from our discussion above, that whereas the historical approach, generally speaking,

89

views the words which constitute the native vocabulary of any language as isolated words which it seeks to link up with other isolated words of kindred languages, the phoneto-semantic approach views the words of the native vocabulary of a language as members of relatively large *word families*. In fact, we go further and formulate explicitly the following concept: *The simple common words of the native vocabulary of any language constitute one large family, that is, an organic whole.* Thus it is asserted that all the simple English or Anglo-Saxon words for example are phonetically and semantically "interlocking members" of a single word family.

The validity of the concept formulated above could be demonstrated by actually exhibiting the phoneto-semantic linkage, that is, the association of sound and meaning, that exists between the native stock of common English words for example. It is not necessary however at this point to proceed to carry out the process in full. The underlying significance of this concept of the vocabulary of any language as constituting an organic whole will become better understood, after we have clarified, in the chapters which follow, the essential character of words and their associated meanings. Even at the present stage of our discussion however it is not difficult to see that such concept is readily suggested by reflecting on the nature of the "vocabulary building mechanism" we have illustrated above. It will be noted in the first place that each of the word families clustered about the "blot idea-complex" or about the "ring idea-complex" is vaguely delimited with respect to the extent of its membership. For, in each family we pass from one word to the next by considering a more or less obviously modified sound with a corresponding modification in meaning associated with the new sound. With words of somewhat similar sounds the meaning modification is obtained by dwelling on or emphasizing some aspect of the meaning associated with the previous word. In the course of the process however, by bridging "shades of meaning" we actually arrive at apparently very different meanings and therefore very different words, although, and this is the essential point, a common conceptual link is still capable of being effected. Thus we linked *ring,* which as a verb has the meaning 'to move in a ring' with *wring* meaning 'to wind or wreathe in coils and convolutions' while we further linked *wring* meaning 'to twist round' with *wrong,* which, as a dialect word, means 'twisted, wry, crooked'. Dwelling on these particular meanings of the words the linkage of *ring - wrong* is rather evident. If however we "mean" the *ring* which is 'a circlet' and we "mean" the *wrong* which is 'not ethically right or just' we shall not off-hand see any semantic association between *ring - wrong.* The association is effected by reflecting on the dialectal meaning of *wrong* just cited and by reflecting further on the meanings associated with such words as *crooked* as 'characterized by a crook or curve', also, 'false, dishonest, fraudulent'.

Thus if we are given two simple words of rather similar sound but of divergent meanings we can not without further analysis, that is, without bridging their meanings through intermediate "word links", jump to the conclusion that they may not belong to the same word family. Similarly, given two words which have a semantic link in common but divergent sounds we can not jump to the conclusion that they are necessarily not members of the same family, that is, that their phonetic linkage may not be exhibited through a bridging process. Thus the pair *ring - turn,* which are evidently linked semantically, may also be linked phonetically by the following "phoneto-semantic chain": *ring* (to move in a ring or rings) - *wring* (to wind or wreathe in coils or convolutions) - *wrench* (obs. to turn or twist suddenly, sharply or violently) - *winch* (a crank with a handle) - *wince* (dial. variation of winch) - *wind* (to twist, twine) - *twind* (obs. twist, twine) - *twine* (dial. to twist, turn) - *ton* (dial. variant of turn) - *turn*. (There is of course no implication of the "uniqueness" of this chain). In each of the "links" of the chain: *wring - wrench, wrench - winch, winch - wince, wince - wind, wind - twind, twind - twine, twine - ton, ton - turn,* a type of phoneto-semantic variant is illustrated which we have discussed in Chapter V and which, as we have seen, is applied in a nonsystematic, largely arbitrary, fashion in conventional etymologies. For example the pair *twind-wind* illustrates the same type of phoneto-semantic variant that is observed (in Webster's) for the pairs *thwack - whack* or *thwittle* (dial. to cut or whittle) - *whittle.* Thus, given any two simple words *of both divergent sound and meaning* we can not, without phoneto-semantic analysis, state positively that they belong or not to the same word family. We conclude therefore that even in our present stage of discussion the concept formulated above, namely, that the native basic vocabulary of a language is to be construed as constituting *an organic body of words,* is not a priori an unjustifiable one or one devoid of significance.

It should be particularly noted that so far in our discussion we have nowhere spoken of the "kinship" of words; we have spoken merely of the phoneto-semantic linkage of words. It may be difficult however for the reader who is familiar with the prevailing concept of word kinship to disassociate his mind from this concept in linking a word pair. The fact that words of quite different sounds but of associated meaning may nevertheless, through a phoneto-semantic chain, as illustrated in the case of *ring-turn* above, be exhibited as phonetically associated he will interpret as equivalent to the statement that the two words are "akin" to each other in the conventional genetic sense. He will then be confronted by the very striking and rather puzzling circumstance that, given any two simple English words, for example of even widely divergent sound and meaning, there is a possibility of "kinship" between them, and if such is the case there does not appear to be too much significance in the whole concept of word kinship as prevailingly understood. This however is precisely the conclusion to which our discussion has led. *Evidently what is implied in the possibility of such linkage is that it is necessary to give up the prevailing concept that is associated with the term "word kinship" as conventionally applied to words and replace it by a different concept.* This we shall now proceed to do.

In the conventional etymology, given any two words (of the same or related languages) they are in general said to be either akin to each other or else to bear no relationship at all to each other. That is, the notion of word kinship is an "either-or" notion. Now the phoneto-semantic viewpoint requires, on the contrary, that we replace the concept of "kinship" by that of "degree of kinship", our attention being focussed on the words within the same language. *The degree of kinship of two native words within a given language is simply the degree of resemblance of the words compared when their sounds and meanings are simultaneously taken into consideration.* With the concept of "degree of kinship" replacing that of "kinship" there will then no longer be anything peculiar or surprising in the statement that the word *ring* for example is apparently "akin" to the word *turn,* or "worse still", to the word *walk.* The statement simply means that we can exhibit the association of these words in the manner above on the basis of the fundamental phoneto-semantic concept. Where the linkage of sound and meaning is more obvious, the two words may be said to be "more nearly akin" than where the sounds and meanings are more divergent. The same word pair may in fact be more akin to each other with respect to certain of their meanings and less akin to each other with respect to other meanings which they possess. Thus the pair *ring - rim* when the former means 'the rim or border of a disk or wheel' and the latter 'the outer circular part of a wheel' are more nearly akin to each other than the pair *ring - rim* when the former means 'an annual ring' and the latter 'the border, edge or margin of a thing'. Furthermore, the "same word" may be to a greater or less degree "akin to itself" with respect to certain of its meanings. That is, we replace the concept of "homonymy", which, like the prevailing concept of kinship is an "either-or" concept, by that of "degree of homonymy". (Words are defined as "homonyms" if they have the same pronunciation 'but differ in origin, meaning, and often in spelling', that is, they are "different words"). An example will serve to clarify our last statement.

The word *blow* meaning 'to flower; to blossom; to bloom' is assumed (in Webster's) to be 'of different origin'and therefore is homonymous with the word *blow* meaning 'to move, as air', also, 'to expand; to inflate; to swell, as cement'. Now the word *swell* means 'to increase in volume; to grow larger, as the buds are swelling' and a little reflection will show that the same idea is contained in the words 'blossom' and 'bloom'. Thus, in accordance with the concept of "degree of kinship" just discussed, the "two blow's" are the "same blow" if by that we mean simply that they can be semantically linked. We may however regard the "two blow's" as "different blow's" and therefore as homonyms. But to be consistent we must then construe the different definitions given after the *blow* one of whose meanings is 'to move, as air' and the other 'to expand; to inflate; to swell' as belonging to "different blow's" so that we have three (or more) different blow's. As a matter of fact, the assigning of a certain group of definitions under one word and other definitions under a different word spelled and pronounced the same way involves, as we shall see even more clearly presently, an arbitrary element associated with the prevailing concept of "kinship" rather than with that of "degree of kinship".

The "vocabulary building mechanism" is a concept that is associated with the interrelationships of the "native" words *within a given language*. The same "mechanism" must, from its very nature, apply to the native vocabulary of any language whatsoever. In a later chapter we shall discuss the full implications of this statement. For the present it will be of interest to show how this concept of "vocabulary building mechanism" provides an insight into the underlying significance of the conventional etymology of words.

In the conventional or historical-approach etymology such simple English words as we have considered above are exhibited as akin to words of "Indo-European stock". Generally the related words will be cited from the Teutonic (or Germanic) subfamily of languages including Gothic, Old Norse, Old High German, Anglo-Saxon, all of which are extinct, and modern Icelandic, Swedish,

Danish, Norwegian, German, Low German, Flemish, Dutch and English. Where possible however the word is "traced" to Latin, Greek, Old Slavic, Sanskrit, Persian, and other "Indo-European roots", the underlying idea being that the ancient word belonging to the "primitive Indo-European stock" has passed, in somewhat modified form, down the generations to the present day English word. Thus for example the simple English *eat* is identified with the ancient Sanskrit root *ad,* Greek *ed,* Latin *ed,* as well as with the Teutonic roots, Old High German *ezz,* German *ess,* Old Norse *et,* Gothic *it,* Swedish *ät,* Danish *aet.* We have already indicated the view that the tracing of English words to such languages as Sanskrit, Latin, Greek, Persian or Old Slavic is open to "considerable suspicion". The grounds for such suspicion lie of course in our general viewpoint. This will be understood more clearly if we focus our attention not on the kinship of English words with any of the above languages but with the languages belonging to the Teutonic group of which English is a member.

One need not delve too deeply into the subject of language kinship to see that the Teutonic languages, whether for example the extinct Gothic or Old Norse or the modern German, Dutch or Swedish, resemble English in a more immediately obvious fashion than they resemble for example Sanskrit, Latin or Greek. Aside from the greater grammatical similarity the resemblance of corresponding words to denote common familiar objects or actions is striking enough not to escape even one not particularly concerned with the linguistic sciences. Thus he can not fail to observe the correspondence of German *Ring* - English *ring,* G.*Hand* - E.*hand,* G.*Finger* - E.*finger,* and with slight modification, G. *Haar* - E.*hair,* G.*Fuss* - E.*foot,* G.*weiss* - E.*white,* G.*Nase* - E.

nose, G.*schlaf*en - E.*sleep,* G.*mach*en - E.*make,* G.*tief* - E.*deep,* G.*Heim* - E.*home,* G.*geb*en - E.*give,* G.*fühl*en E.*feel,* G.*Mann* - E.*man,* G.*Weib* - E.*wife,* G.*auf* - E.*up,* G.*unter* - E.*under.* Similarly the parallels in the Dutch or Swedish vocabularies are of an obvious character. Indeed the resemblance is close enough to make it appear that German or Dutch or Swedish, constitute, together with English, but distinct dialects of essentially the same language. That is, the difference between German and English for example on the one hand and that between English and Scottish on the other is merely one of degree. Since such is evidently the case, a simple question arises, namely, if many common "basic" words of German, for example, like those cited above, correspond, except perhaps for relatively slight and evident modifications, to English words, why do other words, just as common and basic, fail to correspond in the two languages? Thus we find G.*Kopf* - E.*head,* G. *nehm*en - E. *take,* G.*Bauch* - E.*belly,* G.*eil*en - E.*hasten,* G.*red*en - E. *speak,* G.*lehr*en - E.*teach,* G.*anrühr*en - E.*touch,* G. *reiss*en - E.*tear,* G.*Baum* - E.*tree,* G.*lauf*en - E.*run,* G. *scharr*en - E.*scrape,* G.*stoss*en - E.*push,* G.*Berg* - E. *mount,* G.*schneid*en - E.*cut,* G.*klein* - E.*small,* G.*viel* - E.*many,* G.*wenig* - E.*few,* G.*Wolke* - E.*cloud,* G.*wer* - E. *who,* G.*jetzt* - E.*now,* G.*ganz* - E.*whole,* and many others that could be cited. To this question the historical approach provides an answer which may be illustrated by the following example.

German *lauf* for example does not resemble English *run* but if we "hunt around" in the English vocabulary we shall find that the word *leap,* which evidently resembles *lauf* in sound, had the obsolete meaning 'to run; rush' though the modern word is associated with the meaning 'to jump; to vault'. We also find the obsolete (except dialectal) word *lope* meaning 'to leap; to dance', while its modern meaning is 'to go or move with a lope, that is, an easy gait resembling a canter'. We thus pair *lauf,* not with *run,* but with *leap* or *lope*. Similarly instead of pairing *Kopf* with *head,* we shall find if we hunt around that the word may be paired with the obsolete (except dialectal) *cop* meaning 'the top of a thing; the head', with which German *Kopf* is therefore linked as "akin". Similarly we pair German *schneid* not with English *cut* but with the obsolete (except Scottish and dialectal) *snathe* which obviously resembles *schneid* in sound and which means 'to lop; prune'. Our question then is answered, partially at least, by exhibiting the existence in English of obsolete, dialectal, Scottish, or in general less familiar words which have an obvious sound resemblance to the German word in question as well as a similarity in meaning. Our question has not however been completely answered since words will still remain in the native German vocabulary to which it will appear extremely difficult, from the conventional viewpoint, to find corresponding English parallels. This will be particularly the case if instead of considering the Teutonic languages, so obviously resembling English, we consider other languages of the Indo-European stock such as Sanskrit, Persian, Latin, Greek, Welsh, or Armenian.

Now it should be clear that the failure to find corresponding words for the familiar basic objects or notions presents, from the historical-approach viewpoint, a truly puzzling problem. For according to this viewpoint the native basic stock of words of any Indo-European language is, in theory at least, traceable to the primitive Indo-European stock of words. If then we eliminate from consideration any words that may conceivably have come into these languages as borrowings from other stocks it

98

is difficult to explain the existence of the apparently highly divergent basic vocabularies for example of Sanskrit and English or Russian and English. We are forced to assume either that the primitive Indo-European language was endowed with so rich and varied a vocabulary as to bequeath highly diversified vocabularies to its offspring languages or that these latter, to some extent at least, have developed their native vocabularies independently of the mother tongue, that is, the various languages classified under the Indo-European stock are to a very considerable degree "autonomous".

Reflection on the nature of the "vocabulary building mechanism" which we have illustrated above and on the fundamental phonetic and semantic considerations on which it is based leads naturally to the second of the above-mentioned alternatives, namely, that *languages develop their native basic vocabularies independently or autonomously in accordance with the vocabulary building mechanism.* This fact accounts therefore not only for the resemblances *but also the differences* between two such obviously related languages as for example English and German.

Let us illustrate the significance of the statement made above by starting with one of the common German words mentioned above, namely, *Bauch* meaning *belly.* Though the two words are of a "basic sort" they appear to be different words, the only resemblance between them being the possession of a common initial *b.* In accordance with the historical method, as illustrated above for *Kopf - head, laufen - run, schneiden - cut,* the difference would be accounted for by attempting to pair *Bauch* with some isolated, generally more or less unfamiliar, English word which corresponds more nearly in sound with the given German word. Thus it is found

99

that there is in English a word *bouk* which has the obsolete meaning 'a belly or abdomen'. Further, there is a
dialect word *bowk* which means 'a kind of wooden or
iron bucket or pail', and noting that Anglo-Saxon *būc*
meant 'vessel, pitcher' as well as 'belly' the German
Bauch is stated to be akin to the English words *bouk,
bowk, būc, buck* (a basket for catching eels) and *bucket.*
We find then, according to this conventional procedure,
that the idea of a belly is linked in some manner with
that of a vessel, bucket or basket. This meaning linkage
is discovered fortuitously we might say by noting for
example that Anglo-Saxon *būc* which is recognized as
akin to the closely resembling German *Bauch* has both
the meanings of 'a vessel' and 'a belly'. In this process
there is no clear concept either of the character of the
semantic linkage observed or of the extent or scope of
such semantic linkage just as there is no clear concept
of the scope of the phonetic variations of the words.

In contrast to this nonsystematic, essentially arbitrary
method of finding isolated English words that are "akin"
to a given German word we proceed, in accordance with
the vocabulary building mechanism, to "build up the
German vocabulary about the given word". In this process we take fully into account the entire scope of meaning, actual and potential, that is associated with any
word as well as the full range of possibility of phonetic
variation. We proceed to illustrate the operation of this
vocabulary building mechanism in German.

The words *buck* (a basket) and *bucket* were found,
by the historical approach to be akin to *Bauch*. Recalling
the slang reference to the stomach, which commonly denotes also the belly, abdomen, as the "bread basket" and
recalling also our discussion in Chapter V of phoneto-
semantic variants of the type "grab-grasp", etc. we link

bucket - basket as well as *buck - box*. Thus English *box* and *basket* are further "relatives" of German *Bauch*. (It will be noted that the use of "bread basket" to denote stomach or belly is "slang". It is likewise stated in Webster's that the use of "stomach" to denote the "belly" is "common but erroneous". As will however become apparent on reflection upon the character of the concepts here introduced, *it is of the colloquial, dialectal, slang and "erroneous" usage of words that the fabric of the word stock of a language is constructed*).

We proceed to find more English as well as German "cousins" of *Bauch*. The word *bag* means 'a sack or pouch, used for holding anything'. We find however that as a Scottish and dialect word it has the further meaning of 'the belly; the womb of a domestic animal'. We therefore link *Bauch - bag* as well as *Bauch - pouch* (any sac-like organ). Suppose now we dwell on the verbal aspect of *bag* in which it has the meaning 'to swell out like a bag; to bulge'. If we compare *bulge* with German *Balg* meaning 'bag' and take further into account that Anglo-Saxon *belig* or *belg* meant 'bag; bellows; belly' it will be clear that the phonetic difference in the pair *Bauch-belly* exhibits "a switching of emphasis" of the meanings associated with *bag* and *belly*. That is, if we consider *bag, pouch* and *Bauch* as relatively slight phonetic modifications of the "same" word and similarly for *bulge, belg, belly, Balg*, we may say that in German "a bag or pouch (Bauch) is a belly while a belly (Balg) is a bag". If however we take into account what we have already learned on phoneto-semantic variants we find that even in English "a bag is a belly and a belly a bag", that is, the pair *bag - belg*, exhibiting the already familiar relative excrescence of medial liquid *l, r*, are phonetically as well as semantically linked and the same type of variant is exhibited by German *Bauch - Balg*. Thus German *Bauch*, which also means 'paunch', turns out to be "akin" to English *belly* as well as to *paunch*, the pair *pouch - paunch* exhibiting the relative "nasalization" of final *ch*.

It will be instructive to continue somewhat further with our illustration of the vocabulary building mechanism as operating in German. Note that German *Balg* means not only 'bag' but also 'husk; pod; bellows'. Turning our attention to English *pod* we find, besides its meaning of 'a bag; pouch; sac' that it has the dialect meaning 'a large protuberant belly'. Recalling that palatal *ch* mediates between the dentals *t, d* and the gutturals *k, g* the phoneto-semantic linkage between *pod - pot* (as in potbelly) - *pouch - poke* (dial. a bag or sack) - *bag* should be obvious. Further we link *pot - butt* (a large cask) and *butt - bottle* (something resembling or likened to a bottle). The word *bottle* is therefore phoneto-semantically linked with *bag* and we therefore need not be surprised to learn that German *Beutel*, whose phonetic resemblance to *bottle* is obvious, has the meaning 'bag; pouch; purse', that is, whereas in English "a bottle is a bottle", in German "a bottle (Beutel) is a bag".

Let us see if we can still further "bulge" our "Bauch-belly" family. The phonetic relation between *poke - pucker* (a bulge, fold or wrinkle made by puckering) is that between "bat-batter". Noting this meaning of *pucker* and recalling what was said in a previous chapter on the vowel nature and interchange of the liquids *l, r* we link *pucker* with German *Buckel* meaning 'hump; humpback; bump; bulge', at the same time observing that the pair *Bauch-Buckel* exhibits the same type of phoneto-semantic variant as *butt-bottle*. Dwelling on this "bump or bulge" idea, we link *Balg* - *Beule* (bump; tumor; swelling; boil) as exhibiting the same type of phonetic relation as Anglo-Saxon *belg* or English *bulge* and *belly* or *bellow* (s). Thus *Beule* is linked with *belly* and furthermore evidently with English *boil* (a blister), *boll* (obs. a bubble; also a knoblike protuberance), *bowl* (obs. a ball or globe) and *ball* (any round or roundish body or mass) and with German *Bühl* meaning 'hill; humpback'.

Let us pause for a moment and reflect on the "quite general idea" that is associated with the word *ball* which we have thus linked with *belly* and with *Bauch*. It will be seen on a little reflection that the idea of a ball is not a simple or "atomic" one. On the contrary, it is an "idea-complex" in which are involved a multiplicity of associated aspects any one of which may be given prominence by merely emphasizing or reading a particular "shade of meaning" into the word. Thus we may think of a ball as being linked with the qualities of "clumpiness", "roundness", "condensedness", "closedness", "hollowness", "bulginess", "convexedness", "fullness". If we take the verbal aspect the word may be associated, in its "lump or clump aspect", with such ideas as "congealing", "conglomerating", "crowding", "heaping", "forming a knob, knot or mound", in its "bulge aspect", as "bulging", "curving", "bending". In fact one of the meanings given of ball is 'to gather into a ball, as snow; to become entangled so as to form balls, clumps or the like' and additional definitions given after "ball" or "globe" will be found to involve all of the linked ideas mentioned above as well as others. *It is because of the "nonatomic" idea associated with any simple word that we are thus able to introduce a constantly increasing number of new members into any "word family".*

Let us illustrate and bring out the significance of what we have just said by continuing somewhat further with our "Bauch-belly idea-complex". We have found above an English *bouk* having the obsolete meaning 'belly'. There is "another *bouk*" which is stated to be a Scottish and dialectal English variant of *bulk* (magnitude or volume; mass or aggregate; the hull or hulk of a ship). In our view they are the "same bouk" and we further link *bulk-bulge*. We next link, as variants of the "huff-puff" type, *bulk - hulk* (anything or anyone bulky or unwieldly; obs. the hull of a ship) and *hulk - block*. The same type of variant is encountered, as we should expect, in German *Buckel* (hump; bump; bulge) - *Hügel* (hillock; hill; projection; knob). The idea of "a hillock" is thus seen to be linked to that of "a belly" and the word *hillock* itself together with the corresponding German *Hügel* are seen to be members of our "Bauch-belly idea-complex". Recalling what was just said on the idea-complex associated with *ball* we link, as exhibiting the same type of *h-b* interchange, *ball - hill - hull* and further *hull - hole - hollow* (recall the discussion of these words in Chapter IV, Historical Word Linking) as well as *bulk - balk* (obs. a ridge or heap of earth.). (In connection with the pair *hulk - hillock* recall the discussion in Chapter V on the "diminutive ending" *ock*). With German *Hügel* we may further associate English *huckle* (a bunch or part projecting like the hip; huckleback - humpback) while with *Buckel* we associate English *buckle* (a distortion, as a bulge, bend, kink or twist in a beam web, etc.). As of the "hut-cot" type of phoneto-semantic variant we next link *hulk - clog* (a block or lump attached to something). Similarly we link German *Hügel - Kugel* (ball; globe) while we link *Kugel* with English *coggle* (a cobblestone) and with *cudgel* (a short heavy stick). With *coggle* we link, as of the "knob-knag" variant type, the word *cobble*. It will be recalled that the pair *coggle - clog* illustrate the type of phoneto-semantic variant, discussed in Chapter V, in which the final two consonants one of which is liquid *l, r* or *n* relatively interchange. The same type of variant is illustrated in *huckle - hulk, cobble - club - clump, buckle - bulk* and in the German *Buckel - Balg*. Thus the English *clump* or the German *Klump* (mass; clod; lump; cluster; heap; ball) are additional members of our "Bauch-belly idea-complex". As of the "sputter-splutter" type of variant, we next link *club* (a heavy staff of wood wielded as a cudgel) - *cob* (a rounded heap or mass of something; obs. the head of a herring), the semantic relation being the same as that between English *cudgel* - German *Kugel*. Further we link *cob - cop* (a heap or pile; obs. the top of a thing; the head). And now it is seen that we can link *cob - cop - Kopf* (head, top; bowl [of a pipe]). Note that *Kopf* besides meaning 'head' means also 'the bowl (of a pipe)' and recall that *bowl* has been found to be a member of our "Bauch-belly family". Incidentally compare *bowl - poll* (the head, the skull) - *ball*. We can thus further link *Kopf - Kuppe* (top; head [of a nail]) - *Kumpf* (deep basin; bowl) - *Küpe* (large tub; vat), while, as of the "butt-bottle" variant type, we link *Küpe - Kübel* (bucket, pail, tub). We thus find *Kopf* - 'head' to be a member of the "Bauch family". The words are linked by the phoneto-semantic chain: *Bauch* (belly, pouch) - *Buckel* (hump, bump, bulge) - *Hügel* (hillock; hill; projection; knob) - *Kugel* (ball; globe; head of a bone) - *Kuppel* (cupola; dome) - *Kuppe* (top; head of a nail) - *Kopf* (head), each link of which: *Bauch - Buckel, Buckel - Hügel, Hügel - Kugel, Kugel - Kuppel, Kuppel - Kuppe, Kuppe - Kopf* exhibits a type of phoneto-semantic variant discussed in Chapter V. (The linkage could be effected of course by other chains as well).

The word *Kopf* might have been foreseen as being a member of our "Bauch family" for together with *Bauch* it has the semantic aspect in common of denoting a protuberance, that is, a hump or bump of a sort, as is also denoted by the words *bag, hill, bulge, bottle,* etc. and their German equivalents already found to be members of the family, and as recognized in the slang use of the word *knob* to mean 'the head; the nob.' In fact the word *knob* itself, as well as the words *hump* and *bump* are members of the same "Bauch family". For the pair *knob - cob* (a round heap or mass; head of a herring) or *knop* (a projection up or out, as a hill) - *cop* (a heap or pile) illustrate the relative medial nasalization and the same type of variant is observed in German *Kopf - Knopf* (button; knob or ball; head, top; knot). On the other hand we link, as of the "hut-cot" variant type, the pair *cop - heap* and further *heap - hump,* and, like *hulk - bulk* above, we link *hump - bump*. Returning to German we link *Hauf* (heap; pile), which we associate with *heap,* with German *Haube* (cap; hood; top; cupola; dome) and (like *cop-heap*) *Kopf - Hauf*. There is another German word for head, namely, *Haupt,* and reflection for example on the meaning of English *cop* cited above as 'a head', also, 'a heap or pile' should make evident the phoneto-semantic linkage *Hauf - Haupt,* as well as *Haupt - head* (Middle English *hed, heved*).

We could continue in this manner and by dwelling on the different linked "shades of meanings" associated with any concept introduce a still greater number of English and German words into our "Bauch-belly family" or "idea-complex". For example, noting that one of the meanings of "blow" is 'to expand; to inflate; to swell; colloq. to boast' we link *blow - bellow - belly - ball-wheal* (a pustule) and as of the "grate-scratch" variant type, *wheal - swell*. Further we link *blow - bulb* (to take the shape of a bulb; to swell) - *blob* (dial. a bubble or blister) - *plump* (well rounded or filled out) and, as of the "clog-coggle" variant type, *blob - bubble - pimple* (a swelling or protuberance like a pimple; á boil). In connection with this same aspect of blowing or swelling we link, as of the "knot-knag" variant type, *bloat* (to inflate; to puff up) - *bulge - brag - proud* as well as German *Blase* (bubble, blister; bombast) - *bloat,* and as of the "pick-pluck" type, *Blase - Bausch* (pad; bolster; bundle) and *blas*en (to blow) - *bausch*en (swell out, stick out, puff). Further we link *bloat - blast, blast -bluster - blister - bolster,* as of the "sputter-splutter" type, *blast - boast,* also *boast* - German *pust*en (puff, blow) - *bausch* - en (swell out) - *bauch*en (to bulge out) - *Bauch.* (Compare with the same meaning association evidenced in the definition of Anglo-Saxon *belig* - 'bag, bellows, belly'). It is evident therefore that by continuing this process we could "swell" our "Bauch-belly" membership beyond the practical limits that are here available.

From a consideration of the vocabulary building mechanism as illustrated above in connection with German *Bauch* it should be clear now what accounts, not only for the resemblances, but for *the differences* observed in two such "close cousin" languages as English and German in words denoting common objects or actions. The differences are accounted for, namely, by the "autonomous" operation of the vocabulary building mechanism in the two languages. In such process certain secondary "shades of meaning" that may be associated with a word sound in one language are emphasized as "primary" meanings in the other.

Reflection however on the *interplay* of the meaning associations exhibited in our English and German illustrations of the operation of the vocabulary mechanism reveals the significant fact that the association between a word and its "primary" meaning is not in the nature of a "steel link". The so-called "primary" meaning is basically no more the essential meaning of the word than any of the "secondary" meanings. The meanings after a word must rather be construed as possessing essentially equal status and to possess a certain "freedom of motion" which permits them to "hook on" to any word, that is, to a word sound. This freedom expresses itself in the manifold of words that have more or less associated meanings and in the manifold of meanings that attach themselves to a given simple word. We shall learn more about the underlying nature of the linkage by which the word is associated with its meaning or meanings in the chapters which follow.

CHAPTER EIGHT

"STRIKING" ENGLISH WORDS

IT HAS ALREADY been noted in connection with our illustrations of the vocabulary building mechanism of the preceding chapter that some of the members that were found to be included in a word family were words which explicitly involved the idea of striking in some manner or making a striking noise of some kind or other. Thus we found as members of our "blot family" the words *splash* meaning 'to strike and dash about (water, mud, etc.)', *plash* - 'with a plash or sound of plashing'. The word *wrench* which we included as a member of our "ring family" has the obsolete meaning 'to thrust, as a sword, with a twisting or whirling motion'. Again, included in our "Bauch-belly family" was given the word *bump* which, in its verbal aspect has the obsolete meaning 'to bulge; swell' while it has the present meaning 'to strike, knock or thump'. As another member we found the word *blow* meaning 'to expand, to inflate, to swell'. Is this the "same blow" which, nominally construed, means 'a forcible stroke with the hand, fist, etc.'?

It would thus appear that if some of the members of a particular word family involve the idea of striking or making a striking noise of some kind *explicitly* then, because of the semantic linkage, the other members must involve the same general idea at least *implicitly*. We shall see that such is actually the case, that, for example, the words *blot, ring* and *belly* themselves are "striking words". It is necessary however, in order to bring out fully the nature and significance of the concept that is here involved, that we proceed to develop this concept by stages. In the present chapter therefore we shall confine our attention to words which *explicitly* involve the idea of striking, that is, to words which are actually defined (in Webster's for example) in terms of other words that denote a striking action of some kind. It is in connection with this class of "striking words" that we shall formulate a certain concept which, in the following chapters, will be seen to apply to all simple words in general.

It may first of all be remarked that some of the words of the class here considered "strike" us as being of "imitative origin". Thus the words *splash* and *plash* are stated (in Webster's) to be "probably of imitative origin." Similarly the word *bump* is stated as being "probably imitative of the sound resulting from the action". We must therefore first examine the significance of such phrase as "of imitative origin" or "probably of imitative origin" to characterize a certain class of words. Instead of "imitative" the term "onomatopoeic", and more rarely "echoic", is used as a practically equivalent term.

We have already noted that the historical approach to word study attempts to throw light on words and their meanings by seeking to trace them as far as possible to related ancient languages. Thus the English *eat* is traced not only to Sanskrit *ad* but even to Hittite *ad*, the very ancient Hittite language (more accurately one of the Hittite languages) having been discovered, in relatively recent times, to bear apparently some relation to the

Indo-European family. It should be observed now that, as compared with other words, the "imitative" or "onomatopoeic" words, from the point of view of the historical approach, enjoy so to speak a distinct status that sets them quite apart from the other "nonimitative" words. For whereas in the case of a "nonimitative word", such as the word *eat* appears to be, the historical approach seeks to discover the antecedents or ancestry which links the modern with the ancient word, in the case of a word which, like *bump,* is "recognized" as being "of imitative origin" such historical tracing is generally dispensed with. And indeed it does appear as rather superfluous to seek to gain light on such words as *bang, plop, bump* by tracing them through Gothic, Latin, Greek, Sanskrit and even further back. These words and others like them do not appear to present any particular puzzle or mystery as to their origin. Thus, through the process of "recognition" of a word as belonging to the category of "imitative words", the "mystery" that attaches itself to the word is apparently thought to be effectively disposed of. Whatever the mystery therefore that is presented by words presumably attaches itself only to those words, and they of course are taken to constitute by far the larger class, which are not "of imitative origin". Of what origin then are the "nonimitative words" of a language? Just how did they arise in any language and how do they happen to have the meanings associated with them? It is convenient at this point to consider briefly what information we at present possess on this problem.

The origin of language is a subject about which there has been much speculation, more however, as remarked by Otto Jespersen, among philosophers than among philologists. Down to the 19th century there may be said to have existed essentially two schools of thought, that of the naturalists, who claimed the imitative or natural origin of all languages, and that of the conventionalists, who claimed that words are symbols which possess (with few exceptions) purely conventional meanings. Imitative origin theories under the names of "bow-wow", "pooh-pooh", "yo-he-ho", "ding-dong" have been proposed by Max Müller and others.

The latest attempt to solve the mystery is that of Otto Jespersen who thought that the problem "may be approached in quite a new way by starting from languages as we find them nowadays and tracing their history back as far as our material allows, in order from a comparison of present English with Old English (and similarly in the case of as many languages as possible) to find out the great laws governing linguistic development; by lengthening this system of lines on a larger scale backwards beyond the reach of history, we may be able to arrive at uttered sounds of such a description that they can no longer be called a real language". (Quoted from an article "The Origin of Language" by Otto Jespersen, Encyclopedia Brittanica, 14th edition).

The quotation above expresses the generally prevailing viewpoint which we have here referred to as the "historical approach" to word and language study. The method proposed thus rests on the implicit assumption of some regular process in language development which can be extrapolated "beyond the reach of history".

As the reader will by this time have surmised, the approach to the problem in the present book is not that proposed above. We shall not seek to trace historically any primitive form of a word in order to learn about its true nature. We thus do not call upon the historical method to throw light on the basic character of a word.

(This statement does not imply of course that the historical data are entirely set aside). Instead of attempting to trace the origin of words historically we shall *exhibit* the nature of that "origin" on the basis of the phoneto-semantic approach we have introduced, an approach which, as we have seen, rests on certain phonetic and semantic "first principles" applicable alike to ancient and modern words of related or unrelated languages. It will then become apparent that *any evaluation of the significance of the historical method itself must ultimately rest on such fundamental phonetic and semantic principles.*

In connection with our approach to the problem let us now return to consider just what significance is to be attached to such phrase as "of imitative origin". When this characterization is applied to such word as *plop* meaning 'to drop down suddenly' it seems as though the significance of the phrase is quite clear, that is, that *plop* resembles or "imitates" the sound made in "plopping". Yet a little reflection will show that this apparently obvious "imitative quality" of the word is misleading. For suppose by some suitable instrument we obtained a sound record of a "plopping body". We would find that there is *not the slightest resemblance* between the sound of the falling body and the sound "plop". It is not necessary however for the reader to carry out the indicated experiment to convince himself of this fact. The fact that there is no degree of literal "imitativeness" at all about *plop* should appear obvious when it is considered that, aside from the existence of other English words such as *plump, plunk,* which practically mean the same as *plop,* the meaning which in English appears so "naturally" rendered by *plop* is in other languages, even those very obviously akin to English, rendered by quite distinct words. Thus, the Dutch equivalent of *plop!* is *plons!*. On the other hand Dutch *plof!*, which obviously resembles English *plop* in sound, is the equivalent of English *thud!* Thus evidently to the "Dutch ear" *plof* (or *plop*) describes or "imitates" what to the English ear should "properly" be described as the *thud!* of a falling body. Although, upon a little reflection it will become quite clear that there really is not much of a difference after all between a "plopping" and a "thudding" body. And of course such "obviously imitative" words like *plop, bump, splash, thud* possess no "imitative quality" at all to the "Chinese ear" for example which finds quite different words just as naturally describing the "plopping" or "bumping" or "splashing" etc. actions.

We conclude then that the sound of "imitative words" describing a striking action bears no relation to the actual sound that accompanies such action. Why then do we say that these words are "imitative"? Evidently the "imitative quality" that is associated with these words *is not of physical but of psychological origin*. We may say that such words as *plop, bump,* etc. imitate the *imagined sound* that is associated with a "plopping" or "bumping body". Since the sound imitation is an imagined one it follows that *any other sound* might conceivably be appropriated to serve the "imitative purpose" of a given word.

In connection with the statement above we now make the following assertion: *The characterization of certain words as "imitative" (or "onomatopoeic" or "echoic") has no essential significance as a classifier criterion.* (We are in the present chapter confining ourselves to "striking words"). What we are saying then is that every "striking word" may be construed as being "of imitative origin", so that for example the word *strike* itself, which

114

apparently is not (in Webster's) recognized as "imitative" is, according to the assertion above, no less "imitative" than the word *bump;* and the same is true for *every* simple striking word.

The assertion above follows from our general phoneto-semantic viewpoint together with an additional concept, closely linked with this viewpoint, which we shall now proceed to develop.

Let us return for a moment to our "plopping body" above. We have seen that the words *plump* and *plunk* are practically equivalent to *plop* as far as "imitating" the sound of a "plopping body" is concerned. Now it will be observed that the pair *plump - plunk* precisely illustrate one of the frequently occurring phoneto-semantic variant types we have discussed in Chapter V. (Another illustration for example is *chump - chunk*). It might be surmised then that some relation exists between the concepts of a "word variable" and the "imitativeness" of words. As a matter of fact the two concepts are closely interlinked, as will become evident in our further discussion.

We already know that, in accordance with the prevailing historical viewpoint, words, generally speaking, are considered as isolated "static" units of a language. In contrast the phoneto-semantic viewpoint emphasizes the concept of a word as constituting but one "value" of an associated "dynamic" "word variable". If now we consider a "striking word" (it will be recalled that we confine our discussion in this chapter to words of this class only) regarded as a more or less isolated unit the word may or may not "strike" us as possessing the "imitative quality". Thus the word *smite* may possibly strike us as not being "of imitative origin". If however, instead of considering the word in isolation, that is, apart from other native words *in English itself,* we construe *smite* as one of the series of "values" of a "word variable" other values of which are *smot* (obs. smite) - *smash - smack - swack - swash - switch* the question of the presence or absence of the "imitative quality" of *smite* is seen to become somewhat problematical. In fact it will appear after a little reflection that the characterization of for example *swack* and *smite* as "imitative" and "non-imitative" respectively is quite arbitrary and is based on purely subjective factors.

To illustrate further and emphasize the point we have made above we present below a few more examples:

pat - bat - beat - prat (obs. to beat) - *plat* (obs. strike. slap)

plug (to strike, punch) - *plap* (to strike with a "plap") - *blow* (a forcible stroke with the hand, etc.)

hack - hew - whack

flap (obs. to strike, clap; colloq. to drop or fall; to plump, flop) - *flump* (to set, move, or fall suddenly and heavily) - *plump - flop*

slap - clap - plap

clash (dial. to dash, bang, slap) - *plash* (to dash or tumble about) - *crash*

lunge (act of plunging forward) - *plunge - plunk* (Dutch *plons* - plop)

jab - stab - dab - dip (to plunge or immerse) - *dive*

job (to strike, stab or dig with something pointed) - *stob* (dial. to pierce) - *tap*

jab - jag - dig (to thrust; plunge; dive down; poke) - *stick*

At least one word of each word group above is stated (in Webster's) to be "of imitative origin" or "probably of imitative origin", the implication being that the others are "nonimitative". The arbitrariness of such characterization should now be apparent.

But though we have shown, at least for the class of "striking words", that the characterization of some words as "imitative" (and therefore of others as "nonimitative") is arbitrary we have not gone to the "heart of the problem" and stated precisely what is the nature of the link that associates "striking words" with their sounds. Let us consider this problem somewhat more closely.

We have already remarked above that the "imitative quality" of a word is an *imagined* one, a word such as *plop* appearing to imitate not the physical but the *imagined sound* that is associated with "plopping". It might therefore be better, instead of saying that a word is "imitative" to say that it is "suggestive". In saying however that the term "suggestive" is more appropriate than "imitative" it is not at all implied of course that the characterization of words as "suggestive" has any more significance as a classifier criterion of "striking words" than the characterization "imitative". The term "suggestive" is preferable not because it serves to effect a "cleavage" of "striking words" into "suggestive" and "nonsuggestive" words but because it avoids the misleading implication of physical imitativeness although it conveys essentially the same sense that is conveyed by the conventional term "imitative". This may be seen from the following definition of the word *plap* (obviously a close cousin of *plop*): 'to fall or strike with a sound suggestive of the word *plap*'. The substitution of "suggestive" for "imitative" facilitates however the presentation of the concept which we now wish to formulate.

We proceed to do this as follows. We remark, first of

all, that some words at least which involve *explicitly* a striking action of some kind will be found to include within their *explicit* definition *both the striking action as well as the sound itself that is associated with such action.* Thus the word *plash,* a member of our "blot-family" of the preceding chapter, means 'with a plash or sound of plashing' as well as 'to strike and break the surface of (water, etc.)'; the word *splash,* another member, means 'to fall or strike with a splashing noise', while the word *strike* itself has the meaning 'to cause to sound, esp. by strokes'. Other examples are:

clap—'to strike or slap; to strike (the hands) together so as to make a sharp noise'

clash—'a loud sharp sound; collision or hostile meeting'

thump—'a blow or knock, as with something heavy; also the sound made by such a blow'

knock—'to strike sharply or resoundingly as with something hard or heavy'

ring—'to cause to sound, esp. by striking, as a metallic body'

clang—'to strike together so as to make a clang'

whang—'a resounding impact, blow or the like; also its sound; a bang'

bang—'to strike noisily or violently; to make a loud noise as if by striking'

tang—'a sharp twanging sound, as of a single stroke on metal'

twang—'a harsh, quick, ringing sound; a sharp slap or blow, as that delivered by the release of the drawn bowstring'

clatter—'a rattling noise, esp. that made by the collision of hard bodies' *slap*—'to beat, hit, etc. with a slap or the sound of a slap; a click or sharp noise as of slapping'

slam—'dial. to beat or cuff smartly; to make a banging noise'

slash—'a slashing stroke or cut; with the sound of a slash'

smash—'a breaking or dashing to pieces or the sound or result of such'

crack—'a sharp sudden sound or report; colloq. a sharp resounding blow'

thunder—'to strike with a sound likened to thunder'

pop—'to make or burst with a pop or sharp report; dial. to strike or knock sharply'

tap—'to strike with a slight audible blow; to rap lightly'

rap—'to smite or strike with a quick sharp blow'

tick—'dial. to touch or tap a person or thing gently; to make a tick or a continuous series of ticks'

whip—'to strike with a lash, whip, rod or anything slender and lithe; to thrash about flexibly in the manner of a whiplash; swish'

swish—'to make the sound of a swish; to move, strike or lash with a swish (the sound or thing)'

beat—'to strike repeatedly; to knock vigorously or loudly; to make a sound when struck'

flap—'to give a quick stroke; to clap; to sway loosely; usually with a noise of striking'

Still other examples of "striking words" exhibiting this linkage of the striking action with the sound associated with the action could be given. With regard to this "subclass of striking words" we now wish to formulate the following concept:

Every common word denoting explicitly a striking

*action of some kind together with the associated sound
implicitly involves in its meaning the sound itself, given
by the word, that is associated with or is "suggestive of"
the indicated action.* As regards the phrase "suggestive
of" it is here intended to convey no more than is conveyed by the same phrase in the definition of *plap* cited
above. This definition, it will be recalled, read: 'to fall
or strike with a sound suggestive of the word *plap*'. Our
concept, just formulated, then states in effect that for
example:

clap means 'to strike or slap', with the added implication
   'with a sound suggestive of the word *clap*'
knock means 'to strike sharply or resoundingly', with the
   added implication 'with a sound suggestive of the
   word *knock*'
beat means 'to strike repeatedly', with the added implication 'with a sound suggestive of the word *beat*'

Thus within the subclass of striking words which include in their definition some striking action as well as
an accompanying sound we do not distinguish any words
as being essentially different in character from the word
plap whose sound itself is "suggestive of" the action denoted by it.

What about the other "striking words", that is, those
which denote a striking action of some kind but which
in their definitions do not *explicitly* involve any associated sound? An example is the word *hit* with which, as
ordinarily defined, no sound is associated. Other words
of this class are *push* (dial. to thrust against; to butt),
thrust (obs. to meet forcibly; to clash; collide), *butt* (to
strike or thrust), *meet* (to come into collision with or
opposition to), *poke, punch, stick, stab, jab, touch.* To
this class belong of course by far the greater number of

"striking words". But though the definition of such words does not *explicitly* mention any sound associated with the action we conceive such associated sound to be *implied* in the definition. We thus generalize the concept formulated above to *all* "striking words" as follows:

Every common word denoting explicitly a striking action of some kind implicitly involves in its meaning the sound itself, given by the word, that is associated with or is "suggestive of" the indicated action.

The concept just formulated then states in effect that for example:

hit means 'to deliver a blow; to strike', with the added implication 'with a sound suggestive of the word *hit*'

butt means 'to strike or thrust', with the added implication 'with a sound suggestive of the word *butt*'

thrust means 'to push or drive with force', with the added implication 'with a sound suggestive of the word *thrust*'

poke means 'to make thrusts with a stick, sword or the like', with the added implication 'with a sound suggestive of the word *poke*'

stab means 'to thrust or drive, as a pointed implement', with the added implication 'with a sound suggestive of the word *stab*'.

In the same way, in accordance with the concept just formulated, after each definition of the action denoted by *every simple striking word* the implicit phrase is to be added 'with a sound suggestive of the sound of the word defined'.

Our concept then effects a linkage of the sound of any simple, striking word with its meaning, the character of this linkage being precisely the same as that which associates *bang* or *bump* or *plop* or *plunk* or *thud* with their meanings. Thus, all striking words are *by their sounds* "suggestive of" the meaning of the word.

The concept formulated above will now be seen to stand in intimate relation with that of "word variable" and with the concept of the "fluidity of sounds" as exhibited in a word variable and we should now have a deeper understanding of the significance of these concepts. For the fluidity we have found to be associated with word sounds and which is exhibited for example in such groups as *stab-jab, stab-stick, poke-punch, poke-butt-push,* is but another aspect of the "imitative" or, as we prefer, the "suggestive" quality of "striking words". This will be seen clearly in the case of such a word group as *flop-plop-plump-plunk* of the "obviously suggestive" kind. Because of the "unpretentious" character of words of this class the difference in sound exhibited by the group may be ascribed to a rather "careless attitude" toward them. That is, it is not considered significant enough to observe a careful distinction in sound between them and a certain degree of "latitude of pronunciation" is allowed, whereby the word variants arise. Since it turns out now that all striking words are basically of the same "unpretentious" kind as *plop-plump-plunk* that same "careless attitude" with regard to the pronunciation will be observed toward all striking words, or, what amounts to the same thing, the same type and degree of phonetic fluidity will be observed for all striking words.

In particular the underlying significance of the phenomenon of "sound inversion", at least as applied to striking words, should now be clearly grasped. We had discussed this type of phoneto-semantic variant in Chapter V purely on a classificatory basis and had noted that this type of variant was exhibited not only in such obvious case as *tap* - *pat* but that it occurred with a frequency equal to that of the most frequently occurring type of phoneto-semantic variant. The fact that such should be the case may have appeared puzzling since it implied a certain "laxity" with regard to the "direction" in which words were pronounced. We should now see that, owing to the "unpretentious" or "bang-bump" character of words (at least of the "striking class") such "laxity" or "careless attitude" is in fact observed. Thus the difference in sound between *cob* (to beat) -*cuff* -*buck* - *whack* - *puck* (dial. to strike) - *cop* (dial. to strike) - *chop* (to make a quick stroke) - *potch* (dial. slap, strike) - *butch* (dial. to hack) is essentially of a no more "striking" kind than that observed in *flop* - *plump* - *plunk,* the relative inversion not being construed as sufficiently "disturbing" the sound resemblance. A similar "careless attitude" is observed toward *goad* - *dig* - *dag* (obs. to pierce or stab) - *jag* (to stab) - *gouge* (to cut grooves, channels or holes in with, or as with a gouge) - *tuck* (to poke, Scot. to beat) - *cut* (to strike) - *touch* (to hit or strike lightly) - *chuck* (a slight blow or pat under the chin) and toward *every striking word.*

It will thus be seen that the concept we have formulated above is in the nature of a "democratizing" concept in that it reduces all striking words to the rather unpretentious class of "imitative", or as we prefer, "suggestive" words. In so doing the concept at the same time succeeds in resolving, or at least reducing to one of "lower order", the mystery that attaches to the origin of "nonimitative" striking words. For if such words as *bang* or *bump* or *plop* are not considered as endowed with any particular mystery as regards their essential character then neither are any words such as *strike* or *stick* or *push* or *put* or *knock* or any other striking word. Any historical tracing to their "primitive forms" in ancient languages will therefore be of as little value in throwing light on their *essential character* as the historical tracing of such words as *bang* or *plunk*.

But while the mystery surrounding striking words thus appears to have been resolved or reduced to the order of that surrounding such words as *bang, thud, plop*, the mystery surrounding "nonstriking words" apparently still remains. What is the origin of such apparently "nonstriking words" as *hand, book, room, tree, know, cow, bind, leaf, see, child, black, walk* and the other simple words which constitute by far the greater number of the common basic English stock of words? With the "mystery" surrounding such words we shall deal in the next chapter.

CHAPTER NINE

ALL SIMPLE ENGLISH WORDS ARE "STRIKING"

WE HAVE IN THE preceding chapter, in order to develop
our ideas in stages and thereby clarify the discussion,
confined ourselves to "striking words", that is, to words
which in their *explicit* definitions denote a striking action of some kind. In connection with this class of words
we formulated a concept which associates the meaning
of the word with its sound, namely, the concept that all
simple English words which *explicitly* denote a striking
action of some kind *implictly*, if not explicitly, involve
as part of their meaning the sound itself, given by the
word, which is associated with and is "suggestive of" the
striking action. We now wish to extend the concept of
such association of sound and meaning quite generally
to every simple English word. In order to do this we
must show that every common, simple English word
such as forms part of the "basic" stock, is a "striking
word", that is, that its meaning involves, if not explicitly, then *implicitly,* the idea of striking in some manner
or other. If such is the case then the above concept of
the association of the sound with the meaning will naturally apply to the entire basic stock of words.

Now the idea that any simple word such as *boy,* or
black, or *hill,* or *heart,* or *finger,* or *know,* or *is,* or *that,*

or *two,* involves in its meaning a striking action of some kind will no doubt "strike" the reader, at first glance, as a surprising one and apparently contrary to "common sense". To some degree he should have been prepared for such concept however from the remarks in the preceding chapter on the inclusion of explicitly striking words such as *splash, plash, platch* (Scot. to splash) with the "blot idea-complex" and similarly of other explicitly striking words with the "ring idea-complex" and "belly idea-complex" as discussed in Chapter VII. If *platch* is in the *blot* or *blotch* family then evidently the word *blot* itself for example as well as all the words of the "blot idea-complex" must involve at least implicitly the "striking idea".

It is necessary however in order to bring out the full significance of the concept we here wish to formulate that we proceed systematically by approaching it from several different angles. On the one hand we shall see that the idea that all simple words are essentially striking words is intimately related to the ideas of phoneto-semantic variants and vocabulary mechanism. On the other hand it follows as a natural corollary from the concept which we discussed in Chapter II of the "full scope of meaning associated with simple words".

Let us see first in what way the ideas underlying the phoneto-semantic variants and the vocabulary building mechanism are intimately related with the idea of the "essential striking character" of words. If we return for a moment to our "blot idea-complex" it will be recalled that another member phoneto-semantically linked with this family was the word *flat*. This word, particularly when construed as an adjective and viewed in isolation, does not appear to be associated with any striking action of any kind. If however the word is construed in its verbal aspect in which it has the obsolete meaning 'to lay flat, to level, raze' the association with a striking action will evidently be more readily effected. For after a little reflection it will become clear that implicit in the meaning of the verb *flat* (or *flatten*) is the idea 'to strike so as to render flat'. It is this implicit meaning which justifies the linkage of *plat* meaning 'obs. to strike, slap; a buffet, a slap' with *plat* meaning 'obs. exc. dial. flat, level, to fall flat, obs. a flat thing, plank; a small plot of ground'. It is therefore clear that the verb *flat* or the adjective *flat* is a relatively obvious phonetic modification of the word *plat,* as it is also of the words *plot* and *blade.*

We see from the above illustration that the "striking character" of a simple word comes more readily into evidence, if, in connection with the phoneto-semantic variants, we concentrate our attention on the meaning of the word construed as a verb rather than as a noun, adjective, or other part of speech. In the illustration above for example the noun *plat* (obs. a flat thing, a plank; a small plot of ground) may be construed in a sense as the result (in the case considered "a flat thing") of the striking action denoted by the verb *plat* (obs. to strike, slap). Note the parallel semantic linkage between the verbal and nominal aspects in the following pairs:

slap—v. to strike with or as with the open hand; n. *slab*
    —a comparatively thick plate or slice of anything
slat—v. dial. to strike, beat, pummel; n. a slate or piece
    of slate
flap—v. to beat with a flap; obs. to strike, clap; n. any-
    thing flat and thin that hangs loose; a flat piece, slice
    or layer
tap—v. to strike with a slight audible blow; n. *tab*—a

slight flap, tag, strip

tag—v. to touch or hit in or as if in the game of tag; n. a slight flap, tab, strip

stripe—v. to beat, lash, strike; n. a strip

pat—v. to strike, esp. gently with a flat surface, to flatten, smooth, etc. by striking gently with a flat surface; n. a strip or plank of wood or metal

paddle—v. to beat or stir with a paddle; n. a paddle board

bat—v. to strike or hit with or as with a bat; n. *path*—a trodden or beaten way

dab—v. to strike or hit with a sudden motion; n. a flattish mass of anything soft or moist; any flatfish

prat—v. obs. to spank, beat; n. *board* (AS. *bred*)—a plank

plank—v. colloq. to slam down; n. a heavy thick board

In connection with the nominal or verbal character of a word we now wish to formulate a certain viewpoint or concept relating in general to the "parts of speech" to which words are assigned. We say for example that a noun is the "name of a person, place or thing" or that a verb expresses an "action or a state of being". Now although verbs may be distinguished "physically" from nouns by the possession of characteristic endings and inflections, as in Latin, Greek or Anglo-Saxon, it should be noted that the same "root", that is, that part of the word which is divested of any grammatical endings, may be found to occur simultaneously in a verbal or nominal form or even in an adjectival, adverbial or prepositional form. That is, the categories of "parts of speech" do not apply to the "root idea" itself which is not associated with any particular part of speech but which with suitable endings can express itself as any part of speech. If now we consider the English language in particular we find that the isolated word in general has no outward signs by which the different parts of speech, particularly the noun, verb and adjective, are distinguished. Thus such word as *flat*, discussed above, "functions" as a noun, a verb, an adjective or an adverb, the particular part of speech associated with the word being construed *from the context*. We now conceive the English words, which have divested themselves of the grammatically distinguishable endings of the Anglo-Saxon, to be identical with the "roots" themselves. As such they essentially express the "root idea" and are not therefore inherently associated with any particular part of speech. Instead of saying then that a word is a noun, verb, etc. we shall say that the word is "nominally construed", "verbally construed", etc. or that we are dealing with the "nominal aspect", "verbal aspect", etc. of the word. In accordance with this concept, then, any simple verb becomes a noun merely by being "nominalized" or a noun becomes a verb by being "verbalized", the nominalization or verbalization constituting a process in thought.

It should be remarked that we were aided in arriving at the above concept by considering the nature of the words (represented in the written language by single "characters") of the Chinese language. In this language an isolated word as such is not associated with any part of speech whatever, and in fact the categories of parts of speech are not at all essential to the word. A Chinese word (or character) *according to the context in which it occurs* may be construed as any part of speech which gives the proper sense or meaning to the sentence. Alternatively the Chinese words may be construed as "roots" to which the categories of parts of speech do not apply. In accordance with our viewpoint, then, we generalize what is true of Chinese words as essentially applying to the words, or more accurately, the roots, of any language. In particular, with respect to English we thus explicitly formulate the concept: *No simple English word is essentially or preferentially a noun, a verb, or other part of speech.*

Thus, in the example of *paddle* given above it might be supposed that the verb *paddle* is derived from the noun *paddle* which is the more "primitive". In accordance with the concept just formulated however the verbal and nominal aspects have equal status. Similarly the noun *catch* is not construed as derived from the verb *catch*, or the verb *bunch* from the noun *bunch,* or the verb *club* from the noun *club,* etc. although a word may at any time be predominantly construed as a particular part of speech.

Let us see now by further examples how the concept formulated above helps us, in connection with the vocabulary building mechanism, to arrive at the concept we are here primarily interested in formulating, namely, the "essential striking character" of all simple words. Consider such a common "basic" word as English *finger.* A standard dictionary (Webster's) gives this word as related to Dutch *vinger,* Old Saxon and Old High German *fingar,* German *finger,* Old Norse *fingr,* Gothic *figgrs.* For all that we still appear to be as much in the dark about the "true nature" of *finger* as we were at the beginning, that is, we are unable to answer the simple but not insignificant question, namely, "why does English *finger* mean *finger*"? or "why did Gothic *figgrs* mean *figgrs*? Now in accordance with our basic idea that the full scope of meaning associated with a word must be given due weight in any word comparisons we note that besides its immediately suggested meaning as 'a digit of the fore limb' the word *finger* is also defined as 'anything that resembles or does the work of a finger'. Consider now the word *fang* which means 'figuratively, any sharp prolongation or projection of an object', also, as a dialect word, 'talon, claw', while the word "claw" has, as one of its meanings 'the hand, esp. (plural) the fingers of the hand'. We therefore associate, as phoneto-semantic variants of the type "bat-batter", the pair *fang - finger*.

The pairing of *fang - finger* does not yet throw any light on what actually "lies behind" either *fang* or *finger*. Let us proceed to "build the vocabulary around these words". An obsolete meaning of *fang* obviously associated with its meaning as 'a long sharp tooth' is 'a seizing, catch, capture, grip, grasp'. We now link, as phoneto-semantic variants of the type "fuff (Scot. puff, whiff) - huff", the words *fang - hank* (dial. a handle; hold; to fasten with a hank) - *hink* (obs. a reaping hook). Further, as phoneto-semantic variants of the type "pick - pink", that is, illustrating relative nasalization, as is also evidenced in Gothic *figgrs* - English *finger,* we link *hink-hook*. Thus, through a phoneto-semantic bridge our word *finger* is linked in sound and in meaning to the word *hook,* the latter having in fact (in the plural) the slang meaning of 'fingers'.

A *finger* is naturally associated with the *hand*. In fact the two words are phoneto-semantically linked by noting that the pair *hank* (dial. a handle, hold) - *hent* (dial. seize, lay hold of) exhibit the phoneto-semantic variant type "hold (of a ship) - hulk" while the linkage *hent - hand* is obvious. Our "finger family" thus includes *hand* as well as *hook*. In fact it includes such words as *branch, prong,* and *fork,* all associated with "a finger of some kind". Thus the pair *fork* (a prong; branch of a stream) - *fang* evidence the interchange of the "*r* and *n* vowels" as further illustrated by "prick -

pink"; the pair *fork - prong* (a fork; a tine of a fork; hence a slender pointed or projecting part; a fang of a tooth; a branch of a tree) evidence relative medial nasalization while *prong - branch* illustrate relative palatalization. Note how the phoneto-semantic approach draws attention to the "interplay" in the definitions cited in a standard dictionary of words that may in any way be associated in meaning, and to the words themselves that are employed in the definition to define any given word. Words must be defined by employing other words some of which may be "synonyms" of and therefore semantically linked with the word to be defined. Our purpose is to observe whether such words may be linked phonetically as well as semantically.

With the above remark in mind let us note for example that one of the meanings of *prong* given above is 'a tine of a fork'. Considering the word *tine* we link, as phoneto-semantic variants of the type "pain - pang", the pair *tine - tang* (a projecting shank, prong, fang, tongue, or the like). On the other hand we link *fang - tang* as phoneto-semantic variants of the type "tour - whir - veer", while we further link *tang - tong* (dial. tongs) - *ting* (dial. tang, prong). In the same way as *hank - hent* we link *tang - dent* (a toothlike indentation or notch; a tooth as of a gear wheel, etc.), while the pair *dent-tooth* exhibits relative nasalization as is also exhibited by *tang - tack* (a short sharp-pointed nail; any small hooked knobbed or pointed piece of metal for fastening). Further, we link, as exhibiting relative palatalization, *tack - jag* (a sharp projecting part; a tooth; a denticulation; a barb). Our "finger family" is thus expanded to include the word *tooth,* which is one of the meanings of *fang,* which in turn, through another meaning naturally associated with *tooth,* we have linked with *finger.*

132

(From the point of view of words as constituting particular "values" of a "word variable", see Chapter VI, we have limited our "variable field" to the English language. Additional light on *finger* and its relatives is thrown by extending the variable field to the obviously close cousin languages of German and Dutch [recall discussion of German *Bauch* in Chapter VII]. The phoneto-semantic linkage of *finger-hook* may be effected through the intermediary links *hook - haak* [Dutch hook], *haak - hark* [Dutch a rake], *hark - fork* [compare above *hank - fang*]. The pair *hark - harrow* [Middle English *harwe*] are variants of the "holgh [Middle English hollow] - hollow" type. With English *jag* [a sharp projecting part; a tooth], which we have linked with *tack* and with *tang,* we may further link German *Zacke,* meaning 'jag, spike, dent, cog, prong [of a fork]; tooth [of a comb]', while a German variant of *Zacke* is German *Zehe -* 'toe', the linkage *Zehe-toe* being obvious. Thus *toe,* which is "a finger of the foot", is phonetosemantically linked with *finger,* as is not to be unexpected. On the other hand Dutch *teen,* meaning 'toe', we link with English *tine* 'a slender, pointed projecting part, a tooth or spike', while the same English *tine* we link with German *Zahn,* meaning 'tooth, fang, tusk').

It will be noted that so far, in the definitions of the words we have linked with *finger,* we have emphasized these words as nouns. Thus we were primarily concerned with the words *finger, fang, hook, hank, hand, tang, dent, tine, tack, tooth, jag,* in their "nominal aspects". In accordance with the concept we have formulated above however no simple English word is preferentially or essentially a noun or a verb or other part of speech. Let us now continue with our elaboration of the "finger idea-complex" and by emphasizing this time the verbal aspects of the words we cite see how this concept provides us with further insight into what "lies behind" *finger* and its relatives.

We have linked as nouns, in which their meanings as "fingers of a kind" were emphasized, *finger - fang - tong - tack*. Compare now the meaning of *finger*, verbally construed, 'to touch with the fingers; to handle; obs. to lay hands on; to arrest', with the dialect meaning of *fang*, verbally construed, 'to seize, lay hold of, obs. to capture, take', with *tong* 'to take, gather hold of or handle with tongs; to use tongs' and with *tack*, to fasten or attach by tacks'. The words *finger - fang - tong - tack* when taken in their verbal aspects thus emphasize the 'taking idea". In fact the word *take* itself, as well as the words *tag* (to join; fasten to; attach) and *touch* (to put hands upon in any way or degree; to lay a finger on) are additional phoneto-semantic variants of our "finger family", the pair *tong-tag* for example exhibiting the already frequently encountered relative nasalization, while the Scottish and dialectal English *tack* meaning 'to take' is "the same tack" which means 'to fasten or attach by tacks".

It would thus appear that we have gained some additional light on the "mystery of *finger*" by linking it phoneto-semantically to the verbal aspects of such words as *tong* and *take* involving the "taking, seizing or grasping idea". We have not however as yet "hit the nail on the head", that is, we have not answered the question "why does *tong* mean *tong*" or "why does *take* mean *take*", or "why does *touch* mean *touch*".

Turning to the last question, namely, "why does *touch* mean *touch*" note that the word *touch* has in addition to the meaning cited above 'to put hands upon in any way or degree', also the meaning 'to hit or strike lightly'. Thus the word *touch* is a "striking word" of the class we have considered in the previous chapter. This fact provides the needed clue to the "mystery of *finger*". At the same time it provides us as we shall now see with real insight into the peculiarly effective vocabulary building mechanism by which we may apparently link any arbitrary number of simple words into one large word family.

Once we have "struck" on the fact that one of the members of the "finger idea-complex" is a "striking word" we are able to view in a new light the other members of the "idea-complex". Let us now consider some of these words in this new "striking light". It should be clear first of all that the word *tag* which was cited above with the meaning 'to join, fasten to, attach' is the "same tag" which means 'to touch or hit in or as if in the game of tag', just as the word *jag* (the pair *tag-jag* evidence relative palatalization) meaning 'a sharp projecting part; a tooth' is the "same jag" which verbally construed means as a dialectal word 'to prick, stab or jab'. Recalling next the meaning of *dent*, given above in its nominal aspect as 'a toothlike indentation or notch', we now construe the word as the "same dent" which has the obsolete, except dialectal, meaning 'a stroke, a blow' and the present meaning 'a slight depression, or small notch or hollow, like that made by a blow or by pressure'. The latter *dent* is stated to be a variant of the word *dint* meaning 'to dent, obs. to strike or beat' and *dunt*, chiefly Scottish, meaning 'to strike, knock, beat, bruise, etc. with a dull-sounding blow' and is not, like the first *dent*, associated (in Webster's) with *tooth* (and with Latin *dens, dentis* - tooth). Such distinction however, as we now realize, is of no particular significance being based, as in general is the prevailing historical approach, on essentially inadequate concepts with regard to the semantic and phonetic limits of definition of words. In fact further "variants" of *dent-dint-dunt* are *dunch* (Scot. and dial. to strike or shove with a short solid blow; specifically to jog with the elbow) - *tank* (dial. knock, hit, bang) - *dinge* (a dent made by a blow; to make a dinge in; batter; bruise) - *ding* (dial. to knock or beat; a thump or stroke; a push or thrust) and, as of the "titter-twitter" variant type, *dinge - twinge* (to affect with a sharp sudden pain).

The above group of words all starting with a *t* or *d* which we have linked with *tooth* (as well as with *fang* and *finger)* are thus shown to be of essentially the same "striking-suggestive" (or "imitative") class as *ding* (dial. to knock or beat; a push or thrust) which, by the concept formulated in the preceding chapter, is the "same ding" which means 'to ring'. The same phonetic relation moreover, namely the interchange of an initial labial with a dental, that is exhibited by *tang - fang* is exhibited by *ding* (or *dang,* Scot. variant of ding) - *bang,* the word *bang* being similarly of the "obviously suggestive-striking" (or "imitative") type. The phonetic linkage *fang - bang* is obvious. The semantic linkage may more readily be effected by the following chain: *bang - whang* (dial. to beat, thrash, bang; a resounding impact or the like; also its sound) - *ping* (dial. to prick, push, urge) - *ping* (a sharp sound such as made by a bullet striking a wall; to strike with a ping or similar sound) - *pain - pang - punge* (obs. to goad, cause to smart) - *pinch* (to cause pain to) - *punch* (to prod, probe, obs. to pierce) - *pink* (to stab; to pierce as with a sword) - *fang* (to strike fangs into; dial. to seize, lay hold of).

Our word *fang,* therefore, which we have linked with *finger,* is essentially of the same character as the word *bang* which is of the more obviously "suggestive" (or as more commonly but misleadingly denoted "imitative") class. Thus the mystery of "why *finger* means *finger*" is solved, or at least reduced to the order of the mystery of "why *bang* means *bang*". Similarly, because they are all "striking words", explicitly or implicitly, we have answered the question "why *hand* means *hand*", "*hook* means *hook*", "*tooth* means *tooth*", etc.

Moreover, we shall now be able to see what it is that lies behind the peculiarly effective "vocabulary building mechanism" by which these words and a host of others are phoneto-semantically linked into one family. For, if the essential character of these words is to denote "a striking action of some kind" the linkage between a word and its meaning must be of a looser kind than is commonly conceived to be the case, the different striking words, that is, sounds, being "reserved" as it were to limit the "general striking action" to the more specific "shades of meaning" with which they have become associated. (We shall discuss the nature of this link further on below).

What has been shown to be the case for the "finger family", namely, that its members are all striking words, is true of our "blot", "ring" and "belly" families discussed in Chapter VII. Consider for example the "belly family". It will be recalled that we had found via the phoneto-semantic bridge as members of this family the words *bulge, bulb, bump, hump, heap, cop, cob, knob, hill, ball, bowl, poll* (the head), and *head* itself. Although, as there stated, it should not have been too surprising to find these words included in the "belly ideacomplex", since together with *belly, paunch, pouch, bag,* etc. they have the common semantic aspect of denoting "a protuberance of some sort", and although the inclusion of these words was justified by a chain process in

137

each link of which the phoneto-semantic relation exhibited was of a rather obvious kind, the somewhat remarkable and puzzling phenomenon of thus being able to include what appeared to be an almost arbitrary number of words of considerable divergence of sound and meaning within the same family seemed to elude us. The key that solves the apparent puzzle should now be evident. For the words *belly, bulge, bowl, hill, cob, knob* and even *head* are all, like the corresponding members of the "finger family", implicitly, when not explicitly, striking words of the type of *bump* itself which is one of the members. The different members of the family define different "shades" and "gradations" of meaning of the "general striking words" included in the "belly idea-complex". Thus our word *butt* (a large cask) which we linked with *pot, pod* (a bag, pouch, sac; dial. a large protuberant belly) and *pouch* is the "same butt" which verbally construed means 'to strike or thrust'; the word *buck* meaning 'a basket' is the "same buck" which verbally construed means colloquially 'to butt'; the word *poke* meaning 'dial. a bag' is the "same poke" which verbally construed means 'to thrust or prod'; the word *cob* meaning 'a rounded piece or mass of something' is the "same cob" which verbally construed means 'to strike, to thump'. Similarly the "same cop" is given by the definitions 'obs. exc. dial. the top of a thing, the head; a heap or pile; dial. a blow; to strike'; the "same blow" is given by the definitions 'to expand; to inflate; to swell; colloq. to boast; a forcible stroke with the hand, fist, etc.' and the "same plump" is given by the definitions 'with a sudden or heavy drop; well rounded or filled out'.

It will be recalled that we had listed above, in connection with the "blot family" a group of words in which each word, nominally construed, gave the "result", in the case there considered a flat thing of some kind, of the striking action denoted by the verbal construction. It will be instructive now, in connection with our "belly family", to list a corresponding group of words in which the nominal construction gives the result, this time "a lump of some sort", of the striking action denoted by the verbal construction:

bump—v. to strike, knock or thump; n. a protuberance

cob—v. to strike, thump; n. a lump

cop—v. dial. to strike, to thump; n. dial. the top or head; a heap or pile

lump—v. to move or fall heavily; thump. to stump; dial. to thresh; beat severely; n. a mass of irregular shape

stump—v. to strike heavily and clumsily against the ground; n. a clump

stub—v. to beat, drive, crush; n. a stump

club—v. to beat with or as with a club; n. a knob or bunch

clump—v. to knock; n. a cluster

knap—v. to strike smartly; n. a hill, knoll

knock—v. to strike a sharp or resounding blow or blows; n. Scot. a hill, hillock

knoll—v. dial. to knell, toll; the stroke or sound of a bell; n. a little round hill; a mound

toll—v. to sound or strike by tolling; n. dial. a clump of trees

poke—v. to thrust or prod; n. dial. a heap as of hay or corn

pap—v. to make a light tapping noise, Scot. and Ir. var. of *pop* to strike or knock sharply; n. archaic exc. dial. a nipple, teat; anything shaped like a nipple; a rounded nipple-like hill or peak

tit—v. obs. exc. dial. to tap; n. a teat; a pap or nipple

tat—v. dial. to tap, touch; n. *tate* Scot. and N. of Eng. a small piece of something, as wool or hay, a lock

bunch—v. to thump, kick; n. a cluster

slug—v. colloq. to strike heavily; n. a nugget

clod—v. Scot. to throw violently; to hurl; n. a lump or mass

clout—v. colloq. to give a blow to; to strike; n. dial. a fragment

dump—v. Scot. to beat; n. a thick, ill-shaped or shapeless piece

thump—v. to strike or beat; n. *tump* a hillock, a heap

hunch—v. obs. to push, shove; n. a lump, a thick piece

job—v. to strike, stab, jab; n. obs. a lump, a stump

jag—v. dial. to prick, stab, jab; n. dial. a small load, as of hay or grain

butt—v. to strike or thrust; n. the stub or stump of a cigar, etc; a buttock

shock—v. obs. to strike against suddenly; n. a pile or assemblage of sheaves of grain; a heap

click—v. to strike or move with a clicking noise; n. *clique* a small and exclusive set or coterie

clink—v. Scot. and dial. Engl. to strike or beat smartly; n. *clunk* dial. a lump, *clunch* obs. exc. dial. a clump or lump

plug—v. slang, to strike with the fist, punch; n. a piece of wood, metal, etc. to stop a hole; a mass of rock, tobacco, etc.

plump—v. to drop, fall, sink or come in contact suddenly or heavily; n. dial. a cluster, group, flock; clump

Similarly by emphasizing the verbal aspect of the words, taking into account the concept of the "non-preferential status" of words as nouns, verbs, or other parts of speech, all the words of the "ring idea-complex" can be shown to be included within the class of "striking words". Thus the word *gird* or *girth* (obs. exc. dial. Eng. a hoop, as of a barrel) which we linked with *cirque, crook, curve* is the "same gird" which as an obsolete verb means 'to strike', the semantic relation between the verbal and nominal aspects of *gird* being the same as the corresponding aspects of *lace* which verbally construed means 'to beat, to lash', also, 'to interlace or embroider; to twine, draw, thread or pass as a lace; also to intertwine' while nominally construed it has the obsolete meanings 'a baldric or belt, a noose, snare or gin; a net' and the present meaning 'a cord, band or line'. The pair *lace-lash* are phoneto-semantic variants, the word *lash,* which has the obsolete meaning 'to lace' and the present meaning 'to bind with a rope, cord, thong, or chain' being the "same lash" which means 'to strike with a lash; to whip or scourge'. Such association of a "general striking or sounding idea" with a "curving or winding idea" occurs more commonly than would at first be supposed. Consider for example the following group of words:

whip—to lash, beat; to wind, wreathe or bind about something

sweep—to strip or clear by repeated and forcible blows, strokes, gusts or the like; a curving or flowing line or contour; a bend

switch—to strike, beat, whip or flog with or as with a switch; to turn aside, divert, shift, change

twig—to beat as with a twig or twigs, to switch; dial. pull, twitch, tweak

swing—obs. to scourge, beat, whip; to throw with a fling, to hurl; to make rotate or pivot; to move around an axis, on a hinge, etc.

hurl—to throw or cast with violence, obs. to twist or turn, Scot. to wheel or drive in a vehicle

throw—obs. to strike; to fall heavily or violently; obs. exc. dial. to twist, writhe; also to turn, revolve

jerk—obs. to whip, to lash; to throw with a quick motion suddenly arrested; to give a quick and suddenly arrested thrust, push, pull or twist

sling—to throw forcibly away from one; to hurl; to cast; fling; obs. to strike or fell with a missile from a sling; Anglo-Saxon *sling*an—to wind, twist

warp—obs. to throw, cast, hurl, dial. to fall upon with violence, to beat, hit; to turn or twist out of shape; chiefly dial. to weave or interlace

plat—obs. to strike, slap; to interweave or form by braiding or interweaving; to plait

wattle—dial. E. and Scot. to beat or flog with or as with a rod; to twist or interweave with another as twigs; to plat

waddle—dial. Eng. to wattle; to wobble

wallop—dial. and coll. to beat soundly, flog, thrash; to move in a rolling cumbersome manner; to waddle

walk—obs. to thrash, beat soundly; to roll by, also, to circulate around

roll—to beat with rapid continuous strokes, as a drum; to cause to revolve by turning over and over

drill—to pierce or bore with a drill or as with a drill; obs. exc. dial. to turn round; to whirl, twirl, churn

trill—to vibrate, shake or move to and fro so as to cause a trill; obs. to turn, twirl, roll or rock, also, to quiver; to trickle

tirl—chiefly Scot. to knock or tap repeatedly; to patter; to rattle by moving rapidly up and down; to make vibrate by plucking; to cause to revolve, to twirl, whirl, turn rapidly

Reflection on the definitions of the above group of words, in connection with what we have already said on the "blot", "belly", and "finger" families should make it clear that all of the words of the "ring" family are similarly, *implicitly,* if not explicitly, "striking words", and further that it is the essential "striking character" of these words that explains the peculiar effectiveness of the vocabulary building mechanism in "rounding up" so large and diversified a group of words within the same "ring idea-complex". As a matter of fact it will be seen that our families are not independent or exclusive of one another but through their common striking character are interconnected to form one large "striking family" of which they are subfamilies.

We have thus far in our discussion covered a very considerable number of common English words not explicitly denoting any striking action which nevertheless have been shown in fact to be of an essentially "striking character". The idea is therefore at once suggested that all simple English words are of the same character. In order "to clinch the argument" let us shift our attention for a moment from the word as a member, by virtue of its phoneto-semantic linkages, of a relatively large word family and concentrate our attention on the word itself and the nature and scope of the meanings associated with it.

Let us recall the results which we had discussed in Chapter II, The Scope of Meaning of Words. The essential concept we there wished to emphasize (but whose full significance it was not possible at that early stage of our discussion to bring out) was that no single unique meaning was to be associated with any common simple English word. Otherwise expressed, the "limits of definition" of any simple word are essentially "ill-defined".

143

Let us now examine this idea anew in order to bring out its full significance and the relation which it bears to the primary concept that we here wish to formulate.

If we carefully consider the definitions cited of the word group immediately above, namely, *whip, sweep, switch,* etc. we shall find that in addition to the meaning of a striking action of the more specific kind and a "curving action" some words also denote "a throwing, hurling or flinging action", the idea of "throwing" thus being linked in these words with that of "striking". In fact the word *strike* itself has as one of its meanings 'to dash, to cast'. It will be noted further that the word *walk*, because of its obsolete meaning 'to thrash, beat soundly', also, 'to roll by, to circulate around' was included in that group although from its present meaning it would appear at first glance that it does not belong with the others. Now "to throw, dash, fling, etc." constitutes a *motion* of some kind and as a matter of fact practically all of the above group of words have as part of their explicit definitions a meaning which denotes a motion of one kind or another. It will be instructive to cite, in connection with some of these words, specific definitions involving as in the present *walk*, a motion of some kind which we have not included with the definitions cited above.

whip—to move nimbly, to start, go, turn, pass or the like quickly or suddenly

sweep—to move round or about so as to cover a wide circle or extent

switch—dial. to move, run, or fly like a plied switch; to whisk

swing—to march or walk with free swaying movements of the limbs *hurl*—dial. to move or go quickly and impetuously

jerk—to make a sudden motion; to move with a start or by starts

sling—to stride along with a swinging motion

warp—to turn or bend in one's course; to climb or crawl in a zigzag line

plat—obs. to hasten, hurry

waddle—to walk with short steps, swaying from one side to the other

wallop—to waddle

roll—to gad about, wander, roam; to travel on or as on wheels

drill—to cause to flow in drills or rills by trickling

It would thus appear that the idea of "a motion of some sort" is linked in the case of many words with the general idea of striking. In fact one of the meanings of *strike* itself is 'to go, advance, proceed, as to strike into the fields'. What other ideas may be found associated with the "general striking idea"?

Let us return to our above list again. The word *hurl* has the additional meaning 'to emit or utter with vehemence'. Similarly the word *jerk* means 'to utter in a snappy or sharply broken manner; to speak shortly'; the word *throw* has the Scottish meaning 'to quarrel'; the word *warp* has the obsolete meaning 'to emit, give forth, esp. give utterance to'; the word *roll* means 'to utter with a deep sound', also, 'to utter with a trill', while the word *trill* means 'to utter as, or with, a trill'. Thus the idea of "speaking in some manner" is found to be linked to words one of whose meanings is 'to strike in some manner'. It will be instructive to give below a number of words which further illustrate this semantic linkage. In the following list of words we therefore cite that part

145

of the definition which includes 'a speaking action of some kind': (We have already cited several of these words and remarked on the association of speaking with striking in Chapter II).

patter—to strike with a quick succession of pats or slight sounds; to chatter

splutter—to spatter, to splash about; to speak hastily and confusedly

sputter—to splutter; to utter words hastily and indistinctly

clatter—to make a rattling sound by striking hard bodies together; to chatter

chatter—to make a noise by rapid collisions—said of the teeth; shake; to talk idly, carelessly, incessantly or with undue rapidity; to jabber

clack—to make a clack, to clatter; the sharp noise of bodies striking together; to chatter

crack—to strike with a sharp noise, Scot. to talk, chat, colloq. to cry up, to extol, to praise

clank—chiefly Scot. to strike or hit with a clanking blow; to utter or proclaim with a clank

clash—to make a clash by striking against something; to sound or express by a clash; chiefly Scot. to prate or tattle; gossip

clap—to strike vigorously or resoundingly; obs. to talk noisily, to chatter

knap—dial. to strike smartly; to rap, snap, chip; to speak, utter or talk finely or affectedly; to talk

rap—to smite or strike with a quick smart blow; to utter suddenly and forcibly, to deliver with a bang

chop—to cut by striking; to utter in a short or abrupt way

rattle—to make, cause, or emit a rapid succession of

146

short, sharp noises as through shaking or recurrent collisions of hard bodies; to clatter; to chatter incessantly and aimlessly

hack—to cut or mangle, dial. to chatter

ring—to cause to sound, esp. by striking as a metallic body; to announce, proclaim or the like by or as if by ringing; to repeat often, loudly, or earnestly

cut—to strike sharply as in cutting; old thieves' slang to speak, to utter

ding—to sound as a bell, to ring, clang, colloq. or dial. to talk, urge, or impress with vehemence, importunity, or reiteration

tinkle—to make or emit a series of short thin clinking or ringing notes; to chatter idly

peal—obs. to assail or din, as with noise or loud sounds; a stroke or strokes on a bell as a call; to utter or give forth loudly

Thus we have found that a number of words which denote a striking action of some kind are at the same time associated with the meaning of uttering or speaking in some manner. We have already found some of the same "striking words" to be linked with the idea of motion in some manner and, as discussed in our illustrations of the vocabulary building mechanism, with a wide variety of other meanings. The question now naturally arises, namely, *how many different meanings may possibly be associated with words which at the same time denote a striking action of some kind?* To answer this question let us now give some consideration to precisely what is involved in a "striking action" and just what we mean by such term.

In the preceding chapter in connection with the development of our concept that all explicitly striking

147

words involve in their meaning the sound itself, given by the word, which is associated with and is "suggestive of" the action (that is, that all striking words are of the type of *plap* which is defined as 'to fall or strike with a sound suggestive of the word *plap*') we gave a brief list of such words with their definitions as quoted from Webster's. It is now necessary to remark however that we did not there give the full definitions of these words but only the specifically "striking part". In connection with the concept we now wish to develop as to what constitutes "a striking action of some kind" we shall now quote more fully the meanings which are found to be explicitly included after some of these words. In going over the range of definition of each word the reader should note particularly the associative thought process by which one meaning is "naturally" linked to another.

beat—to strike repeatedly; to produce by means of repeated blows; to force or drive as if by a blow or blows; to tread, as a path; to flap; to overcome in a battle, etc., to surpass; colloq. to mystify, astound, puzzle; to measure or mark off by strokes; to scour or range over (a wood or the like); to exercise severely, to perplex; obs. to debate, expound, study; colloq. to cheat, defraud, to come or act with violence; to vibrate, throb; to run or make headway—said of the animal pursued

whip—to move, take, pull, snatch, jerk, or the like suddenly and forcibly; to punish by whipping; to force, urge, or drive by whipping; to belabor with stinging or biting words; to wrap; to wind, wreathe, or bind about something; to seize; colloq. to conquer, to defeat; to move nimbly; to start, turn, go, pass or the like quickly or suddenly; to swish; a stroke or cut

with or as with a whip; obs. exc. Scot. an instant; a
whipping motion; flexibility, suppleness; a circular
swinging motion, Scot. an attack of sickness, a young
unbranched shoot; quickly, in an instant

hit—to reach or touch (an object aimed at); obs. exc.
dial. to cast, throw; to affect in respect of feelings,
reasonings, well-being or other particular; to come
upon, to arrive at, to find; to attain conformity with;
to mimic or reproduce; to set in operation as by
striking or touching; cause to act or function; begin,
turn on; colloq. to suit, agree; to direct one's course,
to betake oneself; a stroke of success; dial. a plentiful
crop of fruit

thrust—to push or drive with force; to shove; to stab;
to pierce; obs. exc. dial. to crowd, press, throng; to
interpose, interject; to push forth; extend, spread;
to push forward, to crowd, intrude; an attack, assault,
onset; obs. a crowd, throng

stick—to pierce with something pointed; to kill by piercing; to push, shove, thrust, poke; to fasten, attach or
cause to remain by thrusting in; to adorn or deck
with things fastened on, as by piercing; obs. to fasten
or close, to shut, also to confine; to set, to fix in; to attach by or as by causing to adhere to the surface;
colloq. to bring to a stand, to pose; colloq. to puzzle;
to adhere; to remain where placed, to stay, abide,
cleave; to be thrust or put; to protrude; to be hin-
dered in progress or operation; to be embarrassed or
puzzled; to hesitate, balk, scruple; a woody piece or
part of a tree or shrub; a log; a stem or stalk; a rod,
wand, staff; a wooden staff, club or the like used as a
weapon; anything resembling or conceived as resembling a stick in shape or use, esp. something long and
slender; slang pl. the legs; of a person one who is dull

inert or lifeless; a portion of liquor or brandy put into water, tea or the like; a thrust with a pointed instrument; a stab; adhesive tendency or adhesion; an impediment or obstacle; hesitation, delay, stop, demur; colloq. a mast

crack—to make or give forth a loud or sharp sudden sound in or as in breaking; dial. to utter vain pompous words; to brag, to boast; Scot. to talk, to chat, to gossip; to fail in tone production, to become discordant or harsh; to burst or open in chinks; to break with or without quite separating into parts; slang to be ruined or impaired, to fail; colloq. to travel by or as if by whipping on; to whip; to rend or burst, as with grief or pain; to empty as if by cracking; to puzzle out, to solve; to utter smartly or sententiously, to tell strikingly; colloq. to move sharply or with a jerk, to snatch; colloq. (with up) to cry up, to extol, to praise; colloq. a sharp resounding blow; slang an experimental attempt; slang a gibing retort, a quip; archaic and dial. a boast, boasting; colloq. a thing or person fit to be boasted of; Scot. and dial. Eng. talk, conversation; a tale or good story, joke; Scot. a talker, a gossip; dial. scandal; mental flaw, a touch of craziness; obs. a crazy or crackbrained person; obs. a pert lively boy, a rogue, a prostitute

touch—to perceive by means of the tactile sense; to bring into contact, conjunction or the like, so as to reach, rest on, examine, stir up, etc.; to take into the hands, to eat or drink; to strike or play on with the hands, as a musical instrument; to play an air, etc.; to sing; to lay the scepter upon as a sign of assent; to rape; to impinge upon; to adjoin; to put hands upon in any way or degree; to disturb or affect by handling;

150

to lay hands on so as to harm; to meddle with; to concern oneself with; to taint, blemish, spoil or otherwise injure in a slight degree; to affect so as to impress, influence, make respond, move, inspire or the like; to stir, as to pity, remorse or love; to melt; soften; to offend or wound, to hurt the feelings of, to sting; obs. to censure, rebuke, accuse; to abrade, scratch, cut, corrode, etc.; chiefly Hist. to test or prove as with a touchstone, to try, assay; to relate to, to concern; to have a perceptible effect or influence upon; to relate, tell, explain, now only to speak or tell of in passing, casually or cursorily; to make allusion or slight reference to; to come to, to reach, to attain to, to attain to an understanding of, to fathom, to guess at correctly, to hit; to compare with, to come up to; to make a light application of, as a salve, to spread thinly on; to make or delineate, as with light strokes of the pencil or brush; to improve, to modify or transform by or as by such strokes; to touch up; to give a delicate tint, line or expression to in a manner suggesting a touching-up pencil or brush; slang to steal or procure by underhanded means, to borrow from; med. to examine by touching or feeling; to come close, approach near, verge; a light stroke, tap or blow; a slight or covert verbal knock, rap or hit; mental or moral sensitiveness; responsiveness or tact; touchstone, criterion, test, trial, proof; a brief mention, hint or reminder; an agreement or covenant; originally the impress of one's race, kind, etc.; characteristic or distinguishing feature, trait or quality; an impression, mark or stamp, a visible effect; obs. harm, injury; a defect, a weakness; a suddenly aroused or transient emotion or impression; rare the power of touching or exciting emotion; something slight of its kind; a small quantity, a trace, a dash; distinctive manner or method; tag (a children's game); a close call; the state of being in contact or communication; slang originally a mean trick, later a tricky, clever, or fitting act or turn

As a last example we shall cite some of the additional meanings of the word *strike* itself:

strike—to touch or hit with some force either with the hand or an instrument; to come in collision with; to injure or destroy with a lightning stroke; to impel or dash, as with a blow; to dash, cast, to separate, knock or hurl with a sharp blow; to smear, daub; obs. to stroke, to move as the hand lightly in or as in stroking; to afflict, assail, attack, punish as if with blows; to cause or produce by a stroke or blow; to cause to ignite by striking, rubbing or the like; to impress with a die or dies, punch or the like; to thrust in; to cause to enter or penetrate; to set in the earth; to make a sudden impression upon, as by a blow; to affect sensibly with some strong emotion; of a thought, idea, etc. to occur to; to affect in some particular manner by a blow, or something acting in a manner suggestive of that of a blow; to transform (a person) into (some other material or form), as by magic; to cause to sound, esp. by strokes; to indicate by sounding; to play (an instrument) by strokes on its keys or strings; chiefly colloq. to hit upon or come or light upon, esp. suddenly; to meet with, find; obs. to fight or wage (battle); to strickle, as a mold in founding; to catch and hold the admiration or love of, to attract; slang to smite with love; obs. to balance (a book of accounts); obs. to unite as in interest or affection; to arrive at by computation; to reach by figuring; to make and ratify; to lower, to let or take down or apart; to remove, efface, cancel or the like with or as with a stroke of the pen; to assume (a posture, an attitude or the like); old slang to take, as money, forcibly or fraudulently; slang to borrow of; to cast in a mold, as a brick, a candle, etc.; obs. to tap, as a cask; to unload, empty, discharge (a vessel) of its cargo; to advance ("struck in years"); obs. to mark a line or lines on, as on paper; to cause (esp. a cutting) to take root; to go, advance, proceed, to take a course, start; to pass quickly or sharply, to dart; now rare to touch, impinge, glance; to quit work in order to obtain or resist a change in conditions of employment; to cause a color to sink in; old slang to steal, esp. money; to thrust oneself forward, as into a crowd, a dispute; to interfere, intervene, join; to break out, as an epidemic; to seize the bait— said of a fish; to run aground as on a rock or bank; to strand; a strickle for leveling; obs. exc. Scot. and dial. Eng. a dry measure; dial. Eng. a strick or bunch of hackled flax, jute, etc. prepared for drawing into slivers

The above are only a few of the more common striking words whose definitions we have quoted extensively (though not exhaustively; for example still other meanings of *strike* are obtained when the word forms part of a phrase as "strike in", "strike off", "strike out", etc.).

It is important that the reader should reflect carefully on *the fact that so large a variety of meanings can be associated with simple striking words such as those cited above*. (Recall also the discussion in Chapter II and the illustration given of the meanings of *cut,* another "striking word"). What accounts for the fact that so large a

153

range of meanings can come to be associated with a word of this character? What after all *is* the essential character of these words? It would appear for example as though the word *strike* itself, *depending on the context in which it is used, could have practically any meaning that would suit the sense of the context.* Instead of conceiving the word as being "basically" associated with a narrowly defined striking action (as with the fist, etc.) it would appear more in accordance with its actual character to conceive the word as essentially vague in its definition so that when isolated it denotes not a specific but a general action whose precise character, that is, whose "more definite definition", depends on the context. In fact we find it useful to formulate explicitly the following concept:

The limits of definition of all simple striking words are essentially vague such that words of this class might properly be construed as "general action words". The explicit (or dictionary) definition of such words is thus conceived as forming only a part of the total "implicit definition".

With the concept formulated above as applying to every striking word it will now be seen that the basic result at which we wish to arrive in the present chapter, namely, that *all* simple English words are essentially striking words, is not as unduly restrictive in character as might "strike" us at first glance. Formally we may now arrive at this result as follows. From our previously discussed principle that no part of speech is inherently associated wih any simple word, we may construe all the simple words of the language (we shall discuss pronouns, prepositions, adverbs and adjectives in Chapter IX, Grammatical Concepts) constituting the basic stock in their verbal aspects, that is, we may "verbalize" any simple word and thereby construe it as an "action word". An action word on the other hand denotes a "striking of some kind" in the vaguely delimited sense we have just formulated above. That is, what we are actually saying is that all simple basic English words are in their essential character "general action words" of the kind typified by the word *strike* itself or any of the words (and others similar to them) whose definitions we have extensively quoted above.

The result we have established will now upon reflection be seen to "tie in" with all the concepts which we have formulated in the preceding chapters, namely, the scope of meaning of words, word variable, phoneto-semantic variants, vocabulary building mechanism, and the "suggestive bump-bang character" of all simple striking words. Thus the "careless attitude" that expresses itself in the phonetic variation of such "obviously suggestive-striking" words as *plump - plunk* expresses itself in the "less obviously suggestive-striking" words *stab - stick*. On the other hand by the process of the vocabulary building mechanism different "shades of striking" associate themselves with the different "values" of the "word variable". The vaguely delimited scope of meaning that is linked with a common word is thus a correlate of the vaguely delimited phonetic variants with which a meaning may become associated.

We shall obtain a still deeper understanding of what is involved in the characterization of words as "essentially striking in character" by viewing the word and its linked meanings from a different angle. We have given above a list of words which denote both a striking action (in the narrow sense) and a "speaking action of some kind". In order to bring out the nature of the concept we now wish to formulate we now add to that list the following group of striking words in which the "censuring" aspect of the speaking action is emphasized:

tap—to strike with a slight audible blow; to reprove, censure

snap—to cause (something) to crack, click or make a report; to utter sharp biting words

slash—to cut by sweeping strokes; to censure unsparingly

drub—to beat with a stick; to abuse with words

lash—to strike forcibly and quickly; to belabor with words, to berate

flash—archaic to rush, dash, or splash as waves, obs. to strike or dash down; to speak suddenly and vehemently

fling—to cast, send or throw from or as from the hand; a violent throw, a kick; to utter abusive language, to sneer, a jibe, a sarcasm

slam—chiefly dial. to beat or cuff smartly, colloq. to criticise vigorously, brutally or recklessly; to abuse verbally

scourge—to whip, lash, flog; to flay by use of satire or criticism

whip—to lash, beat; to belabor with stinging or biting words, to lash with sarcasm, abuse or the like

touch—to hit or strike lightly, to impinge; obs. to censure, rebuke, accuse

In the above group of words the meaning of a "censuring action" appears to be a "figurative usage" of the words, the "literal meaning" being the physically striking action. Thus it would appear for example that the meaning of *drub* 'to abuse with words' is figurative in contrast to the literal meaning 'to beat with a stick'.

Let us now dwell for a moment on the nature of the figurative usage and the splitting of a word's meaning into figurative and "nonfigurative" or literal. The term "figurative", that is, 'representing by a figure or resemblance, transferred in sense from the plain or literal' as applied to the meaning of a word implies of course that such meaning is secondary to the literal or plain meaning which is primary. Such is the implied assumption wherever the definition given after a word is explicitly qualified by such expressions as "by or as if by", "as if", "with or as with", "hence", "used hyperbolically", "figuratively", etc. Qualifying expressions like these occur with extreme frequency in the definitions after a word as given by a large standard dictionary. (Recall for example the definition of *finger* as 'anything that *resembles* or does the work of a finger', or of *fang* '*figuratively*, any sharp prolongation or projection of an object' or of *ring* 'to announce, proclaim, or the like *by or as by* ringing' or of *strike* 'to affect in some particular manner by a blow, or something acting *in a manner suggestive of* that of a blow').

Now while the distinction of the figurative from the plain or literal meaning appears fairly evident in the case of the "censuring words" we have listed above such distinction appears less pronounced in the case of other words. For example in the case of the word *clatter,* one of our "speaking words" already cited, which has the meaning 'to make a rattling sound by striking hard bodies together' as well as the meaning 'to chatter or prattle; to tattle or gossip' it is apparently a little more difficult to decide which is the plain or primary and which the transferred, figurative or secondary. In the case of the word *chatter* whose meaning 'to prate' appears rather more prominent than its meaning 'to make a noise by rapid collisions' there appears to be even still greater difficulty in deciding whether it is the "speaking aspect" or the "striking aspect" of the word that is primary.

Consider now the word *talk* itself, another "speaking word". The idea of a striking action of any kind is nowhere explicitly mentioned in its definition. Similarly the word *speak* is not explicitly associated with any striking action such as is associated with the words *chatter, clatter, rattle* or *patter*. In connection with the words *talk, speak, say, tell, prate,* etc. we now formulate the following concept: Although these words are not explicitly associated with a striking action of some kind *they involve that action implicitly so that the meanings linked with these words themselves constitute the "figurative usage" of the words, the "plain or literal sense" of a striking action of some kind being implicit, that is, unexpressed, in the definition.*

In order to clarify the above formulated concept, as applied to "speaking words" consider the word *prate* 'to talk, to chatter, to babble, formerly to speak boastingly, dial. to scold' which does not explicitly mention any striking action in its definition. Now there is a word *prat* which has the obsolete meaning 'to spank, to beat' and which thus does not explicitly denote any "speaking action". In accordance with the above formulated concept, then, the word *prate* is the "same word", except for the slight phonetic modification, as the word *prat* meaning 'to beat, spank', the word *prate* appropriating to itself the "figurative usage" of *prat*. Similarly the meaning of the word *speak* constitutes the "figurative transfer of meaning" of the word *spank* (one of the meanings of *prat*) which means 'to strike or fall with a spank, to beat or pound with a spanking noise; colloq. with a spanking sound, spang', the pair *speak - spank* exhibiting the relatively common medial nasalization. Whereas now in the words *prate - prat, speak - spank -*

spang (to make a spang, crack) the "figurative speaking action" and the "literal striking action" are "partitioned" among the different phonetic variants, in the word *crack* (one of the meanings of *spang*) the "literal or plain meaning" 'to make or give forth a loud or sharp sudden sound' and the "figurative or transferred meaning" 'Scot. to talk, to chat' are linked with the "same crack" construed as such because of the absence of any phonetic variation corresponding to the "literal" and "figurative" senses.

It is thus seen that the concept formulated above is intimately related to that of phoneto-semantic variants. As a further illustration consider the word *talk* itself, a word which is not explicitly associated with any striking action. In accordance with the above formulated concept the meaning of *talk* constitutes the "figurative portion" of the definition of the word *clack* 'to make a clack; to cackle; to cluck; to chatter', the pair *talk - clack* exhibiting the "tirl (twirl) - curl" type of phoneto-semantic variant we have already discussed in Chapter V. Of course *talk* is not exclusively a variant of *clack* but may be construed as the inverse of *clat* which has the dialect meaning 'to chatter, gossip'; (a similar inversion is exhibited in *prate* [chatter; dial. scold] - *drub* [to beat with a stick; to abuse with words]). We next link *clat - clack, clat - clatter, clat- chat, chat - chatter, chatter - tatter* (obs. exc. dial. to chatter, gabble, tattle, scold), *clack - cackle, cackle - chuckle* (to utter or call with a chuckle, to cluck); *cackle - tattle* (to prate; to chatter), *clack - click* (to utter clicks; to strike or move with a clicking noise) - *clink - clank - clang*, all of which exhibit types of phoneto-semantic variants with which we are already familiar. Our word *talk* therefore is merely a striking word of the "clink, clang, clank" type which has been "elevated" by taking over completely the "figurative" or "transferred" sense of "to talk".

For simplicity of discussion we have confined the formulation of our concept above to words denoting "a speaking action of some kind". It should be clear however that such restriction is quite arbitrary. A speaking action is only one of the possible "transfers of meaning" which may be associated with a word denoting a striking action. From a reflection on the vaguely delimited scope of meaning associated with the words *strike, thrust, touch,* etc. which we have cited above and the concept of a "striking word" as a "general action word", it is clear that any "figurative meaning" may be "read into" the "plain or literal striking meaning". It will be instructive to give one more example of a "homely Anglo-Saxon word" which illustrates this viewpoint.

The word *heart,* being predominantly construed as a noun, does not immediately "strike" us as associated in any way with a striking action. The word in its verbal aspect is however associated with such meanings as 'to fix or seat in the heart; to form a compact center or heart'. Note now that one of the meanings of *heart,* nominally construed, is 'the part nearest the center, as the central part or core of a tree'. The pair *core - heart* exhibit in fact (like the Greek pair *kēr - kardia* to which both *core* and *heart* are apparently "traced") the relative excrescence of a final consonant as discussed in Chapter V (as well as the interchange of initial *h-k*). Reflecting on the meaning of *core* we next link, in accordance with the principle of the vocabulary building mechanism, *core - gore* (obs. to pierce or penetrate with a pointed instrument, as a spear; to stab; to dig or hollow). Further we link, as variants of the same type as *core-heart,* the pair *gore - gride* (obs. to cut or pierce) and *gride - gird* (obs. to strike), noting one of the meanings of *strike* is 'to pierce, to penetrate'. Thus, via a phoneto-semantic bridge, we link *heart* to *gird* which means 'to strike'. We may further link *heart* or *gride* to *cross* which has the meaning 'to traverse'. On the other hand, we may link *gore - core - chore* (obs. core) - *turr* (obs. exc. dial. Eng. to butt) - *through* (Middle English *thurgh, thurh*) - *door*. Further the pair *strike - through* (German *durch*, Dutch *door*) exhibit relative excrescence of initial *s*, as in "grate-scratch", or alternatively the interchange of the unit sounds *st - th*, as in *stamp - thump* (recall discussion in Chapter V). When viewed in this "striking light" the word *heart* is thus seen to be a striking word which has been "elevated" by linking itself to the "figurative transfer of meaning" of the plain, literal, or "common" *strike,* and which furthermore through another "transfer of meaning" becomes *through,* so that the phrase "strike through the heart" is in a sense doubly redundant. The linking of *heart* to *door* which would not surprise us if construed as merely a poetic figure of speech is another simple consequence of the same concept. (A brief discussion of the relation of our viewpoint to the nature of the poetic creation will be given in the final chapter).

We need not of course stop at *door* but, via the operation of the vocabulary building mechanism, could, as already amply illustrated in our earlier examples, draw in more and more words which when not explicitly denoting a striking action in the narrow sense denote a "figurative transfer of meaning" of such action. We may thus express our basic result that all simple words are essentially striking in character in the following alternative form:

All simple words which do not explicitly denote a

striking action of some kind involve such action implicitly, the meanings which are linked to such words constituting the "figurative transfer" of such implied striking action.

From the point of view here developed, therefore, "figures of speech" constitute the very fabric of which are woven the meanings associated with words, that is, with word sounds. This viewpoint has direct bearing on the interrelationship between the "ordinary", the "colloquial", the "dialectal" and the "slang" usage of words. It will be recalled that in our illustrations we did not distinguish as differing essentially in "status" the classifications of meanings under these different categories. Thus in our "Bauch-belly" family we included as a member the word *bag* which has the dialect meaning 'the belly'. This meaning which might be construed as a "transferred meaning" we did not construe as "secondary" to the "primary" meaning of 'a sack, a pouch'. Similarly as another member of the same word family we did not construe the slang meaning of *knob* 'the head' as secondary to its "primary" meaning of 'a round protuberance, a bunch, lump, bump, hump'. What is "primary" about the words *bag* or *knob* or in fact of any simple word is their "essential striking character" such as is more obviously (or explicitly) the case of the word *bump*. That "extravagant fancy" which is characteristic of "slang" words is in fact a manifestation of the same "transfer of meaning activity" which invests words with their "ordinary" meanings.

In our next chapter we extend our discussion to the words of languages other than English or the very closely allied German and Dutch languages.

162

CHAPTER TEN

ALL SIMPLE NON-ENGLISH WORDS ARE "STRIKING"

OUR DISCUSSION THUS far has in the main been confined to the native basic English stock of words although we have now and then extended our "field of word variables" to the closely allied Teutonic languages like German and Dutch and, in connection with our discussion of historical word linking, briefly considered Latin, Greek or Sanskrit words.

In connection with our "Bauch-belly" family discussed in Chapter VII we have already pointed out what is involved in the process of "word tagging" in two such obvious "cousin" languages like English and German. It was seen that what is essential is not that a particular English word resemble very closely in sound and meaning a particular German word but that *the same vocabulary building mechanism operates in each language.* Thus the word *belly* (Anglo-Saxon *belg* - bag, bellows, belly) may be "tagged" to German *Bauch* of the same meaning as well as to German *Balg* meaning 'a bag', while the word *Bauch* may be "tagged" to English *bag, pouch, paunch, bulge* and the entire host of words belonging to the "belly idea-complex" which we there discussed. *What we compare then is not relatively isolated*

163

words but word families which are built in an analogous fashion in each language around the same idea-complex. Such comparison then brings out clearly the full interplay of sound and meaning and the reason for *the differences as well as for the close resemblances* between the common words of two obviously related languages like English and German.

The German language, and the Teutonic languages in general, Dutch, Flemish, Swedish, Norwegian, Danish, Icelandic, ancient Gothic, are so obviously close to English that they might all be construed as "strong dialectal variations" of each other. The Teutonic languages constitute however but one subfamily of the extensive "Indo-European" family which includes besides a wide variety of other languages such as Armenian, Albanian and Sanskrit (and moreover is said to bear certain relations to such other more recently discovered ancient languages as Hittite and Tocharian, "a basically Indo-European tongue"). Now the kinship of English to such languages as Armenian, Albanian or Sanskrit will not, to a student of these languages, be obvious in the same way as its kinship to German, Dutch or Swedish. The kinship of English and Sanskrit for example is based on certain historical considerations but mainly on what is generally assumed to be a very careful comparison by language specialists of "Indo-European" grammar and vocabulary. Implied in the very idea of an Indo-European language stock is of course the concept of a primitive Indo-European mother tongue which must have given rise to the entire family and which moreover is stated to be capable of being reconstructed on scientific philological principles.

It should however at this stage of our discussion be fairly evident to the reader who has followed us all along that such hypothetical reconstruction, based as it is on essentially vague concepts of the scope of meaning association and of the range of sound variation of words and without any grasp of the essential "striking character" of all simple words, is entirely illusory. The question of the genetic kinship of for example English to Sanskrit, a language said to approach closest to the supposed characteristics of the primitive Indo-European mother tongue, must be considered not only in the light of whatever historical information is available and from comparisons of vocabulary and grammar in a wide group of languages but *in the light of the more fundamental semantic and phonetic principles we have discussed. That is, upon any possible genetic kinship that may exist between the two languages must be superposed a "phoneto-semantic kinship" which is common to all languages.*

In order to clarify and further illustrate the meaning of the above statement let us turn our attention for a moment to some of the words that constitute the basic Sanskrit stock. In Chapter II, in connection with our discussion of English *eat*, we have already referred to one basic Sanskrit word (or root), namely, *ad* to which is traced (along with Greek, Latin, and even Hittite roots) the word *eat*. At that early stage of our discussion we were as yet unable to see the full implications involved in this idea of word tracing or "tagging". We now resume our discussion in the light of the concepts we have developed thus far. We first "round up" a number of English words "semantically linked", that is, associated in meaning, with the "eat idea-complex". We note first that English *eat*, in addition to its meaning 'to take in through the mouth as food' has also the meaning 'to gnaw, perforate, or bore into', a meaning which ap-

pears naturally associated with the "plain meaning" of
the word. Now note that English *pick*, in addition to its
meaning 'to pierce, indent or the like by striking with a
pointed instrument' has the colloquial meaning 'to eat',
the word *peck* means 'to strike repeatedly with a pick',
also, 'to bite daintily or nibble, colloq. to eat', while the
word *bite* has the meaning 'to cut, gash, or pierce' and
the obsolete meaning 'to eat'. It should be clear from a
consideration of the "interplay of meanings" and from
our discussion of the preceding chapter that our English
eat is but one member of a family of words built around
the "eat idea-complex" which includes among others the
following English words: *eat, bite, pick, peck, gnaw,
nibble, pierce, cut, gash.* These words are not only
"semantically interlocking" but via phoneto-semantic
chains may be shown to be "phonetically interlocking".
Thus we may link *pick - eat* by the following (not
necessarily unique) chain: *pick - peck - whack - hack -
hash* (that which is hashed or chopped up; meat and
vegetables) - *hatch* (a stroke or line) - *etch* (to corrode
as with acid) - *eat*. We may link *pick - bite* by the chain:
pick - pitch (obs. to pierce with something pointed) -
pash (dial. Eng. to strike violently) - *bash* (dial. beat,
smash) - *butch* (dial. to hack) - *bat* (colloq. a stroke, a
sharp blow) - *bite* (a sharp impact). It is clear, as we
should expect from our discussion of the preceding
chapter, that *eat, bite,* etc. are all "striking words" and
in fact that we may link *bite - beat* in the same way that
we may link *eat - hit*. As striking words we may apply to
them the same kind of relative inversion which we observe in "pat - tap", these two being in fact members of
our "eat idea-complex". Thus we link *bite - chip* (to cut
small pieces from), the *t* of *bite* being palatalized to the

ch of *chip* in the same way as in *tap - chap* (Scot. a blow, rap, knock, stroke). We may further link *chip - cham* (dial. to bite, chew, champ) - *chaw* (to chew; to champ at the bit) - *chew - champ - chop* (obs. to seize with the chops and eat; to snap). We may also construe *eat - chew* as the inverse of each other with palatalization of *t* to *ch*, as observed in *bite - chip* above and in *eat - etch*. The *chop* above is the "same chop" which means 'to cut by striking, to mince', the pair *chop - cut* exhibiting the "knob-knot" type of variant with palatalization of *k* to *ch* as also exhibited in *chop - cop* (dial. to strike) - *cob* (to strike, thump) - *job* (to jab, thrust, peck) - *jab* (to poke, stab). Our words *chew* or *chaw* or *cham* or *champ* are in fact simply variants of *jab*, an obvious, that is, explicit, "striking word". Thus, implied in the meaning of *chew* is 'to strike (or jab) so as to chew', just as implied in the meaning of *eat* is 'to strike (or hit) so as to eat' and in *bite* 'to strike (or beat) so as to bite'.

From our English "eat idea-complex" let us now turn to the corresponding "*ad* idea-complex". We give below a number of Sanskrit words, or rather roots since they are divested of inflectional endings, whose interrelated meanings correspond to those given above. (The definitions are those found in A. A. Macdonell "A Practical Sanskrit Dictionary". In regard to the pronunciation we may note briefly that the letter *h* in *kh, ch, th,* etc. indicates "aspiration", Sanskrit *c* is like English *ch,* ṣ is a "cerebral" *sh,* ś a "palatal" *sh*; similarly ṭ, ḍ are cerebral varieties of *t, d,* ṛ is the "vowel r" pronounced approximately like *ri* in Rig-Veda, ṃ represents the nasalization of a vowel, approximately like French *n* in "enfant", short *a* is like *u* in "but"; confer discussion in Chapter III, The Concept of Sound Kinship). The reader is asked

to note the modification in the sound and meaning of
the words as he proceeds down the list.

ad—eat
aś—eat (bite—obs. to eat)
vyadh, vidh—pierce, perforate, hit, wound
puth—bruise, crush
pīḍ—press, squeeze, wring, give pain to, hurt
piṣ—grind, pound, bruise, destroy, crush, press, touch
piś—hew out, carve
paṭ—split, slit, break through, tear up, cleave, scratch
badh, vadh—smite, slay, kill, destroy, strike down
bādh—repel, press hard, vex, grieve, hurt
bhid—cleave, cut
bhaj, bhañj—divide, share, break
bhakṣ—eat (peck—to strike, break or pick up something
    with repeated small blows; colloq. to eat)
hīḍ—vex, offend (eat—slang to consume with vexation)
khād—chew, eat, gnaw, devour, destroy
ghas—eat
chid—cut, lop off, hew down, tear, bite or gnaw off, sever,
    break, pierce, wound, divide
kṛt (krit)—cut, cut off, out, up or down, cleave
khad, khand—break, cleave
kṣad—carve, slaughter
kuṭ—divide, break up
kuṭṭ—crush, bruise, lacerate
kṣud—pound, crush, pierce, goad
khud—thrust in
chud—urge on, impel, excite
tud—strike, push, pound, sting, goad, strike against,
    peck, bite
tṛd (trid)—split, cleave, pierce
tuj—strike, push, incite, stimulate
168

tij—be sharp, sharpen, urge
taḍ—strike, beat, wound
śas—slaughter, cut down
śat—divide into sections, cleave, sever, cut
daś, daṃś—bite
dabh, dambh—injure, hurt
jabh, jambh—snap at, seize with the mouth, crush, destroy
jakṣ—eat, consume, devour

The above group of Sanskrit words are interlinked in meaning within the "ad idea-complex" in the same way that the English words above cluster about the "eat idea-complex". Further, they are linked in sound, exhibiting the same types of phonetic variants as the corresponding English group. Consider for example Sanskrit *kuṭ* meaning 'divide, break up'. In Chapter II, The Scope of Meaning of Words, we cited extensively the meanings of the English word *cut*. We may link *kuṭ - cut* but the linkage is by no means "one-to-one". For corresponding to the different meanings, which are semantically linked, of English *cut* there are a number of Sanskrit more or less obvious variations of *kuṭ* which have associated themselves with meanings included within the "cut idea-complex". Thus the group *ghas - khād - chid - khad - kuṭ - kuṭṭ - śat - śas - khud - chud - tud - tuj - taḍ - tij* are variants exhibiting palatalization of guttural *k, g* or dental or cerebral *t, d, ṭ, ḍ,* to palatal *c* or *ś,* the palatal sound mediating between the sounds *k-t*. Similar palatalization is exhibited in *bhid* (cleave, cut) - *bhaj* (divide, share) and in *dabh, dambh* (injure, hurt) - *jabh, jambh* (snap at, crush, destroy). The other types of phoneto-semantic variants already discussed in connection with English words of course operate in Sanskrit.

Thus *khad - kṣad* or *kuṭṭ - kṣud* exhibit the interchange of *k* with the unit sound *kṣ*. Again, the pair *bhaj - bhañj* or *khad - khand* exhibit relative medial nasalization (as in English pick-pink) while the pair *chid - kṛt* or *tud - tṛd* exhibit the relative interchange of a medial vowel with the "r vowel" (as in English pick-prick). In the pair *ad* (eat) - *khād* (chew, eat) the "absent" initial aspirate of *ad* has "hardened" to the aspirated guttural *kh* of *khād*, the phonetic relation being the same as in English *hit - cut* or, further, as in Sanskrit *khād - hīḍ* (vex, offend; cf. *eat* - slang to consume with vexation). Instead of hardening to a guttural it may harden to a labial in *ad - bhid,* the phonetic relation between these being that of *eat - bite* (obs. to eat) or *hack - whack - peck.* As obvious variants of *bhid* we may link *bhid - vyadh, vidh - bādh - badh, vadh - pīḍ - piṣ - piś - paṭ - puth.*

It is clear then that if we are to "trace" English *eat* to Sanskrit *ad* we may as well trace *eat* to the entire "ad family". It is not therefore a question of establishing a "one-to-one correspondence" between a relatively limited and arbitrary number of English and Sanskrit words. By taking fully into account, as is logically demanded, the phonetic and semantic relations that are involved in any idea-complex we may in fact find an even closer resemblance of the Sanskrit to the English vocabulary than we had "bargained for". It will be of interest and significance to give below some of the Sanskrit roots cited above followed by closely resembling English words whose meanings are included within the "eat idea-complex".

dabh, dambh (injure, hurt) - *dab* (to strike or hit with a
    sudden motion; to peck) - *thump* (to pound, knock)

jabh, jambh (snap at, seize with the mouth, crush, destroy) - *chop* (obs. to snap) - *job* (to jab, thrust, peck) - *jab* - *champ* (obs. to gnash the teeth)

bhaj (divide, share) - *wedge* (to cleave or separate with a wedge) - *whack* (slang, to divide into shares)

bhañj (break) - *whang* (Scot. to slice, to chop) - *bang* (to cut, to dock)

bhakṣ (eat) - *peck* (to bite daintily or nibble, colloq. to eat) - *pick* (to pierce, indent or the like, colloq. to eat) - *box* (to strike with the hand or fist) - *vex* (to annoy or anger)

bhid (cleave, cut) - *bite* (to cut, gash or pierce) - *pitch* (obs. to pierce with something pointed)

vyadh, vidh (pierce, perforate, hit, wound) - *wedge* (to force or drive as a wedge is driven) - *pit* (to dig a pit or pits) - *fid* (a pin of hard wood or iron tapering to a point)

badh, vadh (smite, slay, kill, destroy, strike down) - *bat* (to strike or hit with or as with a bat, to cudgel) - *beat* - *pat* (obs. exc. dial. to hit with a flat or blunt instrument)

bādh (repel, press hard, vex, grieve, hurt) - *butt* (to strike or thrust)

puth (bruise, crush) - *put* (obs. exc. dial. to push, thrust; to butt) - *push*

piṣ (grind, pound, bruise, destroy, crush, press, touch) - *pash* (dial. to throw violently to hurl, dash, crush, smash, strike violently) - *bash* (dial. and slang, to strike heavily, to beat, to bruise or dent by a blow, to smash)

paṭ (split, slit, break through, tear up, cleave, scratch) - *pitch* (obs. to pierce with something pointed)

piś (hew out, carve) - *butch* (obs. exc. dial. to hack)

pīḍ (press, squeeze, hurt, give pain to) - *bite* (to cause

171

sharp pain or smarting to, to hurt)

hīḍ (vex, offend) - *hit* (to affect to one's detriment) - *eat* (slang, to consume with vexation)

chid (cut, bite or gnaw off, pierce, wound, divide) - *cut* (to wound the sensibilities of) - *chide* (to rebuke, to reprove)

śat (divide into sections, cleave, sever, cut) - *jad* (local Eng. to make a jad or deep groove in) - *dod* (dial. to cut off, to lop or clip off)

śas (slaughter, cut down) - *chase* (to groove or indent)

khād (chew, eat, gnaw, devour, destroy) - *cut* (to fell, to hew)

khud (thrust in) - *cut* (to penetrate)

kuṭ (divide, break up) - *cut* (to sever, divide)

chud (urge on, impel, excite) - *goad* (to urge, instigate)

tud (strike, push, pound, sting, goad) - *thud* (to move or strike so as to make a dull sound or thud) - *jut* (obs. exc. dial. to jolt, to knock against something, shove) - *jot* (obs. exc. dial. jolt, jog)

taḍ (strike, beat, wound) - *tat* (dial. tap. touch) - *tit* (obs. exc. dial. to tap; a return blow) - *dash* (to strike violently) - *dad* (Scot. to strike forcibly, to beat, to knock)

tuj (strike, push, incite, stimulate) - *touch* (to hit or strike lightly; to affect so as to impress, influence, make respond, etc.)

kṛt (krit) (cut, cut off, out, up or down, cleave) - *geld* (to castrate) - *gride* (to cut or pierce) - *curt* (short)

tṛd (trid) (split, cleave, pierce) - *dart* (obs. to pierce or transfix with or as with a dart) - *dird* (Scot. a blow, thump)

daṃś, daś (bite) - *dash* (to strike violently) - *dent* (to make a dent upon, obs. exc. dial. Eng. a stroke, a blow) - *dunt* (Scot. to strike, knock, beat, bruise) -

dunch (Scot. and dial. to strike or shove with a short solid blow; to jog with the elbow) - *dinge* (to make a dinge or dent in)

jakṣ (eat, consume, devour) - *chack* (Scot. to bite with a snapping noise; a bite or small portion of food; a snack) - *jag* (to prick, stab or jab).

It is evident that we are able to find dialectal, colloquial, obsolete or slang English words, all of native and basic stock, which resemble rather closely the ancient Sanskrit roots. And it should be equally evident that the words thus found are not necessarily identifiable with or "tagged" by the corresponding Sanskrit words which resemble them. *What accounts for the resemblance, aside from the question of possible genetic kinship, is the fact that the Sanskrit roots, like the English roots, are all of an "essentially striking character", as is true of the roots of any language.* For, in the first place, where the word is of the "more obviously striking character" (or "imitative") like English *thud* we may expect, from the large number of striking words available, that a similar word will be found to occur in the language compared; we thus find Sanskrit *tud* resembling English *thud* or Sanskrit *tuj* - English *touch,* Sanskrit *taḍ* - Scottish *dad* (to strike forcibly). And in the second place, where the word is not of the obvious but "implicit striking character" the resemblances found will be due to the analogous operation in both languages of the vocabulary building mechanism under which the implicit striking words will assume a "transfer of meaning" or a "figurative sense", as discussed in the preceding chapter. Let us further clarify the meaning of the last statement by considering several additional Sanskrit roots.

The above list of Sanskrit (and English) roots was

173

grouped about the "eat idea-complex". Since the latter
constitutes merely a sub-group of the more general
"strike idea-complex", it is not surprising that we can
"branch off" into what is apparently a quite divergent
idea-complex which is yet semantically (and phonetically) linked with the above. Thus, for example, the English word *wit* meaning 'to know, to have knowledge' of
is "traced" to Sanskrit *vid* -'to become acquainted with,
find out, comprehend, know, perceive' (which is related
to Sanskrit *Veda,* the name for the ancient literature of
the Hindus). Again, as long as we are "tracing" English words to Sanskrit words we must do so in full aware-
ness of the remarkably interlocking semantic and phonetic relationship that exists between the words forming
the basic vocabulary *of any one language,* an interrelationship which in the last analysis is due to the essential
striking character of all simple words. We must thus
link *wit* not only to Sanskrit *vid* but to Sanskrit *vidh,*
vyadh meaning 'to pierce, to perforate' which we had
above included in our "eat idea-complex", and hence to
the entire list of words above. For "to know" may be
construed as a "figurative transfer of meaning" of "to
pierce or penetrate". And in fact we may link English
wit - whet (to sharpen; to make sharp, keen, or eager)
just as we may link English *know - ken* (dial. recognize,
discern, Scot. to know, understand) - *keen* (acute of
mind, sharp, penetrating). There is "another *vid* or
vind" which has the meaning 'find, fall in with, seek
out' which, as should be apparent, is the same *vid* which
means 'to know'. Further, Sanskrit *vind,* which is *vid*
nasalized, may be linked to English *find* meaning 'dial.
to perceive or detect by or as by the senses; to meet with
or light upon accidentally' while the nonnasalized *vid*
may be linked to *meet,* the implicit striking character

174

of *meet* and *find* (and Sanskrit *vid, vind*) appearing explicitly in the meaning of *strike* - 'to meet with, find' and of *hit* - 'to meet with, to reach, to find'. In the same way that Sanskrit *vid* (perceive, know) "appropriates" the "figurative sense" of *vidh, vyadh* (pierce) Sanskrit *paś* - 'see, behold, look at, find, observe' appropriates the "figurative sense" of *paṭ*, included in our "eat idea-complex" above and meaning 'split, slit, break through, cleave'. Similarly Sanskrit *cit* - 'perceive, know' is the "figurative" of *khud* - 'thrust in' or of *chid* - 'cut, pierce', the pair *cit* - *cint* (to think) exhibiting relative medial nasalization.

By continuing in the manner suggested we could draw in the entire basic stock of Sanskrit roots, of which there are somewhat over 800, and exhibit, on the one hand, their phonetic and semantic interrelationship, and on the other, their rather suspiciously close resemblance to English words, which may include obsolete, dialectal, colloquial, or slang words or meanings. We could do the same with native Armenian roots or Albanian roots, which also belong to the so-called Indo-European stock. Could we do the same with Chinese roots or Swahili roots or in general with the roots of languages belonging to other than the Indo-European?

It will be recalled in our Introduction that the concepts presented in this book were arrived at after an attempt had been made to establish if possible the kinship of Hungarian, a non Indo-European language, to the Indo-European stock. We there remarked on the difficulty that is involved in any attempt to establish, or at least render probable, by parallel word lists the genetic kinship of languages provisionally belonging to different stocks, namely, the uncertainty in determining whether a word standing for a common every day idea and bearing a resemblance to a corresponding word in the other language is native or borrowed. The language literature abounds in books and papers in which parallel word lists are cited in an effort to link certain languages with others of provisionally different stocks. The presence of a relatively large number of simple words that resemble each other in what are supposed to be languages of different stock does indeed from the prevailing historical viewpoint present a perplexing puzzle. This perplexity, as we should now realize, is inherent in the very concept of word tracing or "tagging", which is the central concept of the prevailing historical approach. This approach, for all of its notable successes in the past, is, as we already know, based on essentially inadequate and vague ideas relative to the semantic and phonetic definition limits of words and of their basic striking character which account for the operation of the vocabulary building mechanism in any language.

If the reader has carefully reflected on the remarks made above in connection with the Sanskrit roots, which are included within the "Indo-European stock of roots", it will become quite evident to him that the restriction of the concepts here presented to such Indo-European roots is entirely arbitrary. From the very nature of the phonetic and semantic principles we have introduced it is clear that they must be applicable to the words of any spoken language whatever irrespective of the language family under which it is prevailingly classified.

In the remainder of this chapter, in order to illustrate the significance of the above remarks, we shall turn from Sanskrit or other Indo-European languages and devote our discussion, to the extent permissible within the available space, to some of the common words which constitute part of the basic vocabulary of Chinese, a language which has never, to the author's knowledge, been even remotely associated with English as bearing any kind of affinity to it. What we shall do will be merely to apply all of the principles we have presented in the preceding chapters. We shall then discover, perhaps a little to our amazement, that there is an odd familiarity about these "esoteric" Chinese words which makes them strangely reminiscent of our own "homely Anglo-Saxon words".

We shall start first with a group of Chinese words which cluster about the "needle idea-complex". It will be significant to bear in mind, in studying this list, that among the meanings associated with *needle* are the following: 'any slender, pointed object like a needle, as a pointed crystal, a sharp rock, an obelisk, etc.; to pierce or treat with or as with a needle'. The reader is asked as he proceeds down the list to follow carefully the modification in sound and meaning from one word to the next. (It is not essential for our purpose to go into details of pronunciation. In the Wade system of transliteration which is here employed the consonants *t, ch, p, k, ts* are pronounced approximately like English *d, j, b, g, dz* respectively while *t', ch', p', k', ts'* correspond to the unvoiced English sounds *t, ch, p, k, ts*. The number in front of each word gives the page and number down the page of the Chinese character as found in Fenn's Five Thousand Dictionary from which the definitions are cited; the number after the word gives one or more of the four tones with which a Chinese word, in the Peking dialect, which is the basis of the "kuo-yü" or national language, is pronounced. For details of pronunciation the reader may consult any Chinese grammar).

24.3 *chen* 1—needle, pin, to prick
559.7 *tsuan* 4—awl, gimlet
24.2 *chen* 1—to probe, needle
559.2 *tsuan* 3—bore a hole
58.1 *chien* 1—point, sharp
521.1 *tien* 3—dot, point
520.1 *tien* 1—peak of hill (peak—a projecting point, the sharp or pointed end of anything)
69.9 *chien* 4—arrow, dart
78.1 *ching* 1—stalk (stalk—obs. a quill)
528.3 *t'ing* 13—stalk, stick (stalk—a part likened to the stalk of a plant)
80.10 *ching* 4 (*hsing* 4)—the shin bone, shank (shank—obs. the shaft of a column)
103.6 *chuang* 1—a post, stake
238.7 *kan* 1—cane, rod, pole
47.2 *ch'iang* 2—a mast, spar, boom
46.2 *ch'iang* 1—a spear, lance
46.7 *ch'iang* 1—lance, wound
79.10 *ching* 1—thorn
582.8 *t'ung* 3—strike against, punch into
527.1 *ting* 4—to nail (nail—to fasten as with a nail)
526.3 *ting* 4—fix, determine
522.5 *tien* 4—settle, determine
109.12 *chung* 4—hit a mark
111.1 *ch'ung* 1—dash against, rush at
111.2 *ch'ung* 1—rush against, collide
104.4 *chuang* 4—strike against, meet
437.3 *shang* 1—wound, injure
477.2 *sun* 3—wound, injure
111.9 *ch'ung* 4—push, poke at
475.1 *suan* 1—aching, painful muscles
475.2 *suan* 1—sour, distressed, grieved
185.3 *hsing* 2—punish, punishment

178

478.1   *sung* 1—the pine, needle leaf conifers
508.1   *t'eng* 2—pain, ache
583.2   *t'ung* 4—pain, sting
576.4   *tun* 1—strike, thump, jolt

It will be seen that the different words of the above group arise, in accordance with the vocabulary building mechanism, by "reserving" each phonetic modification for a particular "shade of meaning" which, however divergent, is nevertheless semantically linked with the other meanings.

The phonetic variants illustrated above are of the relatively obvious kind. They constitute on the one hand the interchange of initial *t, ts, ch, k, sh, hs* with each other and on the other hand the relative nasalization of final *n* to *ng*. The sound *ch*, as already frequently noted, may be construed either as palatalized *t* or palatalized *k*, the sound thus mediating between *t* and *k*. (The medial character of *ch* was already recognized by the ancient Sanskrit grammarians who placed Sanskrit *c*, pronounced *ch*, between *k* and *t* in the order of the Sanskrit alphabet). Thus the pair *tien* 3 (dot, point) - *chien* 1 (point, sharp) exhibits relative palatalization of *t* to *ch* while *kan* 1 (cane, rod, pole) - *chuang* 1 (a post, stake) exhibits relative palatalization of *k* to *ch*. The latter pair at the same time exhibits relative nasalization of *n* to *ng* as is also exhibited in *t'ung* 3 (strike against, punch into) - *tun* 1 (strike, thump, jolt) and in many other examples that will be noted above. The pair *ch'ung* 1 (rush against, collide) - *chuang* 4 (strike against, meet) may be construed as exhibiting the relative excrescence of medial *w*, *chuang* being pronounced as "chwang". All these types of phonetic variants have of course already been encountered in English words as in the pairs *tingle-jingle*, or *pain-pang*, or *titter-twitter* and illustrate the concept discussed in Chapter III of the fluidity or kinship of sounds.

Consider now the group of native English words below similarly built around the "tine idea-complex":

tine—a slender pointed projecting part; a tooth or spike; a fork or harrow

tine—obs. a brief time, tiny (point—the tapering end of anything; a time or portion of time; obs. a minute part)

shin—Scot. the ridge of a hill

chine—a ridge or crest

keen—sharp, having a fine edge or point

teen—obs. keen, dial. injury, damage, grief, sorrow, pain

tine—pain, trouble, grief, teen

ting—dial. tang, prong

tang—obs. prick, pierce, a projecting shank, prong, fang, tongue or the like, a sting, a pang

tang—sharp flavor or tinge

stang—Scot. sting, pang, spear

stank—Scot. and dial. Eng. variant of stang

junk—obs. a rush or reed

sting—a goad, incitement, stimulus, to pain keenly, as of the mind

sting—Scot. a pole or pike, a post or shaft

twinge—to have a sharp pain

twang—dial. twinge, sharp pain

dinge—to make a dinge or dinges in; a dent made by a blow

ding—dial. push or thrust, a thump, stroke, push

dunch—dial. to strike or shove with a short solid blow

tunk—dial. rap, thump

tank—dial. knock, hit, bang

twank—a sharp slap or blow

twang—a sharp slap or blow
din—to strike wih confused or clanging sound, stun
dun—dial. to din

If the above group of phoneto-semantically inter-locking English words are now compared with the corresponding Chinese group it will be evident that we encounter rather surprising resemblances in both sound and meaning of the Chinese to the English words. Phonetically the above group illustrates the same general type of interchanges as the corresponding Chinese group. Thus, corresponding to the interchanges we noted of initial Chinese *t, s, sh, hs, ch, k* we have in English the interchanges *t, st, ch, k, sh, j* (on construing *st, sk, sp, ts, ks, ps,* as unit sounds see Chapters III and V). Thus we have as "values" of a "word variable" *stank* (Scot. var. of stang) - *shank* - *junk* - *tang* - *stang* which through "denasalization", that is, interchange of *ng* or *nk* with *n*, may be further linked to *keen* - *chine* - *tine* - *shin*. In order to exhibit these resemblances more explicitly and "strikingly" we link the corresponding Chinese and English words as below:

t'ing 13 (stalk, stick) - *ting* (dial. tang, prong)
chien 1 (point, sharp) - *keen*
chen 1 (needle, pin, to prick) - *tine* - *teen* (obs. keen; dial. pain)
chien 4 (arrow, dart) - *tine* (a slender pointed part)
tien 1 (peak of hill) - *chine* (a ridge or crest) - *shin* (Scot. the ridge of a hill)
tien 3 (dot, point) - *tine* (obs. tiny)
ching 1 (thorn) - *ting* (dial. tang; prong)
t'ung 4 (pain, sting) - *tang* (a sting, a pang)
chuang 4 (strike against, meet) - *twang* (a sharp slap or blow)

ch'ung 4 (push, poke at) - *tunk* (dial. rap, thump)

tun 1 (strike, thump, jolt) - *din* (strike with clanging sound) - *dun* (dial. din)

t'eng 2 (pain, ache) - *twang* (twinge, sharp pain) - *twinge*

In the above group of Chinese (and corresponding English) words we have, as already said, given only the more obvious types of phoneto-semantic variants. Corresponding to the other types which we have discussed in Chapter V, for example the type exhibited by *tang* - *fang* we may expect similar variants in Chinese within the limits of "phonetic preferences" characteristic of that language. The word group below is therefore linked through the phoneto-semantic variant type *tang* - *fang* with the group above:

137.7   *feng* 1—butt, push, poke

384.5   *pang* 4—stick

138.2   *feng* 1—point of spear

330.5   *mang* 2—edge, sharp point

330.4   *mang* 2—awn, a point

137.9   *feng* 1—a beacon (beak—anything projecting in a point like a beak; pick—pierce by striking with a pointed implement)

309.6   *p'eng* 4—hit, meet (strike—to hit upon, find; hit—to come upon, find)

138.3   *feng* 2—meet

With these Chinese "feng words" we may link the following corresponding group of English "fang words" which closely resemble them in sound and meaning:

feng 1 (butt, push, poke) - *funk* (Scot. to kick) - *fung* (dial. to beat, kick, emit a sharp buzzing sound) *pang* 4 (stick) - *pink* (stab, pierce) - *ping* (dial. prick, push)

feng 1 (point of spear) - *punge* (dial. goad)

mang 2 (edge, sharp point) - *fang* (a projecting tooth or prong)

mang 2 (awn, a point) - *pang* (a piercing pain)

p'eng 4 (hit, meet) - *bang* (with a bang, smack) - *ping* (a sharp sound such as that made by a bullet striking a tree or wall)

feng 2 (meet) - *whang* (to strike or assail with force or violence; bang)

In accordance with the concept formulated in the preceding chapter a word which denotes a striking action implies, where it does not explicitly express, in its meaning the sound itself, given by the word, associated with and "suggestive of" the "striking action". Thus the English dialect word *fung* above explicitly means 'to emit a sharp buzzing sound' as well as 'to beat, kick'. The word *fung* (or *funk*) is a rather obvious variant of *ping* - 'a sharp sound', which by this concept is thus the "same ping" which means 'prick, push' just as *tang* meaning 'a sting, a pang', is the "same tang" which means 'a sharp twanging sound as if of a single stroke on metal'. By now dwelling on a *tang* as a "twang" we may "branch off" into a group of words all associated with a sound of some kind whether a "sharp sound" or other sound, and still semantically as well as phonetically linked with our "needle or tine idea-complex". To our list of Chinese words already given we may therefore add the following:

168.10 *hsiang* 3—sound, noise
189.4 *hsiung* 1—brawl, scold

18.10 *ch'ang* 4—sing, call out
46.6 *ch'iang* 1—a singing tone of voice
446.5 *sheng* 4—noise, sound
479.5 *sung* 4—intone, recite, chant, read
479.4 *sung* 4—extol, praise
29.1 *ch'eng* 1 (*ch'en* 4)—style, call, name
186.1 *hsing* 4—name

To the above group of Chinese "hsiang words" corresponds a similarly built up group of English "sing words" whose semantic and phonetic resemblance may be explicitly exhibited as follows:

hsiang 3 (sound, noise) - *song* (a succession of unmusical tones or sounds having a peculiar or characteristic tune) - *tang* (a sharp twanging sound) - *twang* (a harsh, quick, ringing sound)

sheng 4 (noise, sound) - *sing* (a small shrill sound as that of a bullet in flight, a whiz; to be filled with a humming or buzzing) - *zing* (a shrill humming noise; a sharp thrill)

ch'ang 4 (sing, call out) - *sing* (call, name) - *ding* (to sound, as a bell, to ring, clang; colloq. or dial. to talk, urge or impress with vehemence, importunity or reiteration; to din)

sung 4 (intone, recite, chant, read) - *sing* (obs. to chant, intone)

sung 4 (extol, praise) - *sing* (to celebrate in song or verse)

hsing 4 (name) - *sing* (call, name)

hsiung 1 (brawl, scold) - *song* (colloq. a clamor, fuss)

Note particularly above how the various meanings associated with the "same" English *sing* are "apportioned" to different Chinese variants of *hsiang* 3 (sound, noise). The different meanings associated with English *sing* may, reciprocally, be construed as associated with "different *sing's*" which are linked semantically and coincide phonetically. (Recall the discussion given in Chapter VII of the concept of "degree of homonymy").

The above group of words was obtained, as already said, by dwelling on the "twang" aspect of a "tang" and the preceding group on its "sting or pang" aspect. Associated with the idea of "sting" is that of "to pierce", "to penetrate" and by a "figurative usage" that of "to stir", "to stimulate", "to excite", "to thrill". We thus have a semantic linkage of "sound words" with "emotion words" as is explicitly exhibited in the meaning of for example *tingle,* which is an obvious variant of *tang, jing* (to ring) and *jingle* 'to cause to ring or tinkle; to stir or stimulate', and of *zing,* another variant of *tang* or *sing,* 'a shrill humming noise; a sharp thrill; vim; spirit'.

By shifting our emphasis this time to such "figurative sense" of the "penetrating idea" as indicated by the meaning of "pierce" - 'to penetrate with the eye or mind; to comprehend; discern; see through; to penetrate so as to move or touch (one's heart; one's feelings), to affect poignantly" we may now add the following "feeling, seeing, understanding words" which branch off from our "needle group" above. (Recall the concept formulated in the preceding chapter on the "figurative usage" of words. In the list below the meanings of words given in parentheses are designed to facilitate the "semantic bridging" of ideas):

580.1 *t'ung* 1—go through, perceive (heart—the understanding, intellect, the part nearest the center)
579.2 *tung* 3—understand
108.1 *chung* 1—center, inside
579.6 *tung* 4—hole, cave, see through, know

185.6   *hsing* 3 (*sheng* 3)—waken, inquire, understand
185.5   *hsing* 31—arouse, wake up
168.8   *hsiang* 3—think, meditate
522.1   *tien* 4—think of, remember
181.1   *hsin* 1—heart, mind, center
 82.5   *ch'ing* 2—feelings, emotions, affections
478.5   *sung* 3—raise, excite, egg on
565.3   *tsung* 1—agitated, excited
579.3   *tung* 4—move, influence, shake, excite
527.1   *t'ing* 14—hear, listen, smell
565.2   *ts'ung* 1—astute, sharp hearing
 61.1   *chien* 4—see, observe
 60.5   *chien* 3—select, choose (see—to discern)
241.2   *k'an* 4—look at, examine, see
240.10 *k'an* 34—spy, watch, seek to find out (see—to make investigation or inquiry)
 78.6   *ch'in* 4—to sound, fathom
183.6   *hsin* 4 (*hsün* 4)—try case, examine
182.7   *hsin* 1—to taste (taste—obs. to test, try, prove)
184.5   *hsing* 1 (*hsin* 1)—fragrant (taste—poetic, to smell, scent)
166.1   *hsiang* 1—fragrant, incense (smell—to detect or become aware of, as if by the sense of smell)
184.3   *hsing* 1—rank, strong smelling
239.4   *kan* 3—to influence, move, affected by

Observe the "semantic interlocking" in the above group of "feeling, understanding, sensing words". The same association in meaning that is observed for example in comparing the obsolete meaning of *taste* 'to test, try, prove' with the "poetic meaning" 'to smell, scent' is observed in the meanings of the two Chinese words *hsin* 1 - 'to taste' and *hsing* 1 (or *hsin* 1) - 'fragrant' which are thus the "same hsin". The entire group of Chinese words above are of course, like the corresponding English words such as "know, see, hear, smell, think, sound, try, seek, etc." striking words which have appropriated the "figurative usage" of the "literal striking action", the different "shades of feeling or sensing" being reserved for each phonetic modification in accordance with the vocabulary building mechanism. (Recall the meanings given of *touch* 'to hit or strike lightly; to affect [one, one's senses, heart, mind, will, etc.] so as to impress, influence, inspire or the like; to make hear, feel, comprehend, etc.'.). Again we find it possible therefore to link with the above Chinese words common English words which resemble them closely in sound and meaning, being similar striking words which have appropriated the analogous "figurative usage":

chien 4 (see, observe) - *ken* (dial. discern) - *keen* (acute of mind, sharp, penetrating) - *know* - *can* (obs. to know, understand)

k'an 4 (look at, examine, see) - *ken* (archaic, look, see)

hsiang 3 (think, meditate) - *think* (to center one's thoughts on) - *twang* (to make a guess or conjecture; to surmise)

hsing 3 (waken, inquire, understand) - *tang* (obs. exc. dial. to sting) - *sting* (to stimulate, incite or urge on as with a sting)

ch'ing 2 (feelings, emotions, affections) - *tingle* (to cause a thrilling, stinging or pricking sensation; to be vibrant or alive)

tung 4 (hole, cave, see through, know) - *chink* (a small cleft, rent, or fissure) - *dinge* (a dent made by a blow; a surface depression) - *sink* (to make a depression by digging, etc.; to enter so as to impress lastingly)

ts'ung 1 (astute, sharp hearing) - *tang* (Scot. and dial.

187

Eng. a pointed knife, pike, foil, etc.)

tsung 1 (agitated, excited) - *zing* (a sharp thrill; vim, energy, spirit, enthusiasm) - *jing* (ring, to be filled with a ringing or reverberating sound) - *sing* (to be filled with a humming or buzzing)

tung 4 (move, influence, shake, excite) - *ding* (to throw violently, to dash, fling, drive)

sung 3 (raise, excite, egg on) - *sing* (to dispatch, force, influence or the like by or as by a song) - *tingle* (to cause to ring or tinkle; to stir or stimulate)

hsiang 1 (fragrant incense) - *tang* (a sharp specific flavor or tinge) - *tinge* (a slight coloring, cast, flavor, etc.)

hsing 1 (rank, strong smelling) - *sting* (stinging force, quality or capacity) - *stink*

ch'in 4 (to sound, fathom) - *chine* (obs. to cleave, chink) - *ken* (obs. cause to know) - *know*

kan 3 (to influence, move, affected by) - *keen* (actuated by sharpened feeling or desire; intense—of emotion, desire, etc.).

By noting for example that *tung* 4 has both the "literal meaning" 'hole, cave' and the "figurative meaning" 'see through' and again emphasizing the former we may further extend our "needle or pierce idea-complex" to include the following "hole, pit, ditch or dig words" which are phoneto-semantically linked with all the preceding words. (Note the meaning of *hole,* verbally construed, 'to cut, dig, or bore a hole in; to pierce' and recall the discussion in Chapter IX on the nominal and verbal aspects of words).

26.7   *ch'an* 2—sink, deep
443.3   *shen* 1—deep
12.9   *chan* 4—dip into, soak
58.4   *chien* 14—tinge, moisten

507.3   *teng* 1—steep
180.5   *hsien* 1—fall into, sink into
77.7   *chin* 1—invade
75.11   *chin* 4—enter, advance
12.1   *chan* 4—sink, soak, deep
80.3   *ching* 3—well, deep pit
18.3   *ch'ang* 2—intestines, bowels
248.1   *k'eng* 1—pit, gully, injure (pit—a surface depression or hollow)
279.1   *k'ung* 1—empty, hollow
280.1   *k'ung* 3—a hole
240.5   *k'an* 3—a pit (pit—to dig a pit or pits, excavate)
247.4   *k'en* 3—break new soil
79.8   *ching* 1 (*keng* 1)—plough, till (plough—to move, cut, or cleave through)
522.8   *tien* 4—till (till—plough; right through to)
76.2   *chin* 4—exhaust, all, uttermost
81.2   *ching* 4—end, finally, to utmost (till—throughout the interval extending to).

Note particularly that the semantic relation between Chinese *ching* 1 (plough, till) and *ching* 4 (end, finally, to utmost) is the same as between English *till* (plough) and *till* (right through to), both pairs being associated with the "through idea". Similarly the semantic relation between *k'ung* 3 (a hole) and *ching* 4 (end, finally, to utmost) is that corresponding to the meanings of *hollow* 'a hole' and 'colloq. complete, thorough'.

With the above group of Chinese words we may as before compare a corresponding group of English words which parallel them closely in sound and meaning:

hsien 4 (fall into, sink into) - *sink*
teng 1 (steep) - *tinge* - *dunk*
k'ung 3 (a hole) - *chink* (a small cleft, rent or fissure)

189

k'an 3 (a pit) - *chine* (obs. a fissure, crevice)
ching 3 (well, deep pit) - *sink* (a depression hollowed out) - *dinge* (a surface depression)
k'en 3 (break new soil) - *chine* (obs. to crack, cleave, chink)
tien 4 (till) - *tine* (to harrow)

We have thus far cited a relatively large number of Chinese words and it has apparently always been possible to "dig up" simple native English words which sound and mean like the corresponding Chinese words. The question arises, namely, to what extent is it possible, given any Chinese word, to find one or more English words resembling it and conversely, given any simple English word, to find one or more Chinese words which resemble it. The answer is that it is always possible to find parallel words within the limits of the "phonetic preferences" characteristic of the languages compared. Let us briefly consider what is the nature of these "phonetic preferences".

Within different areas of the same country we find dialectal variations, that is, differences in pronunciation and often in vocabulary of the same language. The language is "the same" because the variants are mutually intelligible. Thus the same English language is spoken throughout the United States although New England English for example is not quite identical with that of the South. When however the degree of difference is such as to render the speech variants mutually unintelligible we have what amounts to different languages. For example, Castilian and Galician, both "Spanish", are actually different languages, although the resemblance is still close enough so that they are easily recognized as related languages. Castilian and Galician are respectively the languages of the provinces of Castilla and Galicia of Spain, and they may thus be construed as marked forms of "provincialisms" relative to each other, a provincialism implying a speech variant that is found within a restricted area or province of a larger area, which may be a political unit. Now it is found that, aside from historical factors such as invasions or mass migrations, the more remote or relatively isolated two areas or "provinces" are, the greater the difference in speech between the peoples inhabiting them. According to the viewpoint here presented we shift our emphasis from the genetic or "parent-offspring" relation of languages to the "cousin" relation and construe the differences in languages as one of "degree of provincialism". That is, we say that languages differ essentially not in kind but in degree, the difference depending simply on the degree of relative isolation of the "provinces" in which the languages are spoken.

Now what is it that constitutes the difference to a varying degree as we pass from one language to another? Aside from the differences in grammar and vocabulary there is the difference in what we denote as the "sound preferences" that are characteristic of each language or of a group of languages. These sound preferences are simply the choice, variety, and combinations of the sounds which are used to form the words of the particular language in question. Of all the different consonant and vowel sounds that may conceivably be pronounced with the human organs of speech each language selects as it were only a certain relatively narrow range, rejecting all others as "foreign to the genius" of the language. We need not here go into the question as to precisely what the factors are which determine the choice for each particular language. Psychological considerations no doubt play a large part. What interests us chiefly is to formulate explicitly the notion of the existence of such characteristic sound preferences and to note how it fits in with our general phoneto-semantic viewpoint.

In order to illustrate further the meaning of the above remarks and answer the question we have raised on the extent of the possibility of finding word parallels between English and Chinese words let us now return to a further consideration of the Chinese vocabulary. Earlier in this chapter we had found that corresponding to such common English word as *cut* we have a whole series of Sanskrit words *kuṭ, chid, khād,* etc. which resemble the English word in sound and its different "shades of meaning". If we attempt to do the same for Chinese we shall not succeed. The reason is that no Chinese word ends in any of the stops *k, p, t*. As long as by "Chinese" we mean the Peking dialect, which is the basis for the national language, this statement is true and expresses a "phonetic preference" characteristic of that dialect. If however we do not restrict ourselves to the Peking dialect but extend our "word variable field" to Cantonese, Foochow, Hakka or other Chinese dialects then we shall find "Chinese cut's" of various "shades of meaning" in the same way that we found "Sanskrit cut's". We give below a group of Chinese words, including in some cases the Cantonese reading of the Chinese character, centering about the "cut idea-complex" which includes, as we know, the "eating, biting or chewing idea". (Compare with our previously given corresponding group of Sanskrit roots):

249.7   *ko* 1, Cant. *kot*—cut
120.7   *chüeh* 2, Cant. *tsit*—cut off

252.1 *k'o* 1, Cant. *hak*—cut into, carve
120.10 *chüeh* 2, Cant. *kit*—decide (cut—decide a deal)
121.9 *chüeh* 2—pick ax, to pick
89.5 *cho* 4—peck food
96.6 *chu* 4—chopsticks, take up food
89.2 *cho* 2—cut (as gems)
554.9 *ts'o* 4—lop off, file, trim
531.2 *to* 4—chop fine, cut off
545.4 *tsao* 2 (*tso* 4)—chisel
114.8 *chü* 4—a saw, to saw
170.1 *hsiao* 1 (*hsüeh* 14)—cut, slice
54.10 *chieh* 24 (*ko* 4)—separate, parted, partition
548.4 *tse* 24 (*chai* 2)—choose, pick out
549.1 *ts'o* 4—crack, chap
256.1 *k'ou* 1—pick out with knife, carve
41.3 *ch'i* 4—a notch, cut a notch
51.4 *chiao* 2 (*chüeh* 2), Cant. *tsiok*—chew, bite
618.2 *yao* 3, Cant. *gau*—bite, gnaw
71.1 *ch'ih* 1, Cant. *shik*—eat
452.2 *shih* 2, Cant. *shik*—eat

If therefore we extend our field of variables to include Chinese dialects whose "sound preferences" permit ending a word with a stop we may "identify" English *cut* with Pekingese *ko* 1 (to cut) which in Cantonese is pronounced *kot*. Similarly we may "identify" other Chinese words of the above group with such English words as *jag, hack,* etc. as may be explicitly exhibited below:

k'o 1, Cant. *hak* (cut into, carve) - *hack*
chüeh 2, Cant. *tsit* (cut off) - *dod* (dial. cut off, clip, dock)
chüeh 2, Can. *kit* (decide) - *cut* (decide a deal)
cho 4 (peck food) - *chaw* (dial. to chew) - *chew*

chiao 2, Cant. *tsiok* (chew, bite) - *chew* - *tew* (obs. exc. dial. to beat, also to tease, vex) - *jag* (to cut indentations in; dial. to prick, stab or jab)

ch'ih 1, Cant. *shik* (eat) - *chack* (Scot. to bite with a snapping noise)

yao 3, Cant. *gau* (bite, gnaw) - *chew* (to bite and grind with the teeth)

cho 2 (cut, as gems) - *cow* (Scot. cut short, prune, lop off)

tsao 2 (chisel) - *jow* (N. of Eng. to give a blow to, strike)

to 4 (chop fine, cut off) - *taw* (obs. exc. dial. to tew; to beat)

ts'o 4 (lop off, file, trim) - *saw* (to cut, as a saw)

chü 4 (a saw, to saw) - *saw*

hsiao 1 (to cut, slice) - *sheugh* (Scot. to make ditches or drains in; a ditch, trench, furrow) - *sow* (dial. a ditch)

The phonetic relation between the Peking pronunciation of for example *chiao* 2 (chew, bite) to the Cantonese pronunciation *tsiok* is quite analogous to that of English *chew* - Swedish *tugga* (to chew) or English *saw* - German *Säge* (saw), Swedish and German constituting "dialects of English". The final *h* of such word as Chinese *ch'ih* 1 (eat) or *chüeh* 2 (cut off) or a final vowel may be construed as an "unhardened" stop which may harden in the Cantonese or other Chinese dialects. The latter, by extending the range of variables, thus supply us with words like *cut, jag, hack,* etc. which we do not encounter in the Peking dialect.

The phonetic preference of the Peking dialect for a final *h* or a vowel rather than one of the stops *k, p, t* cuts down the number of vocables or separate words thus further extending with each word (or sound) that wide range of meaning which is found so perplexing to the student of the language. For it appears as though a character or its sound may be linked with an almost arbitrary number of meanings, the "intended" one of which depends on the context in which it is used. In this characteristic however the Chinese language merely provides a particularly good illustration of the concept earlier formulated of the essentially vague delimitation of meaning of words, the vagueness arising in the last analysis from the fact that every simple word is an explicit or implicit "striking word" of essentially the same type as "strike", "hit", "touch", whose character we discussed in the preceding chapter. In general the simple English words, in the vague delimitation of their meanings, are thus not essentially different from the Chinese words. Due however to the fact that the sound preferences characteristic of English are much less restricted in scope the vocabulary building mechanism operating in English is capable of producing a greater variety of sounds, that is, words, with which "shades of meaning" of various degree become associated.

The significance of the above remarks will be better understood if we consider the following illustration. The Chinese (that is, Pekingese) word *chih* in its various tones is associated with, among others, the following meanings: *finger, toe, hoof, foot, branch, tooth, limb, wing, fin, grasp, hold, take, finger-nail, hawk.* It will be recalled now that in our discussion of the "finger idea-complex" of the preceding chapter we had in fact included such words as *toe, branch, tooth, take, hand,* with the "finger idea-complex" and by extending our discussion further we could have included *foot, hoof, wing, hawk,* etc. within the same idea-complex. Thus whereas these semantically linked words are in English associated with different phonetic variants they are in the

Peking dialect, because of its restricted sound preferences, associated with a single variant. The dialects however by permitting final stops *k, p, t* give a greater number of variants and therefore of vocables. The vocable
chih has of course other phonetic variants semantically
linked with the "finger or claw idea". It will be instructive to give such a list of words below for comparison
with our discussion in the preceding chapter of the
"finger idea-complex":

256.2   *k'ou* 1—claw, scrape

263.1   *kua* 1, Cant. *kwat,* Foochow *kwak*—scrape, shave

537.1   *ts'a* 1 (*ch'a* 1), Cant. *ts'at,* Foochow *ch'ak*—rub,
      scrape

99.1   *chua* 1, Cant. *chau*—scratch; grab, seize (scratch
      —obs. to seize or gather by or as by scraping with
      the claws)

215.7   *huo* 4, Cant. *wok,* Hakka *fet*—catch, seize, get,
      obtain

42.3   *chia* 1, Cant. *hip*—clasp, pinch

42.4   *chia* 1, Cant. *kap*—pincers, tongs

84.1   *chiu* 1—clutch, pinch

99.3   *chua* 3 (*chao* 3)—claw, clutch, scratch

255.1   *kou* 1, Cant. *ngau*—hook

98.4   *ch'u* 2—a hoe

8.2   *ch'a* 1—fork, hoe

66.9   *chih* 2, Cant. *chi,* Foochow *chi, chieng, pi*—fin-
      ger, toe

67.12   *chih* 2, Cant. *chap,* Foochow, *cheik, teik*—hold
      seize, take

88.4   *cho* 1, Cant. *chuk*—seize, catch

112.1   *chü* 1—seize, arrest

43.9   *chia* 4, Cant. *ka*—marry a husband, attach to

116.8   *ch'ü* 3—take

515.5   *tiao* 1—seize with the mouth or bill
547.1   *ts'ao* 1—grasp
457.1   *shou* 1, Cant. *tsip*—receive
458.3   *shou* 3, Foochow *ch'iu*—the hand
 66.11   *chih* 1—limb, leg
 73.6   *ch'ih* 4—wing, fin
440.2   *shao* 2 (*piao* 2)—handle
516.3   *tiao* 4—hook, to angle
514.3   *tiao* 1—eagle
 68.3   *chih*—hoof, toe, foot
120.8   *chüeh* 2 (*chiao* 3), Cant. *kok*—horn
120.9   *chüeh* 2 (*kuai* 3)—to fork
517.3   *t'iao* 2—branch, twig
 39.12   *ch'i* 2—forked, divergent
 7.1   *ch'a* 1—to differ, unlike
612.2   *ya* 1, Cant. *ga*—fork, crotch
612.3   *ya* 2, Cant. *ga*—tooth, cog
 42.5   *chia*, Cant. *kap*, Foochow *kiek*—jaw
 73.3   *ch'ih* 3, Cant. *chi*—tooth
 71.7   *chih* 4—hawk, falcon

With the above Chinese words we may compare English words of similar sound and meaning as explicitly exhibited below:

ts'a 1 (*ch'a* 1), Cant *ts'at*, Foochow *ch'ak* (rub, scrape) - *jag* (to make ragged as if by cutting) - *jad* (to make a jad or deep groove in)

kua 1, Cant. *kwat*, Foochow *kwak* (scrape, shave) - *check* (to make checks or chinks in) - *chase* (to groove or indent)

chua 1, Cant. *chau* (scratch, grab, seize) - *chafe* (to rub)

huo 1, Cant. *wok*, Hakka *fet* (catch, seize) - *fet* (obs. to fetch) - *hook* (to seize and draw with or as if with a hook)

197

kou 1, Cant. *ngau* (hook) - *gaff* (dial. an iron hook)

chia 1, Cant. *hip* (clasp, pinch) - *hap* (obs. to seize, snatch)

chia 1, Cant. *kap* (pincers, tongs) - *gib* (Scot. a hooked stick)

chia 12, Cant. *kap* (pick up with pincers) - *cop* (dial. to catch)

ya 1, Cant. *ga* (fork, crotch) - *jaw* (a notched or forked part, etc.)

chüeh 2 (*chiao* 3), Cant. *kok* (horn) - *coak, cog* (a tenon or projection) - *gag* (dial. project)

chih 2, Foochow *chi, chieng, pi* (finger, toe) - *toe* - *tang* (a projecting shank, prong, fang, tongue or the like)

chih 2, Cant. *chap*, Foochow *cheik, teik* (hold, seize, take) - *cob* (dial. to catch) - *take*

cho 1, Cant. *chuk* (seize, catch) - *tack* (Scot. and dial. Eng. take) - *chuck* (to place or hold by means of a chuck) - *jaw* (anything resembling the jaw of an animal in form or action; a lathe chuck)

chia 14, Cant. *kap*, Foochow *kiek* (jaw) - *chop* (a jaw) - *chap* (one of the jaws or cheeks of a vise, etc.) - *cheek* (obs. jaw) - *kip* (Scot. a projecting point) - *jaw*

ts'ao 1 (grasp) - *jaw* (obs. to grasp with the jaws) - *chaw* (obs. a jaw)

tiao 1 (seize with the mouth or bill) - *chaw* (to champ as a bit) - *chew*

shou 1, Cant. *tsip* (receive) - *cop* (slang and dial. to catch, capture, get hold of).

The word groups above of the "cut idea-complex" and "finger idea-complex" illustrate in a particularly clear fashion the concept of the fluidity of sounds, discussed in Chapter III, as applying to the end of the word. These groups will be seen on reflection to constitute further branches of our "needle family" with which we started, all the words of which ended in *n* or *ng*. The semantic linkage should be obvious. The phonetic linkage follows from the fact that in accordance with the fluidity concept not only do the final stops *k, p, t* interchange with each other and with a final vowel but because of the vowel-character of the liquids *l, m, n, r* they interchange with the latter as well. In particular the final *n* or *ng* with which the words of our previous groups ended may be construed as a nasalization imparted to a final vowel or consonant. Thus the Foochow variants above *chi* and *chieng* (finger, toe) stand in the same phonetic relation to each other as English *toe* and Dutch *teen* (toe). Similarly the interchange of final *n* with for example final *k* may be construed as a nasalization or denasalization. Thus, through nasalization English *tine* - 'a slender pointed projecting part, a tooth or spike, a prong' becomes *tang* - 'a projecting shank, prong, fang, tongue or the like', then through "denasalization" it becomes *tack* - 'any small hooked, knobbed or pointed piece' and further illustrations are given by *tong* (to take, gather, hold or handle with tongs) - *take, pin - pick*. The words *tine, tang, tong* may in fact be linked to Foochow *chi, chieng* as well as to:

65.3 *ch'ien* 2—pincers, tongs
65.2 *ch'ien* 2—nip, seize
77.9 *ch'in* 2—seize, grasp
179.1 *hsien* 2—to take in bill or mouth
64.4 *hsien* 2—horse's bit

We have thus succeeded in citing a very considerable number of Chinese words which are phonetically and semantically, or "phoneto-semantically", associated by the process of the vocabulary building mechanism into one family of words all linked with our initial "needle idea-complex". As has been seen, by "shifting emphasis" a group can branch off so as to form other groups built around some particular aspect or "shade of meaning" of the same general idea-complex. How many more Chinese words could we have included that are phoneto-semantically related to the words cited? The answer is that we could have included the *entire stock of common Chinese words* within the same idea-complex. The reason for this should be clear. For the "needle or prick or tine idea-complex" is itself included within the more general "strike idea-complex", since all the simple basic words of the language are, as we already know, "striking words". We thus arrive at the concept, already referred to in connection with English words, that *the entire basic stock of words of the Chinese language constitutes a single phoneto-semantically interlinked family, that is, an organic whole.*

It is quite evident that our results are independent of the particular language considered or of the language family under which it is commonly classified. The common stock of words in any language is built up in the identical fashion through the operation of the vocabulary building mechanism. Further, *it is always possible to set up parallel word lists which, within the limits of the phonetic preferences characteristic of the languages compared, will exhibit "striking resemblances" between the words compared.* The common "striking kinship" must therefore be superposed on any genetic kinship that the languages may possess. For purposes of further illustration of the concepts we have presented we have given in Appendix 2 short lists of Swahili, Hebrew, Hungarian and Malay words, all of different genetic stocks as prevailingly classified, extracted from our fuller phoneto-semantic analyses of these languages. These stocks, together with the Indo-European and Indo-Chinese stocks, embrace the major part of the world's languages. As in the case of Chinese it will be found that these words bear a "striking kinship" to the "homely Anglo-Saxon words". We might say that the words of these languages are "disguised English" so that all the world speaks "English of a sort" or with more impartiality "Swahili of a sort".

CHAPTER ELEVEN

GRAMMATICAL CONCEPTS

As INDICATED BY the title of this book, our work is concerned primarily with the lexical aspect of a language, that is, with its words, as distinguished from its grammatical aspect or the interrelations of its words in sentences. We have shown that the simple words which make up the basic vocabulary of any language are of "striking origin" and that it is this fact, in connection with the common word building pattern, that makes it possible to draw up parallel word lists between any two languages (within their "phonetic preferences"). Thus, aside from any conventional or genetic kinship, all languages, insofar as their vocabularies are concerned, may be said to possess a "striking kinship".

In addition however to differing in their vocabularies languages exhibit differences in their grammatical structure, that is, in the grammatical devices by which they combine words to form sentences. Thus, a language like Latin is a highly inflected language, words undergoing declensions and conjugations to express case, tense, mood, voice, etc. and the entire structure of sentences being governed by the elaborate "rules of syntax" characteristic of that language. At the other extreme, a language like Chinese appears to have no grammar, there being no declensions or conjugations or elaborate rules of syntax and the meaning of the sentence appearing to be inferred simply from the position of the words in it. Thus the primary grammatical device in this language is word position.

Though the difference in the grammatical structure of a Chinese and Latin sentence thus appears very striking this consideration taken by itself is not necessarily a criterion for judging the possible genetic kinship of the languages. This becomes immediately evident if we compare the grammar of Anglo-Saxon with that of modern English, the one a highly inflected language of the type of Latin, the other an "analytical language" of the type of Chinese. We have already remarked in our Introduction that besides resemblances in vocabulary there have also been observed grammatical affinities between the nonIndo-European Hungarian and the Indo-European languages. Such affinities in grammatical characteristics, it should be remarked, are not restricted to this particular case. For however unlike languages may appear in their grammatical structure the grammatical distinctions which serve to differentiate languages are by no means as rigid or as clear-cut as, superficially examined, they appear to be. There is in fact an overlapping of grammatical devices in languages belonging to the most diverse linguistic stocks as prevailingly classified. Moreover, just as words are not tied by any " steel link" to their meanings, the linkage being essentially fluid and the delimitation of meaning essentially vague, so within any one language the various grammatical devices, namely, those associated with case, tense, mood, voice, number, parts of speech etc. are essentially fluid in the delimitation of their grammatical functions.

To bring out fully the significance of the remarks

above would involve us in an extended discussion of the comparative grammar of languages in a manner analogous to the discussion of the "comparative vocabulary" of languages and this would require a complete book in itself. We shall therefore, in the present chapter, without going into extensive detail, consider certain concepts in connection with grammatical devices as suggested by our general phoneto-semantic approach.

We start with words as performing the function of certain parts of speech in a sentence. In Chapter VII we formulated the concept that the isolated word or root is not to be construed as inherently associated with any particular part of speech. It is only when the word appears as an element of a sentence that a function, whether as a noun, a verb, an adjective, a preposition, etc. may be assigned to it. In an inflectional language such as Latin such function is "physically" evidenced by the "accidence" or the inflections of words, verbs being conjugated, nouns and adjectives declined, adverbs having characteristic endings, etc. In an "analytical" language like Chinese however the part of speech function of a word in a sentence is not "physically" indicated in any way at all, even the word order not being any reliable criterion. This would appear, at first glance, to render the meaning of a Chinese sentence ambiguous. As a matter of fact however it is not essential for the purpose of grasping the meaning of the sentence as a whole that a word in it be assigned to a part of speech category. Thus the isolated Chinese *tao* 4 is given with the meaning of the verb 'to reach, to come to' and the meaning of the preposition 'to' and we might therefore translate such phrase as *tao⁴ shan¹* as 'reach or come to the mountain' or 'to the mountain'. It will be evident however from the context in which the phrase occurs that whether the word *tao* 4 is construed as a verb or as a preposition is not material to the understanding of the meaning as a whole. In accordance with our concept we say that the same principle is essentially true for any language, the assigning of a word in a sentence to a particular part of speech function not being an essential element with respect to the meaning of the sentence as a whole.

Let us illustrate the last statement above by considering the sentence "I am here". Through the usual grammatical analysis "I" is a personal pronoun, "am" is the "verb of being", "here" is an adverb of place. It would appear, since "am" is the verb, that it forms a significant part of the sentence. In Russian the sentence would be translated "Ya zdyeś", which word for word means "I here". No need is felt for the verb "am" and the same construction is found in other languages. The verb "am" may in fact be omitted from the English sentence (as it might be by a child) and still leave the meaning clear. It should be evident then that in this sentence the word *am* is an "empty word" and is not equivalent to the word "exist". If however the meaning of "exist" is "intended" then *am* is not an empty word but the sentence then possesses an entirely different meaning. In either case, however, what, basically speaking, is the underlying character of the word *am* or of the other "verbs of being", *is, are, be,* etc.?

If we return for a moment to Chinese, from which, as we can see, we may learn more about English, we find that the same "character" pronounced *shih* 4 which means 'to be', 'am', 'is', 'are' means also 'this', that is, the verb "to be" is apparently linked semantically with the demonstrative pronoun "this". This may perhaps strike us as odd at first but as a matter of fact the same semantic linkage of the demonstrative pronouns with the words *is, are,* etc. exists in English itself. That is, in the sentence "It is I" the "verb of being" *is* and the pronoun *it* are fundamentally the same in character, being phoneto-semantic variants of each other; similarly the word *am* is simply a phoneto-semantic variant of *me.* In the sentence "It is I" one of the words *it* or *is* is therefore redundant, the sentence being equivalent to "It I". This is in fact the word for word meaning of Sanskrit *asmi* - "I am", the conjugated forms *asmi, asti* being the juxtaposition of the modified Sanskrit demonstrative pronouns *eṣas* - 'this' or *asau* - 'that' with the personal pronouns *mi, ti.* Similarly the Latin root *es* of *esse* - 'to be' is a phoneto-semantic variant of the Latin demonstrative pronoun *is* (*ea, id*) meaning 'this, that'. Note that the latter means also 'he' ('she', 'it'). The personal pronouns are in fact phoneto-semantic variants of the demonstrative pronouns and it may be stated, without going into detail, that the various forms for the different persons and numbers are akin to each other.

The Chinese *shih* 4 which, as mentioned above, means both 'to be' and 'this' has also the meaning 'such, thus'. In English too the word *thus* is readily recognized as akin to *this* and *that.* It should be clear however that not only *thus* but *all simple common adverbs of manner* such as the words, *as, so, such,* are akin to the demonstrative and personal pronouns and the verbs *am, is, are,* etc. Thus the pronoun *it* is a phoneto-semantic variant of *as* which in turn is *so* reversed (as are also for example *am* and *me, it* and *she* [German *es - sie*]).

We have thus linked as phoneto-semantic variants of each other the demonstrative and personal pronouns, the forms of the verb "to be", and the adverbs of manner. It will be noted now that the word *as,* as a pronoun, has also the meaning 'that, which, the like of which, who' while as a conjunction it also means 'while, when'. In this connection it is instructive to compare *as* with Latin *ut* which is given with, among others, the following meanings: as an adverb of manner, 'in what way', 'as', 'how'; as an adverb of place, 'where'; as an adverb of time, 'when', 'as soon as', 'since'; as a conjunction, 'that', 'so that'. The Latin *ut* is merely a phoneto-semantic variant of Latin *is, id* - 'that, he, it'. Without going into extended details (compare for example Latin *hic* - 'this, hīc* - 'here', *ego* - 'I') it may be stated that the personal, demonstrative, relative, and interrogative pronouns, the definite article *the*, the common adverbs of time, place, and manner such as *when, here, where, how*, and the simple subordinating conjunctions are all phoneto-semantically interlinked.

The fact that the relative pronouns and the subordinating conjunctions are phoneto-semantically linked with the demonstrative and personal pronouns will help us understand more clearly the nature of a "complex sentence", that is, a sentence which consists of a main clause and one or more subordinate clauses in the role of noun, adjective, or adverb. Consider the sentence "He is the man who went". The relative pronoun *who* is, in our viewpoint, simply a phoneto-semantic modification of the personal pronoun *he* and the sentence is equivalent to the two simple sentences "He is the man; he went" which however must be closely associated in thought to convey the meaning intended. Similarly in a sentence like "He knows that I am here" the conjunction *that* is semantically linked with the demonstrative *that* and is equivalent to the closely juxtaposed simple sentences: "He knows that" (namely) "I am here". Of course relative to the meaning of the sentence as a whole the demonstrative force of *that* is barely felt as is also the case with the definite article *the*. (Note that German *der* means 'the', also, 'who' (relative), 'he, 'that'). Thus all complex sentences are, basically considered, simple sentences in close association with each other such that in thought one "predominates" over the other. The intended meaning of the complex sentence is gathered essentially from the close juxtaposition of two or more simple sentences.

In general the *principle of juxtaposition* by which a new or modified meaning is conveyed by placing elements in close association with each other is the *basic grammatical device utilized by language*. In such juxtaposition *the new meaning is always obtained by subordinating one element to the other*. The principle accounts not only for the structure of complex sentences but, in an inflected language, for the conjugations and declensions, in an "agglutinative" language, for the "agglutinations" and in an "analytical" language for the word order and for compound words. The conjugated form of a verb such as Sanskrit *carati* - 'he moves' simply juxtaposes two roots, *car* and *ti* (the *a* is for "euphony", see remarks below) side by side one verbally and the other prepositionally construed, the latter being subordinated to the former. Similarly a declined form juxtaposes two roots, one construed nominally, the other prepositionally, the latter being subordinated to the former. The subordinated form may be reduced to a mere particle. Fundamentally considered, then, there is no distinction between so-called "agglutinative", "inflectional" and "analytical" languages.

Let us dwell a little longer on the nature of such juxtaposition. In the English equivalent of Sanskrit *carati* - 'he moves' the "he" appears to be independent of the "moves" because the two words are not "physically" coalesced as in the Sanskrit *carati*. The dependence however which in the latter expresses itself in the physical coalescence of the two words expresses itself in the former in the fixed order of the words. In general it is not to be assumed that because words are physically separated that they constitute independent elements.

We shall illustrate the idea expressed above further by a consideration of compound words and word phrases. Though the English language possesses considerable "compounding power" it does not appear to possess this power to the same degree as German, an obviously related language. Thus where we say in German "Wärmeüberführung" we say in English "heat transfer" or "transfer of heat". Nevertheless though the words "heat" and "transfer" are thus physically separated there need not be any essential difference in the meaning conveyed. We say "there need not be" because the phrase "transfer of heat", depending on the context or the meaning *intended* by the speaker, may not be precisely equivalent to "Wärmeüberführung". For the one expression may emphasize the "unit idea" of "heat transfer" while the other may for example emphasize the "transfer" element, or the "heat" element, for example, the transfer of heat as contrasted with the transfer of mass (note that *transfer* itself or German *überführung* is a two-element compound). The grammatical structure itself however *does not uniquely determine* the precise meaning conveyed which *must be gathered from the general context*. We shall return to this idea that a grammatical structure or form does not uniquely determine a grammatical function later.

We thus see that the agglutinating process, by which we mean the "physical" joining of elements, while more characteristic of some languages than of others is not an essential characteristic, the agglutination being capable of being carried out "in thought".

Returning to the expression "transfer of heat" we note that it differs from the expression "heat transfer" with which it may be precisely equivalent in meaning by the presence of the preposition *of*. Just what is the function of this word in this phrase and in general what is the nature of prepositions?

Note first that in such expression as "heat transfer" we dispense with *of* and that we can express the "of relation" in other ways, such as "wooden spoon" instead of "spoon of wood". What is the nature of the *en* of *wooden*? Again, in the expressions "time a day" or "John a Gaunt" the *a* is generally construed to be a form of the preposition *of*, the expressions being equivalent to "time of day", "John of Gaunt". This however does not throw complete light either on *a* or on *of*.

It will help us to get a better understanding of certain features of English grammar if we permit ourselves, as we sometimes do, to go far afield and consider languages not generally conceived as having the remotest relation to English. The Hausa language, a native African language "of mixed and disputed relationship but probably of Hamitic origin" declines nouns to indicate possession. Thus *gida* - 'house' is declined as follows:

gida*na*—my house   gida*nmu*—our house
gida*nka* (fem. *ki*)—thy   gida*nku*—your house
    house
gida*nsa* (fem. *ta*)—his   gida*nsu*—their house
    (her) house

The words *na, ka, sa, mu, ku, su* are the personal pronouns. Literally therefore the Hausa says "house I", "house you", etc. the two words being agglutinated whereas in English they are separate. It will be noted however that between *gida* and *ka, gida* and *sa*, etc. the letter *n* is inserted (with feminine nouns this *n* is replaced by *l, r,* or *t*). This *n* (or *l, r, t*) appears to have no special function and is inserted for "euphony". We thus see that when two words stand in juxtaposition to each other such that a relation of some kind is expressed between them a euphonic sound may be utilized to "smooth over" the linkage. It is then natural however to assign to this sound one of the meanings of the preposition *of,* which itself serves essentially as a "blank word" to relate two juxtaposed words in the most general way (consult the definition of the word *of* in the dictionary). Passing from Hausa to Japanese we find the Japanese "postposition" *no* similarly used to indicate possession, as "isha no ie" - 'the doctor's house'. The same "word" *no* is regularly used in quite the identical manner as the *en* of *wooden* to indicate the material out of which a thing is made, thus "mokusei" - 'of wood', "saji" - 'spoon', "mokusei no saji" - 'wooden spoon', and in general after a noun to "convert it into an adjective". We therefore give the *en* of "wooden spoon" the same interpretation as the "euphonic *n*" inserted in the Hausa declension above or as the Japanese "postposition" *no.* That is, the *en* of *wooden* does not inherently "belong" to *wooden* but is a euphonic connecting link between two juxtaposed words "wood-en-spoon" where *wood* may be construed as a noun. (This does not of course prevent the construction as one word which may for example be used at the end of a sentence, as "the spoon is wooden"). In the same way the final *r* of the English possessive pronouns *our, your, their* may be construed as a euphonic *r* to which a possessive significance may naturally be assigned so that for example "our book" is equivalent to "we-r-book", "your book" to "you-r-book", "their book" to "they-r-book".

Returning to the *a* in "time a day", "John a Gaunt" we should now see while this *a* may be said to be akin to *of,* both *a* and *of* are essentially euphonic linking sounds to which the meaning of the preposition *of* is conveniently assigned. If we permit ourselves to compare with still another African language, namely, Swahili (a portion of the vocabulary of which, for the purpose of illustrating the vocabulary building mechanism, is given in Appendix 2) we may see that the *a* in "time a day" is precisely equivalent to the particle *wa* in such phrase as "mtoto wa mtu" - 'the child of the man'. (It should be remarked that *wa* is "modified" to *cha, ya, la, za* and other forms to "harmonize in sound" with the other words of the sentence).

Consider now the Gaelic "sean-a-ghoba" meaning 'old smith'. It should be clear that the *a* in "John a Gaunt" is the "same *a*" that appears in the Gaelic phrase, although in this and similar cases the vowel is construed as an "inorganic" or "parasitic" excrescent vowel and is known more generally by the Sanskrit term "svarabhakti". Now in German the Gaelic phrase would be translated as "alter Schmied" or with the definite article "der alte Schmied" where the *er* or *e* of *alter* or *alte* is generally construed as a declensional ending of the adjective declension. A little reflection should now make it clear that the *er* or *e* of *alter* or *alte* is precisely of the same euphonic character as the linking sounds we have discussed. (For the same reason of "euphony" *alter* becomes *alte* after *der* to avoid the succession of two successive "er's" in "der alter", a succession which relative to the "sound preferences" of the German language is not "euphonious").

The above remarks will now provide us with a better insight into the nature of a predicate adjective or predication in general. In the above German phrase "ein alter Schmied" or "der alte Schmied" the word *alter* or *alte* is used "attributively", which "physically" means in immediate juxtaposition to the word "Schmied". The expression thus represents a "unit idea" about which something may be predicated. In the sentence "Der Schmied ist alt" - 'The smith is old' the word *alt* is used "predicatively" which "physically" means that it is separated from the word "Schmied" by the "verb" *ist*. Now we have already seen the basic nature of the word *is*, namely, that of a simple demonstrative or personal pronoun. The sentence "The smith is old" is thus equivalent to "The smith, he old". (Note that the Hebrew personal pronoun *hū* - 'he' is used in precisely this way to mean 'is'; compare also *hū* with *hōveh* - 'is, exists', *hayah* - 'was'). The predication is therefore effected by the grammatical device of inserting between "smith" and "old" a word *is* or *he* which, as a little reflection will show, is simply equivalent to supplying a "physical pause" between the two ideas of "smith" and "old" so as to indicate that something is predicated about "the smith" rather than about "the old smith". In the German, since the words are no longer juxtaposed the *e* or *er* of *alte* or *alter* is dropped. (A similar difference in the attributive and predicative forms of adjectives is observed in other languages, for example, in Korean, where the attributive generally ends in *n* which is dropped when the adjective is used predicatively).

We have remarked at the beginning of this chapter that the grammatical devices utilized by diverse languages overlap. (We have already given some indications of this in our discussion above). It is this circumstance, in fact, as well as the apparently unaccounted for resemblances in vocabulary, which leads to doubts and difficulties in the conventional classification of languages. It would of course take us too far afield to exhibit such overlapping in detail and would far exceed the scope of this chapter. It will nevertheless be instructive to point out briefly grammatical correspondences between several languages so as to suggest and emphasize the fact that no sharp grammatical cleavages can be effected between the most diverse languages. In accordance with the general viewpoint taken in this book stress is laid on the observed similarities in grammar as well as in vocabulary between languages rather than on the differences. The latter when more closely examined often turn out to be of a superficial character. This point of view moreover provides us, as already indicated in several instances above, with a better appreciation of the nature of English grammatical forms themselves.

Let us first consider such English form as *beating* and inquire into the nature of the *ing* termination. This "suffix", as is known, is used to form the "participle" or "verbal adjective" and the "verbal noun" ending in *ing* (as well as simple nouns ending in *ing*). In the conventional etymology the 'two ing's" are not identified as "the same *ing*" but are stated to have different origins, the participle *ing* being related for example to Latin, *ant, ent,* Greek *ont,* Sanskrit *ant* as well as to Anglo-Saxon *ende,* while the nominal *ing* is traced only to the Teutonic languages, like German *ung* and Dutch *ing.*

Note first of all that the very use of such terms as "verbal noun", "verbal adjective" or "participle", "infinitive", "gerund", "gerundive", "supine", etc. is illustrative of the remarks we had made earlier on the not too clear-cut definition of the parts of speech and in general on the vaguely delimited function of any grammatical form or category. A "verbal noun" may thus in a sense be regarded as a compromise (or even a conflict) between the nominal and verbal functions of the word in a sentence, the greater or less emphasis on the verbal or nominal (or adjectival) character depending on the "intended meaning" of the speaker. Thus in the sentences: "Someone gives the boy a beating" and "Someone is beating the boy" the verb "gives" essentially serves the function of the verb "is" and the construing of *beating* in the former as a noun, the object of the verb "give", and in the latter as a present participle used with the verb "is" to form the present progressive tense, is a mere grammatical formality not essential to the meaning of *the sentence as a whole*.

We shall see this still more clearly when we consider the significance of the termination *ing*. As a participial ending it is used, as already remarked, to form the "progressive tenses" of verbs while as a noun ending it is used to form primarily abstract nouns of action from verbs and also from nouns, adverbs and other verbs "often conveying the idea of process, continuousness, art, or other modification as of time or place". It would thus appear as though by appending *ing* to *beat* the physical continuing of the sound "beat-ing" parallels the continuance or progressiveness of the idea whether as participle or verbal noun. By our fundamental viewpoint this interpretaton of *ing* as denoting continuity is not of course exclusive of other meanings with which the idea of continuity may be associated. (See further discussion below).

The participial ending *ing, ant,* etc. has sometimes

been taken as a grammatical feature peculiarly characteristic of the Indo-European family. Both to illustrate
the remarks at the beginning of this chapter on the overlapping of grammatical forms and to bring out further
the essential significance of the *ing* termination we proceed to exhibit this grammatical feature in several languages other than Indo-European.

The Hungarian word *jövendő* - 'future' is from the
root *jö* or *jöv* - 'to come' and the *end* is a remains of
the ending which with personal suffixes was used to form
a now obsolete Hungarian future tense. Compare this
termination with Latin *and* in "am*and*us sum" - "I am
about to love' where the *and* of the "gerundive" is similarly used with a future meaning. The Latin gerundive
ending *and* is of course simply a phoneto-semantic variant of the Latin present participle ending *ant*. It is
clear that Hungarian *and* or *end* is of the same "continuance character" as the Latin or English termination.
Going still further afield we find that in Songhay, a
West African language (see F. W. H. Migeod "Languages of West Africa") the termination *nte* added to
verbs gives them a participial quality, thus *bei* - 'to
know', *boro* bei*nte* - 'a knowing, that is, prudent, man';
sayi - 'to be rich', say*inte* - 'rich'.

Returning to Hungarian, the present participle end-
ing in the latter is a long *o*, thus *jö* - 'come', *jövő* - 'coming'. Comparing with the African Hausa (one of whose
grammatical features, namely, the declension of nouns
to denote possession, we have already noted above) we
find the present participle ending is *wa*, thus *zo* - 'come',
zu*wa* - 'coming', "ina zu*wa*" - 'I am coming'. It should
be clear that the Hausa participle ending *wa* is of the
"same origin" as the Hungarian *o*, that is, like the Hungarian *end* or *and* discussed above or like English *ing*

it is a suffixed sound which parallels or "suggests" the continuance idea involved. As a matter of fact the participial termination *o* as in *jövő* - 'coming' is merely a phoneto-semantic variant of the termination *end* in jöv*endő* - 'future', that is, "coming". (Recall the discussion given in Chapter III on the relation between the vowels and the consonants; also discussion in Chapter X on the terminations of Chinese words; compare *saint* - Spanish *san* - Portuguese *são* and the pronunciation of French final *ant* as in aim*ant*; compare also Latin *amō* - 'I love', amab*am* - 'I was loving' and the interchange of English *ing* - Middle English *end, and, ind*). The "same *ing*", denasalized, appears as the termination *an* suffixed to Malay verbs to form verbal nouns, thus *tulis* - 'write', tulis*an* - 'writ*ing*'.

It should be clear now, from the overlapping illustrated and from the "continuance origin" of the ending *ing* or *ant* or *and*, etc. that the endings *anza, ant* or *and* found as participial endings in the words of ancient Hittite and cited in partial evidence of the Indo-European character of the language do not constitute a peculiarly Indo-European feature.

It will have been noted that the Hungarian *end* in "jöv*endő* or the Latin *and* in "am*and*us sum", which are of the same "continuance origin" as English *ing*, Latin *ant*, etc. denote futurity. Further, the Hausa sentence "ina zu*wa*" - 'I am coming' cited above may also be translated, *according to the context,* 'I was coming'. Note similarly that English 'I am coming' may, according to the context, indicate a past or future connotation, that is, the general idea of continuity may extend into the past or the future. The tenses are thus not sharply defined grammatically. This is in agreement with our fundamental principle that a grammatical form does not uniquely define a function. Further illustrations of this principle will be found below.

The ending *ing,* as already said, is used to form a "verbal noun". Another form of the verbal noun is the "infinitive" and we shall now give brief consideration to this grammatical form. The modern English infinitive is formed with the preposition *to,* "to go", "to see", etc. The preposition *to,* though not "agglutinated" to the verb is nevertheless practically inseparable from it, so much so, that is it considered a breach of grammatical propriety to "split the infinitive". In the Swahili language, to which we have already several times referred, care is taken (as generally in the Latin alphabet transcription) not to split the infinitive by "physically" agglutinating the preposition to the verb, thus, *piga* - 'strike', 'peck', *kupiga* - 'to strike, to peck' although the Swahili preposition *kwa* - 'to, at, by' is used independently. This is another illustration of the remark made above, namely, that because words are not physically agglutinated it does not mean that they may not be "agglutinated in thought". For the form *kupiga* is precisely equivalent to English "to strike, to peck". In fact, just as Swahili *piga* is of the same "striking origin" as English *peck* or *pick* or *buck,* Swahili *ku* is but "disguised" English *to.* (Compare English *to* with Russian *k, do* - 'to, towards' and with Gaelic *gu* - 'to', Russian and Gaelic being Indo-European languages. Recall discussion of the interchange of the stops *t-k*).

An alternative form of the infinitive in Anglo-Saxon employed the ending *an.* This *an* is phoneto-semantically related to the verbal noun ending *ing* and appears as the Greek infinitive ending *ein,* as in ly*ein* - 'to loose', or *nai,* as in lelyke*nai* - 'to have lost' (note the relative inversion *ein-nai*), the Latin infinitive ending *re,* the

Gaelic preposition *ri* - 'to' and Persian postposition *ra* - 'to, for', the Armenian infinitive ending *el*, or the Swedish infinitive ending *a*, all Indo-European languages, as well as the Hungarian infinitive ending *ni*, the Hungarian suffix *ra* or *re* meaning 'to', the Swahili preposition *ni* - 'to', the Japanese postposition *ni*, used to express purpose, the Hausa preposition *ma* - 'to', the Hebrew preposition *el* - 'to' and prefix *l* (*le*) - 'to, for', and the Korean postposition *ro* or *uro* - 'to'. In fact the preposition *to* which precedes the verb is of essentially the same character as the "termination" *an* which follows the verb. Further, the preposition *to* is *at* reversed and is of the same character as the Latin preposition *ad* - 'to, at' the Gaelic infinitive ending *adh* or *eadth*, the Greek dependent termination *de*, as in oika*de* - 'homewards', and the Lithuanian infinitive ending *ti*, all Indo-European, as well as the Malay prefix *ka* - 'to' the Hebrew preposition *'ad* - 'to, until', the Hungarian termination *ig* - 'to, until', and the Korean postposition *ege* - 'to, for' used with the dative.

In connection with the Latin infinitive ending *re* it is to be recalled that the Latin infinitive, like the English, may be used to denote "purpose", a usage arising from the fact that the ending *re* is of the same character as English *to*. Another Latin form used to denote purpose is the "supine" ending in *tum*. Sanskrit is stated to have no "proper infinitive", a form ending in *tum*, which "is used as an infinitive" being interpreted as the accusative of a verbal noun. From our viewpoint however the distinction between a "true infinitive" and a form "used as an infinitive" is not a particularly significant one. We thus say that the ending *tum* of the Latin supine or of the Sanskrit "improper infinitive" is essentially of the same character as the endings or words we have discussed

219

above associated with the idea of *to*. In fact it is not surprising that the ending *um* is used to form the "accusative" or "objective" case since this case involves the concept "to or towards an object".

We continue with our discussion of the case endings. Since it is not only the accusative but also the dative which involves ideas associated with the words *to* or *for* we may expect that the usages or the functions of the two cases can not be too sharply differentiated. The Latin dative ending *o,* with modifications for the other declensions, is in fact simply a phoneto-semantic variant of the accusative ending *um, em,* etc. and the infinitive ending *re.* (Recall the discussion in Chapter III of the vowel-like character and interchangeability of the liquids *l, m, n, r*).

Since the accusative and dative endings, like those of the infinitive, are simply a form of the preposition (or postposition) *to* juxtaposed in close union with the root (or "stem", the latter being merely a variant of the root modified "euphonically" to effect a "smooth linkage" with the ending) we may expect to find different endings to form the accusative in various languages corresponding to different forms for the preposition *to.* Thus the Hungarian accusative ending is *et* (or *at,* to conform with the "vowel harmony"), for example, *kép* - 'picture', accusative kép*et,* the ending *et* being a phoneto-semantic variant of the already mentioned Hungarian ending *ig* meaning 'to' or 'until'. Similarly the Hebrew particle *eth* which precedes the definite noun to form the accusative, for example, *yad* - 'hand', accusative *eth hayad* is a phoneto-semantic variant of the Hebrew preposition *'ad* - 'to, until'. These words are of course "related" to English *to* or *at* in the sense that they are of the same "suggestive origin".

By dwelling somewhat further on the case endings we shall gain a better insight into the nature of prepositions in general and understand why for example such a concept as a "lost primitive case" is not too significant. We have already noted the Greek ending *de* (occurring also as *se, ze*), denoting 'to' or 'towards' as in oika*de* - 'homewards'. Compare now *de, ze, se* with the Greek "locative" endings *i, thi, si* meaning 'at', as in oik*i* or oiko*thi* - 'at home', and with the "ablative" ending *then* meaning 'from', as in oiko*then* - 'from home'. Note that in Homer there is also found an ending *phi(n)* which expresses various relations including the locative and "instrumental". It should be clear now in comparing these various endings and recalling for example that the preposition *to* is found with a rather vaguely delimited range of meanings including such as 'close against or by', 'dial. at, as to home', 'at or on (a specified time)' and that the word *at* is similarly found with a wide range of meanings overlapping those of *to,* that these various Greek endings are simply phoneto-semantic variants of each other.

The Greek *de, ze, se, thi, phi, then,* etc. mentioned above are of the "same origin" as English *to* as are also the Turkish "locative" ending *de* (or *da,* to conform with the "vowel harmony"), as for example, *el* - 'hand', el*de* - 'in the hand' and the Turkish "ablative" ending *den,* as for example, *siz* - 'you', siz*den* - 'from or of you'. Compare further with the Japanese postposition *de* -'at', as *mise* - 'shop', *mise de* - 'at the shop' and with the Malay preposition *di* - 'in, at', as *di-sini* - 'here (at here)' (compare with *ka-sini* - 'hither, there'). Although Japanese *de,* unlike the Turkish *de* or the Greek *de,* is not ordinarily agglutinated to the noun it rigidly follows it as though constituting a case ending. In fact whether it is construed as a case ending or not essentially involves an arbitrary element.

It should be clear upon reflecting on the illustrations given above that the cases can not be sharply defined in number, the oblique cases simply being "agglutinated" prepositions (or postpositions). To distinguish therefore such Greek forms as oika*de* or oiko*then,* or oiko*thi* from the "true" Greek cases, namely, the nominative, vocative, genitive, dative, and accusative, and the "lost" instrumental, locative, and ablative is seen to involve an element of arbitrariness. Fundamentally speaking, the number of cases is simply the number of prepositions (or postpositions) in the language, although for practical pedagogical purposes it is more convenient to construe a case form if the ending is not "freely shiftable". Thus Finnish, an "agglutinative language" is nevertheless said to possess fifteen "true cases", denoted by such terms as "genitive", "allative", "essive", "adessive", "comitative", "ablative", "illative", "elative", etc. On the other hand, Hungarian, which is classed with Finnish within the "Finno-Ugric" subfamily is rather less determinate in the number of its "true" cases, the endings being somewhat more loosely tied to the root, while Japanese, which is sometimes classed together with the Finno-Ugric group within the Ural-Altaic family, may be said to possess no "true" cases since the prepositions (or postpositions) are not agglutinated to the roots. The distinction however between inflected, agglutinative and analytic languages fundamentally considered is, as already earlier remarked, of a superficial character. It is the order of the words, as is particularly evident in Chinese, that is the basic grammatical characteristic of a sentence. Where the functional relation of two or more juxtaposed words may in some languages be crystallized into inflected or agglutinated forms, the one element being subordinated to the other so that the combined elements may be construed as a single word, such crystallization need not be physically effected in other languages though it may be effected in thought. Essentially then we here encounter the same phenomenon which we discussed in connection with the German compound word "Wärme-überführung" - 'heat transfer' or 'transfer of heat'.

Not only does the assigning of a circumscribed number of cases contain an arbitrary element but the cases themselves are widely overlapping in their functions. This is to be expected since the "case endings" are pre-positions or have prepositional force. All simple prepo-sitions however such as *in, on, by, at, to, for, off, of, till, from, out, up, with,* are essentially vaguely de-limited in their range of meaning since they all partake of the fundamental character of the *a* in "time a day" or of the *en* in "wood*en* spoon" or of the *er* in "alter Schmied" - 'old smith' discussed above. That is, preposi-tions of the above simple type may be construed as "word blanks" whose meaning, that is, the relation they define between the words besides which they are juxta-posed, is to be filled in as required by the context within which it is used. They are therefore closely interlinked and overlapping in meaning. It is in fact this "word blank" character and hence overlapping of meaning which makes the "correct" choice of the prepositions in one's own language, and particularly in a foreign lan-guage, a matter of some difficulty and of a highly "idio-matic" character. (As a simple illustration contrast Eng-lish "*by* someone" - Swedish "*av* någon", English "*for* example" - Swedish "*till* exempel", English "*at* home" - German "*zu* Hause". Such double and triple preposi-tions as "from within", "within", and "out of" further illustrate the essentially loosely defined character of the prepositions).

Without going into any further detailed comparisons and citations from various languages it will be found that what has been said of the vaguely defined functions of the various grammatical categories we have discussed holds true in general for all of the grammatical categories, tense, number, mood, voice, etc. with which grammars conventionally deal. We may express this by saying that the meaning of a sentence is to be inferred, not from a precise grammatical analysis, but from *the sentence as a whole* and from *the context in which it occurs*. This is in analogy with what we have found true for the isolated word whose meaning, apart from the context in which it occurs, is vaguely delimited. We shall add a few more remarks on the nature of a sentence in our next and final chapter.

CHAPTER TWELVE

CONCLUSION; BEARING ON OTHER FIELDS

IT WILL BE SEEN, in reflecting on the results presented in this book, that the general viewpoint assumed turns out to be a "democratizing" one. The mystery with which words are surrounded has been resolved by reducing it to the order of the mystery that surrounds such words as *bang, plop, plunk, splash,* of the unpretentious "obviously suggestive-striking" (or "imitative") type.

But although thus "shown up for what they are" it need not cause too much concern even to those who are accustomed to regard words with a certain degree of awe. For the word itself does not matter; it is the thought behind it that "carries the punch". The word-sound is merely seized as a physical symbol upon which to "hook" an idea, whether the meanest or the most exalted. The meaning with which it is invested, as is of course well known, lies after all in the mind of the speaker who uses it with that meaning and does not reside in the word itself. Our viewpoint however has exhibited the mechanism by which it is made possible to attach meanings to words.

Words differ from algebraic symbols, which are likewise invested with meaning, in that the meanings associated with them are not assigned to them in a purely arbitrary fashion. The word symbols themselves are more intimately related to their meanings in essentially the same way that the sound of *bang* is intimately related to the meaning of *bang*. Furthermore, the word symbols are not independent of each other. They are phonetically and semantically, or "phoneto-semantically", interlinked in a manner which reflects the remarkably complex associative process that is characteristic of human thinking.

The remarks above indicate that our phoneto-semantic approach has a bearing on the field of psychology. In this chapter we propose therefore to touch very briefly on the bearing which our viewpoint has on this field as well as on the fields of logic, mathematical foundations, and several others. It would of course take us quite beyond the scope of this book to do more than briefly suggest the possible application to these and related fields.

It is evident that the concept of word origin as here developed bears an intimate relation with the psychology of the thought process. For in accordance with this concept to denote a thing as a "finger", a "child", a "hill", already implies an idea formed about the thing. That is, all simple common words, from their very nature, to borrow a logical term, "connote", that is, "imply as an attribute" and not merely "denote" or "point out". If words were pure symbols, of the type of algebraic symbols, that is, if objects, ideas, actions, or relations, were named in a purely arbitrary way they could in themselves only "denote". Thus the word *ampere,* the unit of electric current named after the French physicist A. M. Ampère, essentially denotes. But as we have shown, all simple words, being of fundamentally the same character as the words *bang, plop, plunk, splash,* are not of the type of the word *ampere* although the denoting quality in any particular case may have become predominant.

In fact we have seen from our illustrations of the "vocabulary building mechanism" that the range of connotation of simple words such as *finger, head, house, ring,* extends far beyond what is commonly conceived to be the case. For the entire common basic vocabulary of a language, as we have indicated in our chapter on the vocabulary building mechanism and as follows from the essential "striking character" of words, constitutes a single family or organic unit. Since such is the case, these simple words can not in theory be replaced by symbols which stand in a one-to-one relation with them, for example, by letters; the word *finger* can not for example be replaced by *a,* the word *cut* by *b,* the word *touch* by *c,* etc. where the letters would possess a uniquely defined meaning. For, to attain uniqueness, a separate letter would have to be assigned to each of the connotations and "shades of meaning" with which each of the words is associated, and as we have seen, on account of the scope of such connotations, this would be quite impractical. It is therefore clear that we can not use letters to denote words in the same way that letters are used in algebra to denote numbers. (We had not, in our discussion of words included those like *one, two, three* which denote numbers. The word *one* is a phoneto-semantic variant of the indefinite article *a* or *an* and of the word *man.* Compare *an - one - won* [dial. one] - *men* [obs. one] - *mon* [obs. exc. dial. variant of man] - *man* and the German *man* [a certain one] - *mann* [man]. Interesting observations about the other words *two, three, four, five,* etc. for example the similar sounds of neighboring pairs or triplets can be made by extending the discussion to the words denoting numbers in other languages. This would take us beyond the desired limits of discussion. It is enough to remark however that the words denoting numbers are no different in their essential character from other "striking words" the word "count" itself implying "to strike off").

This brings us to a consideration of the possible bearing of our viewpoint on mathematics and, in general, on logic and symbolic logic. We can not of course go into the subject here. We can merely suggest that such bearing must exist and point out certain pertinent facts. Not all symbols of mathematics denote numbers. Some, like $=$, $+$, $<$, ∞ denote relations or processes; in particular the symbols used in symbolic logic largely denote relations. It must be remembered however that such processes or relations must ultimately be defined in terms of words, since the symbols will not of their own accord define themselves. For example a symbol like df/dx or Df is a shorthand way of stating a complete process that is performed on a function of x symbolized by $f(x)$, where the expression "function of x" is itself an abbreviated form of a statement whose significance can only be understood when expressed in one or more sentences. By defining this process once for all and symbolizing it we need not repeat the rather involved verbal statement each time we encounter it. Nevertheless since its meaning must ultimately be given in terms of ordinary words it is clear that *any characteristics which we have found associated with words or with sentences as regards their meanings must in some manner be reflected in the mathematical or logical symbols which are used to represent such meanings.*

We shall give a simple example to illustrate the significance of the statement made above. The algebraic

228

quadratic equation $ax^2 + bx + c = 0$ is a shorthand way of stating a process whose meaning is clear if for example we already know what we understand by positive and negative numbers, raising to an integral power, multiplying (and dividing) two numbers or adding (and subtracting) two numbers. The equation may be construed as a question, namely, what is the number which, as a result of the mechanical process indicated, will give precisely zero? Or it may be interpreted, with a, b, c having specific numerical values, as a hypothetical statement about the existence of such number. As the reader is aware from his elementary algebra, in applying the process by which the solution of such equation is obtained we may come out with a number which has the form $a + \sqrt{-1}\, b$. Since we have initially assumed that we are confining ourselves to positive and negative numbers in relation to which the symbol $+$ was defined while the symbol $\sqrt{}$ had meaning only for a positive number, the symbol $a + \sqrt{-1}\, b$ has no meaning whatever. It will have a meaning only if we assign it one. This on the one hand illustrates the limitations of the symbolic method. For there is no guarantee that any process originally defined so as to have meaning will in every case yield a meaningful result. On the other hand, instead of discarding the meaningless result we may conveniently assign it a meaning which will "fit in" with the other meanings, for example, preserve the rules of the mechanical manipulation process, and in addition turn out to be useful. In the example illustrated, instead of discarding the complex or "imaginary number" (and it must be emphasized that the term "imaginary" is justified since the symbol is quite meaningless with respect to the numbers and operations originally defined) we can "keep it" if we discard instead what we originally "intended" by the term "number", by the term "addition" and by the term "multiplication". Thus we may conveniently change our initial concept of addition, represented by the symbol $+$, by replacing it by that of "vector addition" and assign a $+ \sqrt{-1}$ b a convenient and useful meaning that preserves the rules of the mechanical process if we say that b is "added vectorially" in the $\sqrt{-1}$ direction to a, where the $\sqrt{-1}$ direction may be taken along a line which is neither in the $+1$ direction nor in the -1 direction, that is, along either direction on a straight line. (It need not be in the orthogonal direction but one inclined by any angle θ to the x-axis; the angle θ enters only if we define the "modulus" in the nonorthogonal system as $\sqrt{a^2 + b^2 + 2bc \cos\theta}$ as we naturally would in order to preserve our concept of length).

Similarly we can not guarantee from an equation which was initially set up to describe a relation obtained on the basis of certain concepts on the physical entities involved to come out always with a solution appropriate to the physical situation. For the mechanical process which the equation orders us to perform on the physical entities may "juggle" the relations between these entities by the rules imposed by the process in such a manner that the final relation or solution does not have a physical meaning. Nevertheless the solution may be "rigorous" in the sense that the indicated mathematical or symbolic process has been faithfully carried out according to the initially imposed "rules of the game". We then have as before one of two alternative choices: 1. We may discard the meaningless solution, that is, meaningless relative to the concepts with which we started, 2. We may reexamine our concepts or restate our problem in such a manner that the solution can be assigned a convenient and useful meaning. The mathematical solution does not impose on us the necessity for replacing some ideas by others. Though they may in themselves be meaningless mathematical solutions suggest ideas which they may be usefully assigned and which one might not otherwise have thought of. Thus, a mathematical, or in general a symbolic process, performs the significant function of a mechanism for suggesting ideas.

The theory of relativity is a particularly good illustration of the above remarks. Starting with apparently obvious concepts with respect to space, time and relative motion the application of certain simple transformation equations from one coordinate system to another so as to preserve the experimentally obtained constancy of the velocity of light gave as a result of the mechanical process by which these equations are solved, results such as the "relativity of time", "relativity of space" and the "equivalence of mass and energy". Instead of discarding these results, which it must be emphasized were quite meaningless on the basis of the initial physical concepts of absolute space and absolute time, the latter concepts were discarded and the meaningless symbols were assigned a meaning which fitted in with or "extended" the initial concepts, and which could be subjected to experimental confirmation.

We have in the preceding chapter on grammatical concepts emphasized the idea that a grammatical form does not uniquely define a grammatical function. That is, as in the case of the individual word, there is a vaguely delimited "area of meaning" associated with any grammatical form. The meaning of an isolated sentence therefore is not uniquely or exhaustively determined by its grammatical structure. The full meaning must be gathered not from the grammatical analysis of the sentence

231

but, as in the case of isolated words, from *the sentence as a whole* and from *the general context* in which the sentence occurs. (In saying that the meaning is to be gathered from the sentence as a whole and not from its parts our view bears kinship with the Gestalt School in psychology and other fields in which the psychological events for example are conceived as occurring not through the summation of separate elements but through the functioning of "Gestalten" or functional units). From our standpoint therefore such a concept as a "logical grammar" of language can not be assigned too much significance. That is, in accordance with the general phoneto-semantic approach here presented as applied to individual words or to sentences, the categories of "logical" or "illogical" do not apply to the grammatical structure of a sentence at all. For example, the sentence "I don't see no one" is not illogical grammatically because it has a double negative and is intended to mean "I don't see any one". It simply is not what is regarded as "correct" English. In a different language, for example Russian, it is "incorrect" not to use a double negative for the corresponding meaning. In general, from the viewpoint here developed, the terms "correct" and "incorrect" as applied to grammar have the significance merely of "in conformity with" or "nonconformity with" a standard of usage. Thus, it is only the thought expressed by a sentence and not its form of expression to which the terms "logical" or "illogical" apply.

The above concept of the nature of the relation between the grammatical structure or form of a sentence and its meaning as a whole together with the remarks already made on the purely mechanical characteristics of a symbolic representation and its eventual interpretation in terms of ordinary words have a bearing on symbolic logic as well as on the subject of the foundations of mathematics. Since for example mathematics (and logic) deals with such concepts as *point, line, number, class, continuity, density, member of a class,* etc. it should be clear that the concept here developed of the nature and scope of connotation of simple words bears a relation to the reasoning about such entities. Thus, such a logical paradox as "Least number not nameable in less than 20 words" is not altogether to be unexpected from the very nature of the link between words and their meanings as here presented. The viewpoint here taken agrees in fact with the general trend of recent times to shake some of the absolutism with which the subject of mathematics has in the past been invested. (An extremely significant result in this connection is the theorem of K. Gödel announced in 1931 that it is impossible to prove the consistency of certain basic parts of mathematics, such as common arithmetic, by means of the mathematics adequate for developing those parts). We can not however dwell any longer on the bearing of our viewpoint on mathematics and logic and shall proceed to mention its bearing on several other fields.

As already remarked, the thought is to be gathered not only from the sentence as a whole but from the general context. That is to say, the meaning goes beyond its "physical expression in words" so that the words of a sentence do not exhaustively circumscribe the meaning intended, a part of the meaning always "spilling over" which must be "read between the lines". (This means that such idea as is implied in for example the phrase "the spirit and letter of the law" is of general applicability to any sentence). The fact that the words themselves do not "tell the whole story" is not however to be regarded as a particularly serious defect of language since in any case speech presupposes a sympathetic or "wise" listener to whom "a hint" of the *intended* meaning is sufficient. The significance of this viewpoint is particularly well evidenced in the poetic creation whose bearing on our phoneto-semantic approach will now be briefly considered.

In Chapter IX we formulated the concept that all simple words are "striking words", that is, express explicitly or implicitly the idea of striking in a general way, any meaning which is not explicitly associated with striking, such as that of the word *talk,* being construed as the "figurative usage" of its implied "literal striking meaning". From this concept therefore of the nature of the linkage between words and their meanings, figures of speech like similes, metaphors, hyperboles, allegory, personification, are of the very fabric of which the "prosaic" words of a language are constructed. Now figures of speech are the sort of thing which the poet in his "extravagant fancy" constantly preoccupies himself with. From our viewpoint therefore we find ourselves always "speaking poetry", a fact which may possibly surprise us even more than was the case of the renowned Monsieur Jourdain who was surprised to learn that he had all his life been speaking "prose". The difference is that the poet, "fanciful" soul that he is, feels less hesitant about creating his own "transfers of meaning", thereby delighting us with hitherto unsuspected idea associations, than the more prosaic soul who is generally content to abide by already "well established poetic usage", that is, the ordinarily accepted meanings of words.

Closely associated with poetry is the subject of music which is sometimes referred to as "a language". It is of interest to point out briefly wherein our viewpoint bears on the "language of music". We have already, in our chapter on "striking words", formulated a concept that associates the sound of the word with its meaning, namely, that included as part of the implied meaning of the word is the sound associated with or "suggestive of" the action expressed by the word. (For example, the word *strike* means 'to hit [or any of the other actions denoted by this word] with a sound suggestive of the sound *strike*', just as *bump, plop,* or *thud* are "suggestive of" "a bump", "a plop", or "a thud"). Thus the sound of a simple word is not entirely divorced from its meaning. The "vagueness" of musical meaning is moreover paralleled by that of word and sentence meanings.

Another musical aspect is the "euphony" of language, an element that exerts a considerable influence on the grammatical structure of the language. Thus the rules of "sandhi" of Sanskrit, that is, the various phonetic changes undergone by words in juxtaposition to others to "accomodate" themselves to their "environment", or the "vowel harmony" of Turkish and Hungarian are expressions of the association of language with music, other expressions of which are the "tones" of Chinese or Swedish, the "tonic accent" of Greek and Hebrew or the ordinary "stress accent" of English as well as the "sentence tone". The poet is of course as "extravagant" in his striving for the musical effect by the use of such devices as rhyme, rhythm, alliteration, meter, as he is in the use of figures of speech. Again however the difference is merely one of degree; the poet, being extraordinarily sensitive to the sounds of words as well as their meanings, "exaggerates" the "music" that is already contained in "prose".

In connection with the "music of speech" we may

make some additional remarks on the nature of "phonetic preferences", a subject to which we have already several times referred. We have found for example that within the phonetic preferences it is possible always to set up parallel word lists between apparently the most diverse languages. These phonetic preferences constitute a selection of those sounds and combinations of sounds which characterize the "music" of the particular language in question. Let us give a simple example which will illustrate the significance of this idea.

The names of the week days in the Maori language, one of the "Austronesian languages" of which Malay, a language already mentioned in the Introduction, is another member, are as follows: *manei, turei, wenerei, taitei, parairei, hatarei*. The names of the months are: *hanuere, pepuere, maehe, aperira, mei, hune, hurae, okuhata, hepetema, oketopa, noema, tihema*.

If any of these names, say *taitei,* or *tihema,* is pronounced at random it is not likely that it will be "recognized" but if the names are pronounced in succession it will become apparent that they are "somewhat disguised" forms of the corresponding English names from which they have evidently been borrowed. What effects the disguise is the phonetic preferences characteristic of this language which restricts the "admissible" consonant sounds to *h, k, m, n, p, r, t, w, wh, ng.* Thus there being no such consonants as *g, s, d,* or combinations *st, mb,* the nearest approach to *August* is *okuhata,* to *December - tihema,* to *Tuesday - turei,* etc. It is clear then that because of the very distinctive "music of the language" it will in general not be possible to set up a list of word parallels between this language and for example English, as is possible with Malay, another Austronesian language with sound preferences more nearly akin to those of English (see Appendix 2).

It has been possible to mention only briefly the bearing of the phoneto-semantic viewpoint, as presented in this book, on such fields which are associated in some manner with language. Since the language factor enters a wide field of intellectual human activity other fields besides those mentioned above will more or less directly have some relation with the viewpoint presented. Thus it has a bearing on the interpretation of ancient classics. Such works for example as the "Analects" of Confucius abound in difficult passages. These difficulties can often be resolved for example by realizing that the interchange of one Chinese written character for another having the same or similar sound but which is more commonly used in a different meaning context is more common than would be supposed. This is of course a consequence of the nature of the link between a word, that is, a word-sound, and its meaning, as illustrated by the Chinese words cited in Chapter X. In accordance with the viewpoint here presented it is *the sound* of the Chinese character rather than the written character which is to be emphasized in seeking a plausible interpretation.

Again, turning to a different field, since language considerations are sometimes adduced in judging inter-relationships among certain ancient peoples, such considerations will have to be reexamined in the light of what we have here presented as the basic character of all words of all languages and the overlapping of the grammatical features of languages. It is already known that peoples, whether ancient or modern, speaking languages of the same stock are not necessarily racially akin. From our viewpoint not only is this true but the concept of the cleavage of languages into sharply differentiated linguistic stocks loses much of its significance. It may in fact be remarked, in concluding this book, that the statement that "all mankind speaks one language" turns out, as a consequence of the viewpoint here developed, to have an unsuspected degree of philological, as well as poetical, truth.

APPENDICES

TYPES OF ENGLISH PHONETO-SEMANTIC VARIANTS

A LIST IS HERE presented illustrating the different types of English phoneto-semantic variants. Although the list is not intended to be exhaustive but merely illustrative it is of sufficient scope to include the greater representative part of the basic English vocabulary.

The variant types are arranged in the order of occurrence of the phonetic change at the beginning, middle, or end of a word. The definitions given after a word, which may be a dialectal, Scottish, obsolete, slang, or in general less familiar word or meaning, are quoted from Webster's New International Dictionary, 2nd edition. It is not practical of course to cite the full definition of a word, only that part being cited which indicates the semantic linkage between the words compared. It is well for the reader in some cases to consult the dictionary for the more complete definition of the word as well as for comparing its conventional or historical-approach etymology with the "phoneto-semantic etymology" here given.

1. COBBLE - PEBBLE, TROOP - GROUP (that is,

illustrating the interchange of the stops *p* [and its modifications b, m, v, f, w, h] - *t* [d, th, s, sh] - *k* [g, ch, dg, j]):

tour - whir - veer - chare (obs. to turn, esp. away) - *gyre - sheer* (turn aside)
cobble - pebble
curl - whorl - tirl (twirl, turn) - *purl*
cuddle - huddle
clap - frap (obs. strike) - *drub - drum - thrum*
dart - bolt - flit
grit - dirt - filth
gabble - babble - jabble - jabber - fable (obs. to talk)
fang - tang (a projecting shank, fang, etc.) - *shank*
ping (to prick) - *pang - ting* (dial. *tang*, prong) - *tinge*
troop - group - globe - blob (a globule, lump) - *bulb* (a rounded mass)
keen - peen (sharp edge of hammer) - *teen* (obs. keen) - *fine* (keen) - *pin*
dark - black - murk
puff - whiff - guff (Scot. puff) - *huff*
pinch - hinch (dial. scrimp, pinch)
probe - drive - delve - grave (to dig) - *groove - drob* (Scot. to prick) - *brob* (dial. to pierce with or as with a bodkin)
toll (obs. pull, drag) - *pull* (to pluck) - *cull* (select, pick)
pod (dial. protuberant belly) - *cod* (obs. the belly)
clog - plug - block
cap - top
spirt - squirt - start (to move suddenly) - *sprit* (sprint, dart)
push - dush (Scot. push) - *joss* (dial. to jostle, crowd) -

dash (to move or advance violently) - *butt*

bunt (to strike or push with the horns or head, butt) - *dunt* (Scot. strike, knock, beat) - *punch* - *dunch* (dial. a short solid blow or shove) - *pound* - *punt* - *dint* (obs. to strike or beat)

gauze (a haze or mist) - *haze* - *fuzz* (fine light particles)

hatch (a stroke or line) - *gash* - *dash* (a stroke or line) - *pash* (dial. to dash: strike violently) - *bash* (dial. a heavy blow) - *bat* - *butch*

cub - *pup* - *bub* (a little boy) - *babe* - *bob* (a very young calf)

quill - *twill* (dial. a quill) - *pile* (obs. dart, shaft)

cot - *hut* - *house* - *booth* - *case*

plump (dial. clump, group) - *clump* - *group*

an - *one* - *man* - *mon* (obs. exc. dial. variant of man) - *won* (dial. one) - *men* (obs. one).

2. **GRATE - SCRATCH** (that is, illustrating the relative excrescence of initial sibilant *s*):

dab - *stab* - *dub* (to poke)

dig (to thrust, poke) - *stick* - *tick* (a light quick audible beat: a tap)

broad - *spread*

flat - *splat* (obs. to spread or flatten out) - *blade* - *plate*

lank - *slank*

well - *swell*

track - *streak*

drag - *stretch*

draggle - *straggle*

lap - *slab* - *lamp* (obs. a lamina)

lath - *slat*

lash - *slash* - *slat* (dial. to strike)

lam (slang, strike) - *slam* - *lamp* (dial. beat)

lag - slack

bar - spear - bore - peer - spar - spell (dial. a bar) - *pale - pole*

plunge - splunge (Scot. to plunge) - *plunk*

pat - spat (dial. a light blow)

wiggle - swiggle (dial. sway or swag)

wet (wetness) - *sweat*

wheel - sweel (Scot. swirl)

dam - stem - stop

lime - slime - slub (dial. a mire)

scrimp (wrinkle) - *crimp*

quash - squash - squeeze

deer - steer

curve - screw

limp - slump

peg - spike

whip - swoop - sweep

ken (archaic, look, see) - *scan*

crush - scruze (dial. squeeze, crush)

gird - skirt

tour - steer

dip - steep - dive

wad (dial. a mass) - *swad* (slang lump, mass) - *mass - mat* (a piece of material)

dart (shoot out suddenly) - *start*

platch (Scot. to splash) - *splash - plash*

flash (archaic dash, splash) - *splash*

brod (dial. a sprout) - *sprout*

warp (to swerve) - *swerve*

beal (dial. swell) - *swell - weal* (obs. wealth, pomp) - *ball*

pod - swad (dial. pod, shell)

tirve (Scot. strip) - *strip*

patch (a small piece, a bit) - *bit - spot - piece*

nock (dial. knock) - *snock* (dial. knock, tap)

cuff (to scuffle, box) - *scuff* (dial. to cuff)

flutter (to vibrate or move quickly) - *splutter* (to hurry noisily, to bustle).

3. LUMP - CLUMP, RIM - BRIM, WIDDLE - TWIDDLE (that is, illustrating the relative excrescence of initial stops *p, k, t* and of their modifications).

rough - *gruff*

ring - *clang* - *clink*

reap - *lop* - *clip* - *lip* (obs. to clip)

rock - *crag*

cling (adhere tenaciously) - *link*

break - *wreck* - *wrack* - *crack*

leam (Scot. gleam) - *gleam*

log - *block* - *lug* (obs. a big or clumsy bow)

lout - *clout* - *clod*

lock - *flock*

lab (dial. to blab) - *blab*

roll - *crull* (obs. curly) - *curl*

rude - *crude*

drag - *lag* - *lug* - *rack* (to stretch or strain by force)

lag - *flag*

widdle (dial. wriggle, waddle) - *twiddle* (twirl, wriggle) - *wattle* (to twist or interweave) - *waddle*

fiddle - *twiddle*

rap - *clap* - *lamp* (dial. to beat) - *lap* (a sound of or as of lapping) - *flap* - *frap* (dial. to strike)

rubble - *crumble* - *crumple* - *rumple*

leer - *glower* - *lour*

rumble - *grumble*

rattle - *prattle*

rim - *brim* - *limb* (a border or edge) - *lip* (rim or margin)

rundle (something which rotates about an axis) - *trundle*

(a rolling motion)
look - *gleek* (an enticing look or glance)
robe - *garb* - *drape*
ram - *cram*
ward - *guard*
waver - *hover* - *quiver*
quap (obs. heave, quaver) - *heave, huff*
well - *quell* (a spring)
latch (to shut with a latch) - *clitch* (dial. close or clench)
   - *lock* - *close*
hurl - *whirl* - *twirl* - *swirl* - *querl* (twirl)
ramp (dial. climb) - *climb* - *grimp* (climb)
rod - *prod* - *reed*
rase (rub, scrape) - *graze* - *grate* - *raze*
lap (a loose part) - *flap*
lob (to throw or toss heavily or slowly) - *plop* (to drop
   or throw with a plop)
wrinkle - *crinkle*
rill - *prill* (dial. a rill) - *drill* (obs a rill)
ring - *crink* (dial. a bend or twist) - *rink*
rake (to scrape or scratch as if with a rake) - *creak* (to
   make a prolonged sharp grating or squeaking sound)
   - *cratch* (obs. to scratch, claw, grab).

4. STUMP - CHUMP (that is, illustrating the interchange of the unit sounds *st, sp, sk,* with each other and
with single consonants *ch, j, sh*):

scatter - *spatter* - *shatter*
stab - *jab* - *dab*
shoot - *scoot* - *scud* - *jet* - *spit* - *spout*
stamp - *thump* - *champ* (mash, trample)
stammer - *jabber*
strip - *slip* - *scrap* - *slab* - *shrip* (dial. to shred)
strum - *thrum* - *drum* - *drub*

244

strew - *throw*

skimp - *jimp* (dial. skimp)

steer - *sheer* (turn aside) - *chare* (obs. to turn, as aside or back)

slew (turn or twist) - *screw*

stir - *spur* - *scare* (to alarm) - *skirr* (to move hastily) - *jar*

stem - *dam* - *jam* - *stop*

stutter - *chatter* - *tatter* (dial. chatter) - *sputter* (utter indistinctly)

stick - *jag* - *spike* - *tack*

scuffle - *shuffle* - *jumble* - *squabble* (disarrange type)

stump - *chump* - *stub*

shell - *scale* - *skull*

strip - *slip*

screak - *screech* - *shriek* - *chark* (obs. exc. Scot. to grate, screak)

scuff - *shove*

strike - *scourge* - *slug* - *sledge*

shin - *stem* - *jamb* (a projecting part)

strait - *throat*

sklander (obs. slander) - *slander*

sklent (Scot. to slant) - *slant*

sklinter (Scot. splinter) - *splinter*

skirl (Scot. a shriek, a shrill sound) - *shrill*

splunge (dial. to plunge) - *slunge* (Scot. plunge, splash)

splother (dial. splash, splutter) - *slatter* (slop, splash) - *splutter*

slart (dial. splash, spatter) - *splurt* (dial. spurt) - *spurt* - *spread*

5. DUB - DRUB, SPUTTER - SPLUTTER (that is, illustrating the relative excrescence of medial liquid *l* or *r*):

cuff - *cluff* (Scot. cuff, slap) - *club* - *cob* (to strike,

    thump)
dub - drub
wheel - whirl
patch - blotch - plotch (obs. a blotch)
puff - bluff - blub (dial. to puff, swell out) - *bleb* (a blister, bubble)
bubble - burble
*pobb*y (dial. swollen, puffed up) - *plump - pomp*
bag - bulge - belg (Anglo-Saxon bag, bellows, belly) - *belly - bug* (colloq. *bulge*)
withe (a willow: to wind or twist like a withe) - *writhe - wreath*
skew - screw
flit - flirt (obs. to flick)
gowl (dial. howl, yell) - *growl*
pick - prick - pluck - pilch (dial. to pick or pluck) - *filch* (to pilfer)
babble - blabble
sag - slack - sick
sump - slump
big - bulk - bulge
weed - wort
pack - flock - block
dive - delve
squash - squelch
wiggle - wriggle
pat - plat (obs. strike, slap) - *pet - bat - prat* (obs. beat) - *beat*
daggle (to draggle) - *draggle*
quill (a roll, spindle) - *curl - querl* (twirl, coil)
dag (obs. stab as with a dagger) - *dirk*
seek - search
cob (a rounded mass) - *club - gob* (dial. a mass or lump) - *globe*

tug - *drag* - *tag* (colloq. to follow after) - *chug* (dial. pull, tug)

egg - *urge* - *irk* (annoy, bore) - *edge* (urge or egg on)

cop, cob (dial. catch, capture) - *grab* - *clip*

bush - *brush*

cut - *curt* (curtail, cut off) - *geld*

stamp - *stramp* (Scot. stamp)

wabble (dial. boil) - *burble* - *bubble*

hit - *hurt* (obs. to strike)

kid (colloq. a child) - *child*

till (to plough; cultivate; through to) - *thirl* (obs. exc. dial. to pierce, drill) - *drill* (to pierce; to train one-self)

dap (to drop, or fish by dropping, the bait gently on the water) - *drop* - *dip* (to drop down)

chat - *clat* (dial. chatter, gossip)

queeve (dial. bend, twist) - *curve*

catch (to capture or seize) - *clutch*

batch (the quantity of bread baked at one time; to bring together into batches; to mass) - *bread* - *plot* (to press into cakes) - *pellet* (a little ball, esp. of food, medicine or the like).

6. PICK - PINK, CLUB - CLUMP (that is, illustrating the relative nasalization of *k, p, t* to *nk, mp, nt*):

pick - *pink* (to stab; to pierce as with a sword) - *pinch* (to cause pain to) - *ping* (obs. exc. dial. to prick, push, urge)

hook - *hink* (obs. a reaping hook) - *hitch* (to hook) - *hank* (dial. a handle)

hent (archaic or dial. to seize; to lay hold on) - *hand* (obs. to seize; to lay hands on) - *hitch* (to hook)

put (to thrust, to push) - *punt* - *butt* - *push* - *punch* (to strike or thrust forcibly against) *hit* - *wound* (to hurt by violence) - *hunch* (obs. exc. dial. to push or jostle, esp. with the elbow; to thrust)

clog (a block or lump attached to something) - *clunch* (obs. exc. dial. a clump or lump) - *clunk* (dial. lump)

lock - *link* (something which binds together or connects things)

kit (a kitten) - *kid* (a young goat; colloq. a child) - *kind* (kindred, progeny; obs. to beget)

tooth - *dent* (a toothlike indentation or notch) - *dint* (to dent)

chock (dial. a block of wood) - *chunk* (colloq. a short thick fragment) - *cake* (a mass of matter concreted, congealed or molded into a solid mass of any form)

loaf (obs. exc. dial. bread; any thick lump or mass) - *lump*

cob (a lump or piece of anything) - *chump* (a block)

batch (the quantity of bread baked at one time; to bring together into batches) - *bunch*

bubble - *pimple*

crook - *crink* (dial. to bend or twist) - *crank*

wriggle - *wrinkle* (obs. a winding) - *wringle* (obs. to writhe)

wind - *withe* (to wind and twist like a withe) - *wand*

lag - *lank* (languid, drooping)

lag (obs. exc. dial. coming tardily after or behind) - *lang* (Scot. long) - *long* (acting, protracting, delaying for a long time)

flag - *flinch* (to withdraw from any suffering or undertaking)

tick (dial. to touch lightly, esp. to tag) - *tank* (dial. to knock, hit, bang) - *touch* (to hit or strike lightly) - *tag* - *tang* (obs. to prick; to give point or force to)

tat (dial. tap, touch) - *dunt* (Scot. to strike, knock, beat, bruise, etc. with a dull-sounding blow) - *thud* (to move or strike so as to make a dull sound or thud) - *dunch* (Scot. and dial. Eng. to strike or shove with a short solid blow) - *touch*

flick - *fling* (to throw; toss)

split - *splint* (obs. to split into splints)

plaque (any flat thin piece of metal, clay, ivory or the like used for ornament) - *plank* - *planch* (dial. a plank, board or slab)

whack - *whang* (dial. a blow; whack; bang) - *bang*

stick - *sting*

wag (to sway or swing shortly to and fro) - *wing* (to traverse with or as with wings) - *wink* (to move flickeringly)

widdle (dial. wriggle; waddle; struggle) - *windle* (Scot. and dial. Eng. to whirl around; to meander) - *wander*

wabble (to waver or vacillate between different courses of action) - *wamfle* (Scot. to flap) - *wample* (Scot. to wind, intertwine) - *waver* (obs. Scot. to wander, roam, stray; to sway one way and the other) - *hobble* (to wobble, as a hoop)

clutch - *clinch* - *clench*

7. TITTER - TWITTER (that is, illustrating the relative excrescence of medial semivowel *w* or labial *v, f, p*):

sote (obs. sweet) - *sweet*

sag - *swag*

sump - *swamp*

suck - *swig* (obs. to suck)

tirl (Scot. twirl, whirl) - *twirl*

curl - *quirl* (a curl)

son - *swain* (obs. a youth, boy)

titter - *twitter*

tit (dial. tug, twitch) - *twitch* - *tweak*

tinge - *twinge*

sock (slang to beat) - *swack* - *thwack* - *twich* (obs. touch) - *touch* (to hit or strike lightly) - *twig* (to beat as with a twig or twigs; to switch) - *switch* - *smack*

tour - *twire* (obs. to twist)

soar - *spire*

kill (obs. strike, beat) - *quill* (to pierce as with a quill) - *gore*

twattle (chatter) - *tattle* - *chatter* - *chitter* - *twitter*

toil - *tweil* (dial. toil, struggle) - *twire* (obs. curl or twist) - *twill* (to quill, or flute, as cloth)

ton (obs. exc. dial. turn) - *twine* (obs. to turn round; to revolve) - *time* (obs. an hour; also, a year)

chare (obs. exc. dial. Eng. return or coming back or round; turn, occasion, time) - *twire* (obs. to curl or twist) - *gyre* - *year* (Anglo-Saxon *gēar*)

8. BALL - BUBBLE, FLARE - FLUTTER, TRILL - TRICKLE (that is, illustrating the relative excrescence of the medial stops *k, p, t* and their variants before final liquid *l, r*):

wheel (AS. *hwēol, hweogul, hweowol*) - *wobble* (a hobbling or rocking uneven motion, as of a wheel) - *waggle*

pool (a puddle) - *puddle*

ball - *bubble* - *pill* - *pebble* - *boll* (obs. a bubble)

boll (the pod or capsule of a plant) - *bottle* - *bowl*

twire (obs. to curl or twist; a twisted filament, a thread) - *twitter* (Scot. to spin unevenly, as thread) - *twiddle* (to twirl; twitter) - *twill* (quill)

mull (colloq. anything muddled, a failure) - *muddle*

mell (dial. meddle, mix, mingle) - *meddle*

heel (to incline) - *huckle* (dial. bend, stoop)

tell (dial, to talk, chat) - *tattle* (talk idly; tell tales or secrets)

brawl (to utter clamorously) - *prattle* - *brall*en (Middle English cry, make a noise)

smile - *smicker* (obs. to smile amorously; to smirk)

flare (obs. to stream or flutter) - *flutter* - *flicker* (wave or undulate like a flame in a current of air) - *flacker* (dial. flutter, tremble, throb)

flurr (to flutter, flit) - *flutter*

skirr (to move, fly, etc. hastily; to scurry; a whirr) - *skitter* (to pass or glide lightly or hurriedly)

scare - *scatter* (to disperse, rout; hurl or drive about, esp. in confusion)

spire - *spider*

spar (obs. to spurt out, as blood) - *sputter* - *spatter*

spill (scatter, colloq. to throw out or off accidentally) - *spittle* - *spatter* - *spattle* (dial. to spatter, sprinkle)

jar - *jitter* - *chatter* (to make a noise by rapid collisions)

tear (dial. split or shatter by impact) - *shatter* - *tatter* - *shear* (obs. to pierce, cleave, carve)

tail (AS. *taegel*) - *taggle* (to tag or follow) - *daggle* (to draggle)

frill (to curl or crimp like a frill; wrinkle) - *frizzle* (curl or crimp; crinkle)

rile (colloq. to roil) - *roil* (to have an undulating form; to turn from side to side) - *wriggle* - *ruffle* (to swagger) - *ripple*

trill (to flow in a small stream; to trickle) - *trickle* - *dribble* - *drizzle*

crull (obs. curly) - *curl* - *crookle* (dial. to bend, twist)

gule (obs. the gullet) - *guggle* (dial. the windpipe)

nill (dial. Eng. needle) - *needle* - *neel* (darnel) - *nail*

still (to stop, cause to become quiet) - *stifle* (to stop, extinguish, deaden) - *stopper* (to plug up) - *stopple* (to stopper) *soil* - *suddle* (Scot. to stain, soil)

cull (to choose and gather or collect) - *cuddle* - *gather*

jar (to shiver) - *shiver* - *shimmer* (to shine with a tremulous light, glimmer) - *sheer* (bright, fair, shining)

mole (obs. to spot, stain) - *mottle* (to spot, blotch) - *moil* (obs. to soil oneself in the mire or wet, dial. mud) - *muddle*

sweel (Scot. swaddle) - *swaddle*

sprawl - *spraddle* (dial. sprawl) - *sprattle* (Scot. sprawl) - *spartle* (Scot. to kick about, sprawl)

glare - *glitter* - *glimmer*

fire (fever) - *fever*

peel (the blade of an oar) - *paddle*

knoll (a little round hill) - *knobble* (a little knob) - *knar* (a knot in wood) - *knuckle* (obs. a joint of a plant; a node)

fur (hairy covering of mammal) - *feather* (a feathery tuft or fringe of hair) - *hair*

gore (obs. to dig or hollow) - *gutter* (to form into small longitudinal hollows) - *core* (to form by means of a core, as a hole in a casting)

swill (to shake, swash or swish about) - *swiggle* (dial. to swig or sway)

troll (to roll, trundle) - *truckle* (to roll or move on casters; trundle)

scull (Scot. a large shallow wicker basket) - *scuttle* (obs. a broad shallow dish) - *shell* (any slight hollow structure) - *scale* - *shale* (obs. a shell or husk) - *sheel* (Scot. shovel) - *shovel* - *shoal*

slur (dial. to slip, slide) - *slidder* (dial. slide, slip)

smear (to daub; spread all over or in patches) - *smatter* (obs. to spot, spatter) - *spatter*

sneer - *snicker*

hull (dial. to throw) - *huddle* (to drive, push or thrust

252

hurriedly or in disorder, obs. to hurry in a disorderly
manner) - *whir* (*hurry*, commotion) - *hubble* (Scot.
hubbub, uproar) - *haggle* (to wrangle, dispute)

bull - *buffle* (obs. a buffalo)

ball (slang to confuse, muddle) - *baffle* (bewilder, con-
found) - *boggle* (Scot. baffle, foil) - *foil* (baffle)

fool (a person deficient in judgment) - *feeble* (weak;
not strong or effective, as in character or mentality) -
fickle (not fixed or firm)

bar (to mark with stripes, to stripe) - *batter* (to beat
with successive blows) - *wale* (to mark with wales or
stripes) - *wattle* (dial. to beat or flog with or as with
a rod)

bill (the beak of a bird; a kind of military weapon; obs.
to strike, peck) - *beetle* (to beat with a beetle) -
peckle (to peck slightly or repeatedly)

feel - *fumble* (to feel or grope about clumsily or per-
plexedly) - *fimble* (dial. to feel with the fingers moving lightly over anything)

full (obs. to beat down, trample) - *fettle* (dial. to beat,
thrash, strike)

pell (obs. to pelt, knock about) - *pummel* (to pommel,
thump) - *pommel* - *paddle* (colloq. to beat with or
as with a paddle)

hill (a heap or mound) - *huddle* (a conglomeration) -
*huckle*back (humpback) - *hubble* (a hub or protuberance) - *hull* (obs. a hulk)

steal (dial. a stalk, a stem) - *stubble* (stumps of grain
left after reaping)

stell (dial. a support, prop; shelter for sheep or cattle) -
staple (obs. a post, a supporting frame) - *stall* (a
stable, obs. a stand) - *stable* (fixed, steadfast) - *still*
(obs. constant, continual)

wale (to weave the web of) - *wattle* (to twist or interweave; to plat) - *wicker* (wickerwork) - *waggle* (to move one way and the other)

churr (a vibrant or whirring noise such as that made by some insects) - *chatter* (noise made by collision of teeth as in shivering) - *shiver*

hurl - *hurtle* - *hurdle*

wile (to beguile, allure) - *wheedle* (to entice by soft words or the like)

rail - *rattle* (obs. to scold, rail at) - *rackle* (dial. rattle, clatter)

lil (dial. little) - *little*

smore (Scot. to smother) - *smother*

roll (to utter with a deep sound) - *ruckle* (dial. to make a hoarse rattling sound) - *rattle* - *rackle* - *roar*

toll, tole (obs. to pull, drag) - *taggle* (to tag or follow) - *daggle* (to draggle)

trail - *draggle* - *drabble* (to draggle) - *drawl* (to drag out)

tool - *tackle* (instrument used for work or pastime)

scrawl - *scribble* - *scrawm* (dial. Eng. and Ir. scratch; scrawl)

broll (dial. child, brat) - *brother* (Swedish *bror, broder*)

birn (Scot. burden) - *burden*

curl - *curble* (obs. curb) - *curdle* (dial. curl)

whirl - *wirble* (whirl, eddy)

purl (to eddy, swirl) - *burble*

9. KNOT - KNOB - KNAG (that is, illustrating the interchange of the final stops *k, p, t* and their modifications):

slap - *slug* - *slat* (dial. a resounding slap or blow) - *slam*

whack - *whap* (dial. a stroke, blow) - *wham*

plug (to strike, punch) - *plap* (strike with a plap) - *plat* (obs. strike, slap) *slab* - *slat* (a lath, dial. a slab of stone) - *slug* (a strip of metal) - *slate*

slick - *slide* - *slip* - *sleek* - *slive* (dial. to slip; slide)

flick - *flip* - *flit* - *flitch* (a flip, flick)

slug (sluggish, slow) - *slack* - *slow* - *sloth* - *slouch*

strip - *stripe* - *streak* - *stream* (obs. to streak, stripe) - *streek* (Scot. stretch, extent) - *stretch* (a continuous line or surface) - *street*

puff - *pock* (a pustule) - *pout* - *bag* - *poke* (dial. a bag) - *pouch* - *bowk* (dial. a kind of wooden bucket or pail) - *butt* - *vat* - *buck* (a basket) - *pod*

card (to comb with a card) - *grate* - *graze* - *crab* (of hawks, to scratch or claw)

knot - *knob* - *knag* (a knot in wood)

flap - *flack* (dial. to flap) - *flit* (to flutter)

late - *lag* (dial. slow, late) - *laze* - *lob* (go heavily or lumberingly)

leave - *let* - *loose* - *lax*

sop - *soak* - *sot* (to guzzle)

crimple - *crinkle*

shrimp - *shrink*

hump - *hunch* - *hunk* (colloq. a hump, hunch)

peck - *pat* - *pop* (dial. strike sharply) - *bob* (to tap) - *buff* (dial. strike, beat) - *beat* - *bash* - *pash* (dial. to strike violently) - *potch* (dial. slap, hit, strike)

dribble - *trickle* - *drizzle*

bulge - *bulb* (to swell) - *bulk* - *bulse* (a purse) - *purse* - *belg* (AS. belly, bag, bellows) - *belly* - *bellows*

snap - *snack* (dial. snap, snatch) - *snatch*

smack - *smite* - *smash*

lick - *lap* (to lick, splash gently upon) - *lash* (strike quickly)

waggle - *waddle* - *wobble*

gulp - *glut* - *gorge* - *greed* (to crave) - *gorb* (Scot. greedy)

- *crave*

clog - *clot* - *clod* - *club* - *clump* - *globe*

sprig - *sprit* (a shoot, sprout) - *sprout* - *spurt*

track - *tread* - *trip* (a light step) - *tramp*

probe - *prod* - *prick* - *brod* (to goad or poke) - *brob* (a brad shaped spike) - *brad* - *brog* (dial. prod, prick)

button - *buckle* - *pebble* - *pimple*

pound - *punch* - *bump* - *pink* (stab, pierce) - *punt* (to kick, hit)

trot - *trig* (dial. to trot) - *tread* - *trip*

flat - *plaque* - *plat* - *flap* (a flat piece or slice, as a flap of bread) - *flake* (a lamina)

huddle - *huggle* (dial. to hug)

shred - *shrip* (dial. to shred, clip, trim) - *trim*

rabble (dial. babble, gabble) - *rackle* (dial. rattle, clank) - *rattle*

limp - *lank* (languid, drooping) - *lent* (obs. slow, mild, gentle)

dab (strike) - *dad* (Scot. strike) - *dag* (obs. stab)

wilt - *welk* (dial. fade, dry up)

shuttle (to move backwards and forwards) - *shuffle* (to move one way and the other) - *shoggle* (dial. joggle) - *shamble* (to shuffle along) - *jiggle* - *joggle* (to shake slightly to and fro)

draggle (to drabble) - *drabble*

log - *lob* (dial. something thick or heavy) - *lout* (an awkward fellow, a bumpkin) - *lad* (obs. a man servant; a man of low station) - *lass* (Scot. a maidservant)

lug (obs. a big or clumsy bow; that constitutes or contains a lug, or reasonable load) - *load* (a cargo, pack) - *lead* (a heavy metallic element, German *lot* - plummet, small weight) - *lump* (colloq. a sluggish or dull person; a heavy set or sturdy person; the whole aggregation, lot) - *lot whisp* - *whisk* - *whiss* (obs. to whistle; whizz; hiss) - *whizz* - *whist* (archaic and dial. to hush)

sweep - *switch* - *swish* - *swack* (dial. strike or beat violently) - *swat* - *swap* (dial. a blow, stroke) - *swoop*

spring - *sprint* - *springe* (dial. supple, agile)

rind - *ring* - *ramp* (a short bend or curve where a handrail etc. changes direction) - *rung* - *round* - *rink*

dip - *dig* - *ditch* - *dive* - *duck*

jab - *jag* - *jut*

scream - *screak* - *screach*

sigh - *suff* - *sock* (dial. sigh)

peep - *peek*

tab - *tag* - *dash* (a stroke, a mark) - *dab* - *daub*

sink - *sound* (to fathom) - *tinge* - *dunk*

stub - *stock* - *stud* (obs. a trunk, stem) - *stem* - *stump*

slag - *slud* (dial. slush) - *sloke* (slime in water) - *slime* - *sludge* - *slut* (obs. to befoul) - *slub* (dial. a slushy mess) - *slop* (soft mud, slush) - *slutch* (dial. mire, slush) - *slush*

jerk - *jolt* - *jert* (obs. exc. dial. jerk)

break - *breach* - *bruise* - *part*

brittle - *brichel* (obs. exc. dial. brittle)

cobble - *coggle* (dial. cobblestone)

squash - *squab* (dial. crush, squash) - *squat* (dial. squeeze) - *squeeze*

pluck - *ploat* (Scot. pluck, fleece) - *pilch* (dial. pick or pluck)

tick (touch, tap) - *tap* - *touch* - *tag* (touch or hit) - *tat* (dial. tap, touch)

chit - *chick* - *tot* - *kid* - *toad* (dial. a child) - *tad* (a small child)

jot (a tittle) - *teat* - *dot* - *tip* - *tick* (a dot or speck) - *dod* (Scot. summit of a hill) - *tit* (a small horse) - *touch* (a small quantity)

257

skimp - *scant*

pud (colloq. paw, hand) - *paw* (foot of an animal; an ungainly hand) - *peg* (a pointed prong or claw, colloq. foot or leg) - *pad* (the foot of certain animals) - *pat* (slang, foot or paw) - *foot*

huck (dial. hip, haunch) - *hip* - *hook* (dial. haunch)

midge - *mite* - *mib* (dial. a marble) - *mig* (a marble) - *pit* - *pip*

bub (small boy) - *boy* - *buck* (the male of deer, goats, etc.; a dashing fellow) - *pug* (obs. an elf, sprite; a very small dog; dial. Eng. anything short, thick and rounded) - *pup*

strake (obs. proceed, move, go) - *strike* (go, proceed) - *stride* - *stream* (to move forward with a continuous motion)

smitch (dial. spot, smut) - *smut* - *spot* - *speck* - *spat* (a light splash) - *smot* (Scot. a stain) - *smit* (dial. a spot, stain)

tickle - *tiddle* (dial. tickle)

tit (dial. pull, tug, jerk, twitch) - *tug* - *tic* (a twitching)

dunt (dial. a blow or thump) - *tunk* (dial. thump) - *thump* - *dunch* (dial. a short solid blow or shove) - *dump* (Scot. to knock heavily or beat) - *tamp* (to drive in by a succession of blows) - *tank* (dial. knock, hit, bang) - *ding* (dial. to knock or beat) - *dint* (obs. strike or beat) - *dint* (to dent) - *dent* (obs. a stroke or blow) - *dent* (a toothlike indentation or notch; a tooth) - *tang* (something that pricks or spurs one on; a fang)

hank (dial. a handle; a hold) - *hand* - *hent* (dial. to seize, lay hold on) - *hink* (a reaping hook)

plump (obs. blunt) - *blunt* (abrupt, bluff) - *plunk* (to drop or sit down suddenly or heavily; to plump) - *plunge* (to pitch or throw oneself headlong or vio-

258

lently forward and downward) - *plumb* (in a plumb direction or condition; vertically)

blab - *blat* (colloq. talk inconsiderately) - *prate* - *bleat* (to utter or give forth with a bleat)

stab - *stick* - *stitch* (obs. to prick) - *stob* (dial. stab) - *stoush* (dial. to strike, beat)

stow (to put away, hide) - *stuff* - *stock* - *stop*

snip (to clip suddenly or by bits) - *snick* (to snip, nick) - *snathe* (obs. exc. Scot. and dial. Eng. to lop, prune)

catch - *cotch* (dial. to catch) - *cop* (slang and dial. to catch, to capture) - *gaff* (dial. an iron hook; to strike or secure with a gaff; slang, to take in, deceive) - *get*

10. KNOT - KNAR, KNOB - KNOLL (that is, illustrating the relative interchange of the stops *k, p, t* with the liquids *r, l*):

peek - *peer*

knock (to strike sharply or resoundingly) - *knell* (to ring) - *knoll* (archaic and dialectal Eng. knell)

knock (Scot. and Ir. hill, hillock) - *knoll* (a little round hill, a mound)

knot (a node) - *knar* (a knot or burr in wood)

hud (dial. husk or hull) - *hull* - *hill* (obs. exc. dial. to hide, cover) - *hide*

pot (a rounded vessel) - *bowl* - *ball* - *pod*

hut (a rude small house, hovel or cabin) - *hole* (dial. Eng. a house) - *house* - *home*

cut - *kill* (obs. to strike, beat) - *gore* - *gut*

jag (dial. to prick, stab or jab) - *jar* (to drill by repeated percussion) - *jad* (to make a jad or deep groove in) - *dig* - *till*

beak - *bill* - *pike* - *pile* (obs. a dart, a shaft; also, its head)

tug - *toll* (obs. to draw by tugging)

pick (to separate and remove or pull away) - *pull* - *pill* (obs. to pillage)

spike - *spire* (a slender tapering blade or stalk) - *spear*

nick (to make a nick or nicks in; to notch) - *nill* (dial. needle) - *nail*

shriek - *shrill* - *sharp* - *skirl* (Scot. to utter in a shrill tone)

grate - *grill* (obs. to offend, irritate, vex) - *chark* (obs. exc. Scot. to grate; creak) - *creak* - *growl* - *gride* (a harsh scraping or cutting)

creep - *crawl* - *creek* (obs. to run as, or form, a creek; also, turn, wind) - *career* (to move or run rapidly)

spread - *sprawl* (to spread out)

rock (to roll or sway backward and forward; to reel) · *roll* - *reel*

mud - *mire*

smooth - *smear* - *smeir* (a glaze)

smack (rare, to perceive by taste or scent) - *smell*

choose - *cull* (to choose and gather or collect)

speck (a small piece or object; a bit) - *spell* (obs. exc. dial. a splinter or splint; a chip)

stick (colloq. to bring to a stand) - *still* (to stop, as physical motion or agitation) - *stop* - *stem* - *stell* (obs. exc. Scot. to fix)

wave (a ridge or swell on the surface of a liquid) - *well* (an issue of water from the earth) (German *Welle* - wave) - *heave* (to rise and fall with alternate motions)

pat (to strike or beat gently) - *pell* (obs. to pelt, knock about) - *fell* (to cut, beat or knock down) - *fall*

spit (to throw forth or out; sprinkle) - *spill* (to let out; colloq. to throw out or off accidentally) - *spout* (to utter magniloquently)

speak - *spell* (obs. exc. dial. to speak, utter, say)

tweak - *twill* (to quill, or flute, as cloth)

heap - hill (to form into a hill, heap or mound) - *head* (the top)

peak (a headland or promontory; the top of a hill) - *poll* (the head) - *pole* (either extremity of an axis of a sphere) - *pile* (a heap; obs. a spike, nail or spine; a dart, also its pointed head) - *mull* (Scot. a promontory)

dumb (colloq. dull, stupid) - *dull* (heavy, gross, cloggy)

brat (a child, an offspring) - *broll* (obs. exc. dial. child; brat)

buck (the male of deer or antelopes, or of goats, hares, rabbits, and rats) - *bull* (the male of any very large quadruped, or of certain other animals) - *male*

11. BUTT - BOTTLE, BEAT - BATTER, HULL - HULK, BALL - BULB (that is, illustrating the relative excrescence of final consonants):

vat - vessel - butt - bottle
tour - turn - tirl (twirl)
scale - scalp - shell
score - scrape - scratch
heel - heald (dial. incline)
bud - button
ball - bulb - bulge
foal - whelp
coop - cove - cover - hovel - cave - chamber - home - haven
lean - lank - long
rim - ring - rink
brim - brink
mar -mark
hull - hulk - bulge - bulk
stir - start - startle
roam - rove - ramble

chill - cold

veer - verge - ward (avert)

pull - peel - pilch (dial. pluck) - *pluck*

hear - heark - hearken

pin - pine - pang - pain - punch (prod or poke) - *ping* (a sharp sound such as made by a bullet striking a wall, etc.) - *pink* (to stab; pierce)

wire (to wind about) - *warp* (swerve, turn or bend)

jar - jolt - jerk - jarg (dial. to jar)

peck - peckle - pecket (peck repeatedly)

feel - palp (touch, feel)

bore - burrow - furrow - hole - hollow

tine (a tooth or spike, any slender pointed part) - *tang* (a fang, any projecting part) - *dent* (a tooth)

beat - batter - battle

win (dial. wind) - *winnow - wind - fan*

tell - talk

score (scold) - *scold*

class - cluster

well (obs. boil) - *boil - wallop* (dial. boil)

grime - ground

shin - shank

tire (obs. seize, pull) - *draw - drag - toll* (to draw)

12. TWEAK - TWIST - TWITCH (that is, illustrating the interchange of the final unit sounds *sk, sp, st,* with each other and with single consonants *ch, j, sh*):

tag - touch - taste (a touch or stroke)

fit - fix - fast

tweak - twist - twitch

hut - hud (dial, husk or hull) - *husk - hutch* (a hut, hovel) - *house*

late - last

fresh - brisk - brash (colloq. impudent)

wit - wist (to know)

keg - cask - jug - gotch (dial. jug)

break - burst - breach

grab - grasp - clasp - grip - clutch

hap (obs. to seize, snatch) - *hasp - haps* (dial. hasp)

cop (slang and dial. to catch, capture) - *cop*s (obs. to fasten or shut in) - *cosp* (AS. fetter)

thrust - strike - slug - sledge

bathe - bask (obs. bathe)

wet - wash - moist

beat - baste (to beat, cudgel) - *box*

joke - jest - josh (slang chaff)

gird - girth - crust

tooth - tusk - jag - tush (a tooth)

haste - whisk - whish

paste (any soft mixture) - *mash* (a mass of mixed ingredients) - *mass - mix - batch* (mixture of raw materials)

god - ghost

laze - lash (obs. exc. dial. lax; loose) - *lax - loose - lask* (obs. a laxative)

pout (to swell out, as lips) - *boast* (to brag)

bloat (to inflate; puff; make vain) - *blast* (obs. exc. dial. to become inflated) - *blaze* (obs. to blow as with a trumpet) - *breathe*

flit - flisk (obs. exc. dial. to frisk; whisk; to flick) - *flick - flash*

hush - whist (archaic and dial. to hush) - *whisht* (Scot. to be silent) - *whisk* (obs. exc. dial. whist) - *whisp* (a low sound as of puffing, rustling or sprinkling) - *whoop* (to utter, etc. with a whoop) - *whiff*

guff (Scot. a puff; a whiff) - *gasp* (act of gasping; a gasping utterance) - *gust* (a violent blast)

263

13. SPUTTER - SPURT, CACKLE - CLACK (that is, illustrating the relative interchange of the final two consonants one of which is a liquid *l, r, n*):

bubble - *bleb* (a bubble)

pebble - *blob* (dial. a bubble or pustule; a pimple; a small lump of something viscid or thick) - *pimple*

cobble - *club* - *clump*

coggle (a cobblestone) - *clog* (Scot. a short thick piece of wood; a block or lump attached to something) - *cudgel* (German *Kugel* - a ball)

wattle (to plat) - *plat*

guggle (dial. the windpipe) - *gorge*

kittle (to kitten, bring forth young) - *child* (obs. to produce young) - *kitten* - *kind* (obs. to beget) (German *Kind* - child)

flitter (dial. flutter, flicker) - *flirt* (to move jerkily, obs. to flick)

sputter - *spurt* (to spout forth; obs. to sprout, shoot up) - *sprout*

spatter (to scatter by splashing; to sprinkle around) - *spread*

batter - *prat* (obs. to spank, beat) - *patter* (to strike with a quick succession of pats)

paddle (to beat or stir with a paddle) - *plat* (obs. to strike, slap) - *pelt*

peckle (to peck slightly or repeatedly) - *plug* (slang, to strike with the fist; punch)

plum (obs. to fall like a plumb; dial. to plump) - *pummel* (to thump)

waggle - *walk* (obs. to toss to and fro)

wabble - *wallop* (to move in a rolling cumbersome fashion; waddle)

waddle - *waltz* (German *walzen* -to roll)

264

dagger - dirk
daggle - drag
jigger (colloq. to jerk) *- jerk - jiggle*
fickle (not fixed or firm) *- flick - wiggle - waggle*
smicker - smirk
fimble (dial. to feel with the fingers moving lightly over anything) *- palp* (to touch, feel)
chatter - clat (dial. chatter)
cackle - clack
babble - blab
batter (a mixture as for cake or biscuit) *- bread*
button (a small knob or piece resembling a button in shape) *- bunch* (a protuberance, hump, swelling)
bottle (something resembling or likened to a bottle) *- bloat* (to inflate; to puff up) *- purse*
puddle - plud (obs. exc. dial. a puddle; a pool)
gather (come together; to congregate) *- crowd* (to press together or collect in numbers) *- clot - clod - cuddle*
huddle (to crowd together) *- herd*
gobble (to gulp) *- gulp*
goggle (to look obliquely) *- gleek* (obs. exc. dial. an enticing or ogling look or glance)
cover (an envelope or wrapping) *- crib* (a hut or hovel) *- curb* (an enclosing frame, border or edging)
cotter (Scot. to congeal, clot, coagulate) *- clot - close* (to unite or coalesce, as the parts of a wound)

14. TAP - PAT, CLUB - BLOCK (that is, illustrating the relative inversion of the sounds of words):

pin (to seize and hold fast) *- nip*
peak - cap (the top or uppermost part) *- pike* (a sharp point)
gab (obs. project, as teeth) *- buck* (as in buck tooth)
cleave - break - crumb (to break into crumbs)

265

cuff - peck - cob (strike, beat) - *whack - puck* (dial. strike, butt) - *peg* (colloq. to hit, hammer) - *paik* (Scot. to strike; beat; pommel)

cluff (Scot. cuff, slap) - *flog - club - clap - plug* (slang, to strike with the fist, punch)

beat - tap - bat - dab - pat -daub - pet - jab

sleek - gloss - slick - glaze - glass

goad - dig - dag (obs. to pierce or stab) - *jag* (to stab) - *tuck* (to poke)

flock - group - block - club - clump

tup (dial. to butt as a ram, a ram) - *butt - dub* (to poke)

keen (pungent or stinging) - *nick* (to notch, to cut) - *notch - nag* (gnaw, dial. to ache as if from gnawing) - *gnaw - chine* (obs. to cleave, chink)

wick (twisted or braided cord) - *queeve* (dial. bend, twist) - *wogh* (obs. crooked, perverse)

shirt (to cover or clothe as with a shirt) - *dress*

lick (dial. quick stroke) - *kill* (obs. strike, beat)

whisk - scuff (brush aside, wipe off)

cart - drag

blow - flap - flop (colloq. to flap, clap or strike clumsily)

wet - ooze (obs. juice, sap) - *weeze* (dial. to ooze) - *sap - sob* (dial. soak)

catch - get - tag (fasten to, attach, to touch or hit) - *touch* (to lay the hands upon) - *tack* (to attach or secure in a hasty manner) - *take - tack* (Scot. take)

call (to shout or cry out; dial. to abuse) - *rag* (slang, to scold or rail at) - *cry*

mite - whit - mote - wad (a little mass, tuft or bundle) - *bud - bit - tip* (an end piece or part) - *chip - chob* (a broken spike of grain) - *boss - job* (obs. a lump) - *mass*

mig (a marble) - *gob* (dial. a lump) - *midge - gem* (obs. a bud) - *mad* (obs. a maggot) *bean* (a nipple or similar device in an oil-well line to restrict flow of oil) - *neb* - *nub* (knob, knot, lump) - *bun* (a round loaf)

mount - *tump* (a hillock) - *mound* - *tomb*

wire (coil about, wind about) - *rove* - *err* (archaic wander, roam, stray) - *roam* - *mar* (obs. err, wander)

lump - *lob* - *lobe* - *loaf* - *ball* - *pill*

knip (variant of nip) - *pinch*

murk (dial. darkness, gloom) - *gloom* - *black*

dark - *cloud* - *grit* (dial. soil, earth) - *clod* (soil or ground) (Middle High German *terk*en - to make dark, to soil)

mag (colloq. chat, chatter) - *gab* - *wag* (colloq. chatter)

gleet (obs. to flow slowly) - *drag* (draw along) - *glide*

sip - *booze* (colloq. drink) - *swipe* (a long drink, draft)

peg - *gaff* (dial. an iron hook) - *hook* - *gab* (a hook or notch) - *wedge* - *gib* (dial. a hooked stick)

fetch - *cop* (dial. to get hold of) - *chap* (Scot. to choose; to fix upon) - *jab* (to poke, stab)

butt - *tub* - *vat* - *pod* (a bag, pouch) - *pouch*

boat - *tub* (slang a boat)

furrow (Middle English *furgh*) - *groove*

prat (obs. to spank, beat) - *plat* (obs. to strike, slap) - *slap* - *drub* - *drum* - *trim* (colloq. to beat)

cut - *dock* (to cut off) - *gash* - *jag* (to notch; archaic and dial. a shred; rag; tatter; scrap)

tuck (Scot. to beat) - *touch* (to hit or strike lightly) - *cut* (to strike)

clout (dial. to strike) - *slug* - *clash* - *sledge*

hatch (hatchet) - *hack* - *whack* - *buck* - *potch* (dial. slap, strike) - *butch* (dial. to hack) - *bash* (dial. beat, smash) - *chop* - *chap* - *cuff*

bite - *chip* (to cut small pieces from) - *cham* (dial. to bite, chew, champ) - *chaw* (to chew; to champ as a bit) - *bit*

champ - *munch*

chew - *eat* - *etch*

patch (a small piece, a bit) - *piece* - *bit* - *dab*

scrub - *brush* - *shrub* (to scratch)

glime (dial. a sidelong glance) - *blick* (fulguration, German *blick* - flash, glance) - *gleam* - *flick* - *glow*

gore (obs. dig, hollow) - *ruck* (dial. a rut or furrow) - *rake* (obs. to bury) - *core* (the central part of anything)

hole (a cavity in a solid body or area; a place where the water is comparatively deep, as a swimming hole) - *loch* (Scot. a lake) - *lake* (obs. a pond or pool; a pit or den)

dip (to penetrate) - *pit* - *deep* - *dive*

bulge - *globe* - *bulk* (obs. aggregate or mass) - *clump* - *block* - *club*

knob - *bunch* - *chump* (a block) - *bung* (a bundle of stalks) - *knop*

kid - *tyke, tike* - *chick* - *kit* - *dog* - *cat* - *chit*

cub (a whelp) - *cob* (a round and plump mass) - *cow* - *pig* - *hog* (a sheep about a year old) - *sheep* - *chub*by (like a *chub*; plump and round).

ILLUSTRATIONS OF THE VOCABULARY
BUILDING MECHANISM

THE ILLUSTRATIONS GIVEN are abstracts from more complete phoneto-semantic analyses, made by the author, of the basic vocabularies of these languages. They are designed to exhibit the generality of the principles developed in the book, these principles having already been illustrated in Chapter X for the Chinese vocabulary. The languages cited, Swahili, Hebrew, Hungarian, and Malay are, together with English and Chinese, representative of the most widespread language stocks under which they are prevailingly classified.

It is not essential for our purpose more than to indicate briefly the pronunciation and we can not moreover at this place go into any detail on the phonetic characteristics or "preferences" of each of these languages. It will be sufficient to make the following remarks with respect to each of them:

a. SWAHILI:

This is an African language of the widespread "Bantu" family. Madan's Swahili dictionary was used as a basis for the definitions but other books and grammars were consulted. Note the prevalence of the sounds *ng, nd, mb,* that is, of the nasalization of the voiced stops *g, d, m,* which is characteristic of the "phonetic preferences" of this language. Another phonetic preference is the ending of words in a vowel, which is characteristically *a.*

b. HEBREW:

The Hebrew alphabet in its customary order has here been transliterated as follows:
', b, bh, g, d, h, w (or v), z, ħ, ṭ, y, k, kh, l, m, n, ṡ, ', p, ph, ts, q, r, s, sh, t, th. The letter ' (aleph) represents the "smooth breathing" of Greek; bh is pronounced like v, ħ and kh are pronounced alike, that is, like the guttural ch in German "ach" (in the Western or Ashkenazi pronunciation; in the Eastern or Sephardi pronunciation ħ is a guttural variety without "friction" of h); t and ṭ are pronounced alike (in the Ashkenazi pronunciation; in the pronunciation influenced by Arabic ṭ is an emphasized variety of t); th is like s in the Ashkenazi and like t in the Sephardi pronunciation; ṡ is like English s; ' ('ayin) is like aleph though it may be given a more guttural sound in analogy with the corresponding Arabic letter.

The Hebrew words, in the case of verbs, are given as is customary in the form of the third person masculine singular of the "perfect" tense. This form is justified for exhibiting the root since it is actually the latter without the inflectional endings. Although this form "qaṭal" appears to be disyllabic it may be construed as monosyllabic, the first vowel (qamats) being essentially of the nature of a neutral vowel and akin to Hebrew "sheva" which indicates the absence of a vowel or the presence of a short neutral vowel, or to Sanskrit short *a* which is essentially a neutral vowel. This can be shown through further discussion and comparison (compare

270

for example with the corresponding Aramaic form *qĩal*
pronounced "qeĩal") which can not be entered into
here. Thus for example the word *paraq*—'break' bears a
close resemblance to *break* even as regards the number
of syllables. This is in accordance with our concept that,
as a striking word, a root is essentially a "unit sound".

c. HUNGARIAN:

Hungarian c is like English ts, cs like English
ch, s like English sh, zs like English s in "pleasure",
gy like English d in "endure", j like English y, ly like
English y, ny like n in "onion", sz like English s, ty
like t in "tune". Accent is on the first syllable. With
regard to the vowels of a root note the remarks above in
connection with Hebrew roots. Thus the root *csavarol*
of *csavorol*ni—'to screw' is construed as essentially monosyllabic like the corresponding English *twirl* or *quirl* or
the German *zwirl*en—'to twirl'. The final *l* of a root
such as in *gördül*ni—'to roll', 'to trundle' is precisely of
the same sort as the *l* (*le*) in English *girdle* and is an integral part of the root, although shorter roots are found
relative to which the final *l* is excrescent. The same is
true in general of all final consonants. (Cf. discussion in
Chapter V of the relative excrescence of final consonants
and of the "diminutive" or "frequentative" interpretation of final syllables like *en, l* [*le*], *ock, et*).

d. MALAY:

The definitions are quoted from Richard Winstedt's
"Dictionary of Colloquial Malay". With regard to the
construing of the words as essentially monosyllabic and
the character of the final consonants in such words as *bengkil*—'knob', *bengkak*—'bump', 'swelling' as compared
with English *bunch, bundle* see remarks above.

271

SWAHILI

Group I: "Knot Idea-Complex"

funga—tie, bind, gird, close, shut (*bunch*—to gather in a bunch; cluster; *bung*—a bundle of hemp stalks)

fundo—knot (*band*—a fastening)

bindo—knot, fold (*bind*—that which binds or ties)

pinda—bend (*bend*—a curve, crook, bow; *wind*—to effect by or as by bending or turning)

pinga—hinder, thwart (*pinch*—to confine or limit narrowly)

ki*pingo*—bar, pin, peg (*pin*—to enclose, confine)

ki*fungo*—button, knob (*bunch*—a protuberance, hump, swelling)

mango—round stone, pebble, cobble

u*punga*—bud (Old Norse *bunga*—tumor, protuberance)

fumba, bumba—hunch, *hump* (*bump*—a protuberance; *bob*—dial. a bunch; a cluster; *pump*—obs. bilge)

ki*vimba*—ulcer, protuberance (*pimple*—a swelling or protuberance like a pimple; *pimp*—a small bundle of kindling wood, a fagot)

ki*bumba*—lump, clump, ball

bonge—lump, clump (*bing*—dial. a heap or pile; slang a bindle)

m*fugo*—flock, fold (*pack*—a bundle; a group, *fag*—a knot or tuft in cloth, dial. a tuft of grass)

wingi, ungi—multitude, many (*hunk*—a large lump or piece, *bunch*—a group, flock)

m*pango*—rank, troop (German *Menge*—multitude, Danish *bunke*—heap)

tonge—lump, ball (*chunk*—colloq. a short thick fragment; lumpy)

ki*donge*—lump, clump, clot, ball, pill (*junk*—a chunk, lump) ki*donda*—ulcer, protuberance (*junt*—Scot. chunk)

ki*tungu*—onion, bulb

tango—pumpkin, gourd

ki*tangu*—round cucumber

ki*jongo,* ki*gongo*—humpback (*knock*—Scot. a hill; hillock, *knag*—a short projection or spur; a knot in wood, *kink*—a close loop; a twist or turn, *chunk*—colloq. a short thick fragment)

m*kungu*—bunch (*knitch*—dial. a bundle, a fagot)

gongo—club, hump (of camel) (Swedish *knagg*—a protuberant twig or knot)

gogo—log, clog, block, trunk (*chuck*—dial. a log or lump; a *chock,* a *chunk*; *yoke*—a frame or piece resembling a yoke)

m*ganda*—bundle (*knot*—a cluster of persons or things: a band)

changa—collect, gather (*chunk*—to gather and pile)

kanda—knead (*knit*—to form into a knot)

kunda, kunja—fold, wrap, tangle, wrinkle, crimp (*knot* —to entangle, *knit*—to contract into wrinkles)

konde—fist (Swedish *knyt*näve—clenched fist, Dutch *knuist*—fist, Dutch *knots*—club, cudgel)

ganda—congeal, curdle, freeze (*knit*—to become compact; to consolidate)

kundi—flock, herd, crowd (*knot*—a group; clique)

songa—press, crowd, throng; throttle (*snug*—to lie close)

m*songe*—crowd, throng (*snug*—compact, close, tight)

Group II: "Hollow Idea-Complex"

chumba—room, chamber (*coop*—a cage or small enclosure)

u*kumbi*——hall (*cove*—Scot. a *cave* or den)

komba—scrape, hollow, scoop (*cope*—to form a cope or arch; to bend; arch, *cave*—to make hollow, excavate) *chimba, timba*—dig (*chop*—obs. to thrust quickly and forcibly, *scoop*—to dig out; to make hollow)

kuo—furrow, hollow, hole (*cave*—obs. any hollow place or part)

chombo—utensil, vessel, boat (*cup*—a thing resembling a cup in shape or use, *tub*—slang, a slow-moving boat or vessel, Swedish *skepp*—ship, German *topf*—pot, German *Kumpf*—basin, bowl)

sambo—vessel (*sump*—a cistern or reservoir; a pit, depression, tank, etc. serving as a drain or receptacle for fluids)

m*tumbwi*—canoe (*tub*—a bucketlike vessel)

jombo—large vessel, jug, tankard, butt (*coomb, coom*—obs. a brewing vat)

m*tungi*—water pot (*tank*—a large basin, cistern or other artificial receptacle for liquids, slang *tank*—the stomach)

chungu—cooking pot, crock (*knag*—Scot. a keg, *junk*—a kind of sailing vessel)

kombe—shell (*keeve*—a vat or tub)

kombora—shell, bomb (*chamber*—a compartment or cell, *cover*—an envelope or wrapping)

kopo—cup, *gob*let, pipe (*cob*—dial. a wicker basket)

kwapa—armpit (*cave*—obs. a cavity)

ki*kombe*—cup (German *Kuppe*—vaulted arch, German *Küpe*—large tub, vat)

m*kaba*—pocket, wallet (*comb*—a valley, dial. *comb*—a hollow in the side of a hill, *cub*—dial. a *coop*)

chamba—hiding place, den, cave (*coombe*—Scot. a hollow in the side of a hill)

n*govi*—skin, hide (*chaff*—the glume or husks of grains and grasses separated from the seed)

ma*kapi*—*chaff* (*cope*—something likened to a cope, a concealing or covering over)

274

jumba—house (*chap*—a cleft, crack or chink, as in the surface of the earth, *cove*—Scot. a hollow in rock; a *cave* or den, Low German *schup*—a shed)

timbo—hole, pit, hollow (*dip*—a depression or hollow among hills, *dimple*—a slight indentation on any surface)

ki*tundu*—cage, nest (*dent*—a slight depression or small notch or hollow like that made by a blow)

tumbo—womb; stomach, belly (*deep*—that which is deep, *tub*—something likened to a tub, *tomb*—a house, chamber or vault formed wholly or partly in the earth or entirely above ground for the reception of the dead)

tupa, chupa—bottle (German *topf*—pot)

tupu—empty, void (*toom*—Scot. empty)

Group III: "Wave Idea-Complex"

wimbi—wave, billow (*heave*—an upward motion; a rising, as of the breast in difficult breathing, of the waves, etc.)

pofu, povu, bofu—foam, froth, *bubble* (*fob*—dial. froth; to foam or froth, *bub*—to bubble)

yumba—sway, bend, bow (*weave*—to move to and fro or up and down, *hobble*—to bob up and down)

pepea—wave, fan, blow (*waff*—Scot. to wave, flutter, wag, flap)

papa—tremble, palpitate, flutter, throb (*wobble*—colloq. to tremble or quaver, dial. to boil vigorously, *bob*—to move with a bob, *waver*—to sway one way and the other)

ki*pepeo*—butterfly (Dutch *wipp*en—to shake, move up and down)

ki*popo*—bat (*buff*—dial. to strike, beat; *beat*—to strike [the wings] vigorously against the air or the sides;

275

to flap; to *buffet* against)

bembea—swing, rock, *bob* (*whop*—dial. to move quickly; to strike quickly, *wimple*—to cause to ripple or undulate)

fuma—weave (*weave*—to *move* to and fro or up and down; *whip*—to wind, wreathe or bind about something)

wayawaya—sway, waver (*wey*—obs. to move, agitate, *wag* —to sway or swing shortly to and fro, Dutch *waaien* —blow, fly, flutter in the wind, G. *wehen*—blow, flutter, wave)

punga—swing, rock, bob (*wangle*—dial. to totter, to shake, wiggle)

yonga—sway, bend, bow (*hinge*—to *hang* or turn as on a hinge, obs. to bend, *yank*—dial. to move actively and quickly, *wingle*—to wind in and out)

angaa—hang, suspend (*hang*—hover; dangle)

engaenga—falter (*hink*—obs. hesitation, faltering, German *wanken*—falter)

enda—move generally, go, walk, *wend*, budge, (*wind*— to move in a curved path or course, *wand*—obs. Scot. to wander; *haunt*—obs. to go)

mwendo—motion, gait, trip (*wind*—a turn, bend; any movement of air, *windle*—dial. to whirl around)

vuma—blow (*whiff*—to *puff* or blow away, *whiffle*—to blow unsteadily or in gusts; to make a whistling or puffing sound; to *wave* or shake quickly)

vimba—swell, *puff*, bulge, be bloated (*pump*—to fill with air by means of a pump or bellows)

pamba—adorn, deck out (*puff*—a vainglorious exhibition; a boast, *bombast*, *pomp*—ostentatious display)

vuvia—breathe (*whuff*—to emit a violent *whiff* or series of whiffs; *fuff*—Scot. *puff*, whiff; *huff*—dial. to puff, to blow; *heave*—to pant) u*pepo*—wind, breeze (*bub*—obs. Scot. a blast or gust; *waff*—Scot. a *puff*, gust, *whiff*; *puff*—slang wind; breath; life)

HEBREW

Group I: "Gather Idea-Complex"

qabhats—gather, collect, assemble, (*quat*—dial. lying close)

kawats—gather together, shrink, contract (*quat*—dial. squash, press down; dial. *squat*—*squeeze*)

qamats—compress, grasp, take handful (*quash*—to crush; dial. quelch—to squelch)

kabhash—press, suppress; pickle (*quash*—to suppress or extinguish summarily and completely; to crush out)

qaphash—clench, grab, snatch (*cops*—obs. to fasten)

kaphash—press down (Anglo-Saxon *cwēsan*—*squeeze*; *quench*—subdue, suppress)

ḱabhas—crush, press (German *quetschen*—crush, squeeze)

ḱabhaq—embrace, clasp

ḱabhash—bind, bind up (*quease*—obs. to squeeze)

'*abhaī*—give or take a pledge (*wed*—Scot. pledge; *wedge*—to push or be forced or fixed as or as if a wedge)

kaphath—tie, bind (*cops*—obs. to fasten or shut in; a shackle)

qawats—shrink, be dried up (*quat*—dial. collapsed, shrunk)

qaphats—shut, draw together (hand, mouth) (*quash*—to smash or crush against something)

'*aphats*—fix closely, make contiguous (*wedge*—to crowd)

gamad—contract (*queaze*—obs. to *squeeze*)

tsamaq—dry up, shrink, shrivel (*smock*—to gather in lines so as to produce a shirred effect)

qamaz—squeeze, contract, curl (*crush*—to squeeze; *quash*—to crush) *qamaī*—wrinkle, shrivel (*crease*—to become creased or wrinkled)

kamash—wither, wrinkle

tsamath—press, oppress, shrink, gather together (*swat*—dial. to squat; to strike with a smashing blow; *smash*—to crush; *smite*—to strike)

tsaphad—cling, shrink, shrivel, press, contract (*tweeze*—Scot. to squeeze; *swathe*—bind or wrap, swaddle)

tsabhath—join, associate (*twitch*—dial. to fasten or tie tightly; to squeeze)

tsebhath—pair of tongs (*twitch*—obs. pair of *tweezers*)

tsebheth—bundle of sheaves (*swathe, swath*—a bandage; a bond)

tsamad—join, couple, bind (*swathe*—a bond, a fetter, a shackle)

kanas—gather, collect, assemble (*knit*—become compact, consolidate; *knot*—obs. to gather in a group, assemble)

ganaz—gather, hoard, hide (*knitch*—dial. a bundle, fagot)

kamas—store up, hide

gabhash—crystallize, consolidate (*quash*—to crush)

kabhats—make butter (German *quatsch*en—crush, squash)

gebhes, gephes—plaster, gypsum (*quash*—a *squash, cheese*—the consolidated curd of milk)

gūsh—clod, lump of earth; bulk, group, block (*gad*—billet of metal; *cud*—Scot. cudgel)

gadad—gather in bands

qashash—assemble, gather (*cot*—dial. a confused mass)

gadash—heap, pile up

kaddūr—ball, globe (*cotter*—Scot. to congeal, clot; *gather*—to compress)

qarash—become solid, congeal (*crush*—to press or cause to press closely; to squeeze; *clot*—to concrete; *close*—

278

ħagar—gird, gird on, bind (*wicker*—to incase or cover with wickerwork; a withe, Anglo-Saxon *hacele*—cloak, mantle, German *wickel*n—roll, roll up, wind, swaddle)

ħāg—draw round, make a circle (*hedge*—to enclose or separate with a hedge, German *hege*n—to hedge or fence about)

'*āg*—draw a circle (*hook*—to crook; *hedge*—to surround as for defence; *hag*—an enclosed wood)

'*agal*—make round, roll, make a circle (German *kugel*n—roll, make globular, German *wickel*n—roll, twist, wind)

kalīl—wreath, crown (*coil*—to form a coil)

kalal—complete, make perfect, comprise, include

kāl—comprehend, include (*coil*—to encircle and hold with or as with coils)

kōl—all, whole

kalah—be complete, finished

galīl—ring, circuit, region, zone (*curl*—a coil; *whorl*—a coil; *whirl*—a rapid or violent turn; *wheel*—a circular frame or body)

karakh—bind round, wrap; wind around (*crook*—to bend, to curve, to wind; *cloak*—to cover with or as with a cloak; *quirk*—a sudden turn, twist, or curve)

galgal—wheel, circle, whirl, whirlwind (*goggle*—to turn to one side, to roll)

galal—roll, roll up, revolve (*chare*—obs. to turn; *coil*—to wind)

dūr—circle, rim (*tour*—obs. circle)

zōr—circle, wreath, crown (*tire*—a hoop)

zēr—frame, edging

tōr—turn, course; row; line (*tour*—obs. a round; a circuit, an endless series)

šār—turn aside, depart (*sheer*—turn aside, swerve)

zār—be a stranger, turn aside (*chare*—obs. to turn, esp. away)

gār—sojourn, dwell

dār—dwell, lodge (*tour*—to make a tour of)

dōr—generation, period, age, cycle (*tour*—obs. a course around; *turn*—a period; Anglo-Saxon *gēar*, Old Saxon *jār*, *gēr*—year)

HUNGARIAN

Group I: "Turn Idea-Complex"

kör—circle (*chare*—obs. exc. dial. Eng. return or coming back or round; turn; occasion; time)

kor—age, era, time (*gyre*—to turn round, Anglo-Saxon *gēar*—year)

karika—circlet (*crook*—a bend, turn, or curve)

kerék—wheel, circle (*cirque*—a circle or circlet; *quirk*—a sudden turn, twist, or curve; *jerk*—a sharp twitch, throw, etc.)

göröncs—potter's wheel (*crank*—obs. any bend, turn, or winding)

*kering*eni—circulate; whirl about (*crink*—dial. to bend or twist, Dutch *kringe*len—curl, coil, wreathe)

gyűrű—ring (*gyre*—a ring; *tire*—a hoop)

karima—brim, border (*curb*—an enclosing frame, border, or edging)

gyürem—brim (of a hat) (*crown*—a wreath, garland, or fillet about the head, Dutch *krom*—curved)

*gurol*ni—to roll, trundle (*curl*—to move in curves)

*gurog*ni, *görög*ni—to roll (*crook*—to bend, to curve, to wind)

*gurit*ni—to roll (*gird*—to encircle; dial. to move or act quickly or energetically; obs. to strike)

*gördül*ni—to roll, to trundle (*girdle*—to encircle)

gurgulázni—to *gargle*; to roll (*gurgle*—to run or flow in a broken, irregular, noisy current; obs. to gargle; *guglet*—a small whirlpool)

gyűrüzni—to ring, to girdle (trees) (*girdle*—to make a circular cut around a tree, etc.; *girse*—obs. exc. dial. *girth*)

görbe—*curv*ed, crooked (*curb*—obs. to bend or curve)

*görbűl*ni—to bend; to become crooked (*curble*—obs. curb)

keret—frame, border, halo (*girt*—to encircle; *girth*—circumference)

kert—garden (Anglo-Saxon *geard*—yard; *garth*—dial. a close; yard)

kéreg—rind, crust, bark (*cork*—cortical tissue; obs. the torus of certain fruits)

térni—turn (*tour*—dial. turn one's steps, go)

torzítani—distort (*jirt*—dial. jerk; *tort*—obs. twisted; *torse*—twisted spirally)

*sérit*ni—twist, twirl, roll out (*jert*—obs. exc. dial. jerk)

serdülni—turn around (*sward*—dial. rind; *turret*—obs. a small metal ring)

csürni—wring, writhe (*twire*—obs. to turn or twist; *chare*—obs. to turn)

*csavarol*ni—screw (*twirl*—to writhe in a twisting motion, German *zwirl*en—twirl; German *quirl*en—to whirl about)

*csavarg*atni—to twist; to screw (*twirk*—obs. twitch or twirl)

*csavarog*ni—to gad about; to stroll about (*quirk*—to progress or move with jerks)

*facsar*ni—wring, wrench, writhe (*feak*—dial. tweak, fidget; *feeze*—dial. turn, as screw; *wattle*—to twist or interweave; to plat)

*forog*ni—turn, revolve, whirl (*frike*—obs. exc. dial. to

move or dance briskly or nervously; *flick*—to flutter, flit; *wrig*—dial. wriggle; Anglo-Saxon *frician*—to dance; *walk*—obs. to roll; to toss to and fro; to roll by; to circulate about; *wrack*—obs. rack)

*bolyg*ani—rove, roam (*walk*—obs. to roam; ramble; wander)

féreg—worm (*worm*—to move, go, or work slowly, etc. in a manner suggestive of a worm; *wriggle*—writhe, twist)

forgódni, forgolódni—to busy oneself about, to bustle about (*work*—to be engaged in some occupation; to be in or as if in agitation)

fordítani—turn (*-ward*—suffix denoting course or direction to; motion or tendency toward, German *wälzen*—trundle, roll)

ferdítni—warp, pervert (*writhe*—to twist or turn so as to distort; Swedish *vrida*—turn, wring, wrench)

bordázni—warp (*wreathe*—to twist; to entwine; *braid*—to entwine together; *plat*—to interweave; to *plait*)

borda—rib (*vault*—arch)

boltos—*vault*ed

barka—*willow* (Dutch *wilg*—willow)

perge—spiral, helix (*bark*—obs. rind; *whelk*—any of numerous large marine snails)

*pereg*ni—twirl, whirl, roll (*firk*—obs. to move quickly; *walk*—obs. to roll by, circulate around; *flick*—to flit; a light jerky stroke)

*burk*olni—wrap (*bark*—outer covering; to cover or enclose with bark, or as with bark)

Group II: "Knot Idea-Complex"

gömb—globe, sphere, orb, knob (*cob*—lump, bunch)
gomb—button, knob (*gob*—dial. lump)

göb—hunch, knot (knot—bud; lump; *job*—obs. a piece; a lump)

gumó—tubercle; bump; knot; knob; bulb (*gum*—a pimple; German *keim*—germ, bud)

gomoly—lump, clump (*cobble*—a cobblestone)

golyó—ball, globe (*clew*—obs. a globe, a ball; *glome*— obs. a ball or clew, as of thread)

*gyül*ni—gather, assemble (*geal*—obs. exc. dial. to congeal; Scot. ice, also jelly; *jell*—colloq. jelly)

*gyülem*leni—gather into a mass (*clump*—to form clumps)

göröngy—glebe, clod (*clunk*—dial. lump; *clunch*—dial. a lump or clump)

*gyülöng*ni—gather (*cling*—to stick together or cohere in a solid mass; *clinch*—obs. to set or shut fast together; *clink*—Scot. clinch)

*gyülek*ezni—gather, assemble (*clog*—to unite in a mass; *clique*—colloq. to associate together)

gyülde—assembly, club (*guild, gild*—an association of men belonging to the same class; *clot*—a mass, a rounded lump; *clod*—a lump or mass)

család—family (*class*—a group of individuals ranked together, etc.; German *kloss*—a *clod*, lump; German *klotz*—a block, lump)

*gyüjt*eni—collect, *gather,* assemble (*gad*—a bar, billet or ingot of metal, *cot*—dial. a confused mass)

*köt*ni—bind, knit (*cot*—dial. to mat, as wool)

gáncs—obstacle; *knot* (*knot*—an intricacy; a difficulty; Norwegian *kank*—a twist; knot)

göcs—knot (German *knoten*—knob, tangle, tubercle, German *knüttel*—cudgel, club; *cud*—Scot. cudgel)

csög—knot, knop, gem, bud (*chuck*—dial. a log or lump; a *chock*, a chunk; *chuck*—Scot. a checkstone [pebble]; *check, chack*—dial. a small pebble; *cock*—a small conical pile of hay; *shock*—a cock, as of hay)

kéve—*sheaf*, bundle, pack (Anglo-Saxon *scēaf*—sheaf; *chump*—a block; *cop*—dial. a heap or pile, a shock or stock of grains, peas, etc.; *goaf*—dial. a stack of grain; *cob*—dial. a small stack of hay)

csomó—knot, node, package (*chump*—a block)

csomag—bundle, parcel, package (*knitch*—obs. exc. dial. a bundle; a fagot; German *knocke*—a bundle of flax)

csömek—*knag* (German *knagge*—a knot in wood; *chunk* —dial. a log, stump)

görcs—knot, knarl (*knar*—a knot or burr in wood; obs. exc. dial. a rough rock or stone; *crag*—a steep rugged rock; *clog*—Scot. a short thick piece of wood)

könyv—book (*book*—a bundle [of silk]; German *knebel*n—bind [sheaves]; German *kniffen*—fold; German *band*—volume, binding [of book])

csombók—knot

tömeg—crowd (*knot*—a cluster of persons or things)

tömb—crowd, throng (*tump*—a tumulus, heap, clump)

domb—hill, mound (*knot*—a knob-shaped hill; *tump*—hillock)

dombocs—hillock (*tummock*—dial. hillock)

dombor—boss, bulge (*tuber*—a protuberance; *tumor*—a protuberance)

csoport—group, heap (*chump*—a block)

hoporcs—*hump*, hunch, lump, bunch (Low German *humpel*—a hill, hump; Dutch *homp*—lump, hunch, chunk)

Group III: "Flutter Idea-Complex"

*lóbál*ni—sway, swing (*lop*—to flop or sway about loosely; *leap*—to throb, beat high; *lope*—to go or move with a lope)

*lógáz*ni—to swing to and fro (*log*—dial. to rock, oscillate)

286

*lóg*ni—to dangle; to hang down (swing—to hang, to suspend)

*leng*eni—wave (in the wind), flutter blow gently (*linge* —dial. thrash, flog; flog—flap violently; thrash—swing, beat, or strike in the manner of a rapidly moving flail)

lenge—light, slight, fickle, fluttering (Old High German *lungar*—light; lights—the *lung*s)

*lend*ítni—cause to wave or sway, put in motion (*lunge*— to move or cause to move with a lunge; a leap)

láng—flame, blaze (flame—to have a flamelike appearance or motion; flap—to sway loosely; *link*—a torch)

lob—flame (*leam*—obs. exc. Scot. flash, blaze, glimmer, gleam; Anglo-Saxon *lēoma*—light, brightness; *lamp*— a torch)

*lebe*gni—float in the air, hover, hang over or about (*loom*—obs. to rise and fall, as the sea or a vessel; to come into sight, esp. above the surface of either sea or land, in indistinct form; *lop*—to be pendent)

levegő—air (Dutch *lucht*, German *luft*—air; *loft*—obs. the sky; the air; German *lüft*en—*lift* up; air)

*lobo*gni—blaze, flare, flicker; wave in the wind, flutter in the wind (*low*—dial. flame, blaze, glow, light)

lebke—flitting, flightly; light, swift-winged

lepke—butterfly (*leap*—to move swiftly, to throb)

*legye*zni—fan (Dutch *lucht*en—air, ventilate; fan—obs. flap, flutter; to blow, as the wind; force to glow or flame up)

lég—air (Dutch *lucht*—air, German *licht*—light, bright; light, thin, open)

*lehe*gni—breathe heavily (German *lech*zen—pant [for a thing])

*lehel*ni—breathe, blow (blaze—obs. to blow as with a trumpet; German *loh*en—blaze or flare up, flame) *villog*ni—*flash,* glitter (*flake*—a flash; German *blick*en—glance, shine, German *blitz*en—flash, lighten; *flicker*—a scintillating light)

világ—light, world (*flick*—a streak)

villám—lightning, flash of electricity; *flame*—any flame-like condition or appearance, as a light ray; *flimmer*—glimmer)

*billeg*ni—wag, waver, oscillate, swing, sway (*flick*—flutter, flit)

*pillang*ani—glitter, sparkle (German *blink*en—gleam, twinkle, wink, sparkle)

*pillant*ani—cast a look at, glance, wink (German *blinz*en—blink, wink, twinkle)

*pillog*ni—wink, ogle; glitter (German *flacker*n—flare, flicker; *flack*—dial. a stroke, blow, flap; to flap or flutter; *fllick*—a slight jerky stroke or blow; a streak)

MALAY

Group I: "Pile Idea-Complex"

bentok—a curve (*bend*—a curve, crook, bow)

buntar—rounded (*bunt*—obs. to swell out; *paunch*—a potbelly)

bengkok—bent, crooked, curved (*binge*—Scot. to bow low; to cringe)

mangkok—bowl, cup (*bung*—obs. slang a purse)

pongkis—basket, hamper (*bunker*—a large bin or other storage place; *bunk*—a case or frame which serves as a bed or sleeping place)

bakul—basket (*buck*—a basket for catching eels; *bowk*—dial. a kind of bucket or pail; *bouk*—obs. the belly or abdomen; *beaker*—a large drinking cup; German *pokal*—goblet; drinking cup)

bonkol—hump (on camel); knoll (*bank*—dial. an elevation or hill; *bing*—dial. a heap or pile; *buckle*—to bend; to warp; Swedish *puckel*—humpback)

bengkak—bump, swelling (*bunch*—a protuberance; hump; swelling)

bongkok—humpback (Old Norse *bunga*—tumor, protuberance)

bunchit—potbellied (*paunch*—a potbelly)

bongkak—proud, pompous (bloat—to inflate; to puff up; to make vain; proud—dial. protuberance; growing or swelling to excess)

bongkat—proud (*bunt*—obs. to swell out; *bung*—obs. slang a purse)

bengkil—knob (knob—a rounded protuberance or mass; German *buckel*—boss, stud, knob; *buckle*; Dutch *bonk*—chunk, lump; Dutch *peukel*—pimple)

buku—knot, node, knarl; *book* (*wick*—a bundle of fibers for use in candles; *book*—a bundle of skeins of raw silk; Dutch knot—knot; skein of yarn)

bungkus—bundle, bunch (*bing*—slang a bindle; *bung*—a bundle of hemp stalks)

pungut—collect, gather (*bunch*—to group; *bank*—to group in a bank; a flock or group)

beku—congealed, curdled, clotted (*pack*—to crowd together; to become compressed so as to form a compact mass; packed, as pack ice)

bukit—hill (hill—to gather in a heap; to amass; *pack*—to mass compactly; a great collection or group; *packet*—a small pack or package; *package*—a packet, a bale)

busut—ant hill (*butt*—a mound of earth; *pout*—a protruding)

busong—dropsical swelling (*pouch*—a cyst or sack containing fluid)

butang—button (*button*—a small knob or piece resembling a button in shape; a bud) *kuntum*—a bud, blossom (*knot*—a bud; German *knoten* —knot, knob, growth, tubercle)

kenchup—budding

kanching—button (*knot*—a knob, lump or protuberance)

kuncha—bale, bundle (*knitch*—dial. a bundle; a fagot; Swedish *knyte*—bundle)

kuntau—fist (Dutch *knuist*, Swedish *knyt*näve—fist, German *knüttel*—cudgel, club; clog)

gumpal—clod, lump, clump (*cobble*—a cobblestone; *cob* —a lump)

gemal—cluster, bunch

kumpul—gather together, collect (*chump*—a block; *cumber*—to lumber up)

himpun—collect, gather together (*hump*—a mound or hummock; *heap*—accumulate)

simpul—to knot, tie into a knot (*semble*—obs. to assemble, gather)

kampong—assemble together, collect (*cop*—dial. a heap or pile)

tompok—a small heap (*tummock*—dial. a hillock)

tambak—to bank up (earth) (*dump*—to deposit something in a heap; *tump*—a heap; a hillock)

jambak—cluster, bunch (*job*—obs. a lump; a stump; *gob* —dial. a mass or lump)

keping—lump, clump (*cob*—a lump or piece of anything; *chump*—a short thick heavy piece of wood)

kelapa—coconut (*clump*—a lump; *club*—a knob or bunch)

kepala—head (coconut—slang the head; nut—slang the head; knob—slang the head; *chump*—slang the head, *cop*—a heap or pile; obs. exc. dial. the top of a thing, the head; *cob*—the head of a herring; Dutch *koepel*— dome, cupola; German *Kopf*—head)

Group II: "Dig Idea-Complex"

gali—to dig (*gore*—obs. to dig or hollow)

galah—a pole (Anglo-Saxon *gār*—a spear; *goal*—a stick to mark a goal)

ber*gala*—stab, butt, punt (*gore*—to stab, of horned or tusked animals; *kill*—obs. to strike, beat)

chula—horn of rhinoceros (*gore*—an angular piece of planking; German *keil*—wedge; wedge-shaped piece)

cherok—corner, nook (*crook*—an angular bit of land; a knee)

gerek—to bore (*grig*—Anglo-Ir. to tantalize; irritate; annoy; *jarg*—Scot. to jar)

keris—dagger, dirk (*crotch*—a fork; *fork*—a barbed point; *gride*—to cut or pierce; to cut or scrape raspingly or with a grating sound)

korek—bore, dig (*dig*—a thrust; a punch; a poke; *creek* —a cleft, crevice; *crack*—to strike with a sharp noise; *crig*—a blow)

kerbok—bore into, gnaw (*carve*—to cut; to cleave; *grub* —to dig in or under ground; slang to eat)

cholek—to pick out with a pin or pointed tool (*dirk*—to stab with a dirk; German *dolch*—dagger, poniard)

jolok—poke with a stick (*click*—dial. a sharp unexpected blow, rap, or the like; *jerk*—to give a quick and suddenly arrested thrust, push, pull, or twist; *jolt*—obs. to butt or to nudge)

tolak—repel, push away

duri—thorn (*jar*—to affect painfully; *turr*—obs. to butt; *shear*—obs. pierce)

jarum—needle (German *dorn*—*thorn*, prickle; spine)

garu—scratch, excavate (*gore*—obs. to dig or hollow)

chari—search for (German *scharren*—scrape; rake)

garok—scratch a hole, excavate; scratch with finger nail (*cratch*—obs. to scratch; claw; grab)

jari—finger, toe (*claw*—a sharp nail on the finger or toe of an animal; [pl.] the hand, esp. the fingers of the hand; a scratch from or as from a claw; Sw. *gräva*—to dig; grub)

garis—to scratch, make a mark (Dutch *krassen*—scratch)

garau—hoarse, strident (*gruff*—hoarse, harsh; German *krähen*—to *crow*, screech; *cry*—to make a loud call or cry)

kerit—scrape, scratch (*graze*—to scratch or abrade as by rubbing on a rough surface; *coarse*—harsh, rough, or rude; *screed*—Scot. scratch; German *kritzen*—scratch; scrawl)

jerit—shriek (*grate*—to utter in a harsh voice)

turis—scratch a line or mark (*trace*—to draw; to write; *track*—a trace; streak—to form streaks or stripes on; *chart*—to delineate)

tulis—write (Old Saxon *wrītan*—to write; to tear; to wound; *slash*—to cut by sweeping strokes; *slit*—to slash; *slice*—to cut across something with or as with a knife)

Group III: "Slack Idea-Complex"

lembek—soft, pulpy (*limp*—flaccid; flexible)

lempong—spongy, light

lembut—soft, flexible, gentle (*limber*—dial. *limp*, flabby, weak)

lampai—slim, slender (*limp*—lacking firmness or strength)

lemah—weak, soft, debilitated (*lame*—feeble, infirm)

lumpoh—lame from paralysis (German *lahm*—lame; languid; loose)

lambat—slow (*lame*—limping, halting; *lob*—go heavily or *lumber*ingly; *lamper*—dial. to go or walk heavily) *lama*—long, ancient, old (*loaf*—to lounge or loiter about or along; *limp*—to halt; to proceed slowly)

lecheh—slack, dawdling (*lag*—dial. slow; late; last; slug —obs. sluggish; slow; to rest idly, to loiter; *lug*—to drag along)

lega—easeful, comfortable (*lash*—obs. exc. dial. *lax*; loose; relaxed; flabby; *lask*—obs. a laxative; German *liegen* —*lie*, be recumbent)

longar—loose (in socket) (*lank*—languid; drooping)

leteh—tired, weary (*late*—dial. slow, sluggish; tedious)

lesu—worn out (*loose*—lax; German *lass*—weary; *lazy*, lax; loath; slack; slothful)

lenda—dawdling (*lent*—obs. slow; mild; gentle; German *lind*—soft, gentle)

lunjor—stretch oneself (*linger*—to protract, prolong; to move slowly; to dawdle; *lounge*—to move or act in a lazy or listless way; to stand, sit, or recline in relaxed indolent manner; German *längen*—*lengthen*; stretch; slacken)

lanjor—protracted (*lank*—slender and thin; lean; languid; *slang*—dial. a narrow strip of land; *slank*—dial. lank, lean; *leng*—obs. to lengthen; delay; *linger*; abide)

lanjut—long, lengthy

INDEX

INDEX

INDEX

298

INDEX

Logic, 66

Malay, 4, 217, 219, 221, 236, 271,
    288 ff
Maori, 236
Mathematical
    concepts, 233
    symbols, 229
Meaning
    assigned, 229 ff
    association of, 13, 19, 36, 74 ff, 81
        ff, 91, 103, 139, 141, 144 ff, 226,
        234
    "basic" and "derived", 11 ff
    in context, 17, 129, 195, 209, 217,
        223, 231 ff
    delimitation of, 36, 203
    emphasis, 209
    figurative, 156 ff, 185
    intended, 205, 208, 209, 215, 225,
        230. 234
    interplay of, 64, 66 ff
    linked to sound, 1, 118 ff
    "nonatomic" character of, 103
    not residing in words, 225
    poetical aspect of, 161
    relativity of, 11
    scope of, 6, 9 ff, 71 ff, 153 ff
    of sentence, 205 ff
    "shades of", 71, 77, 108, *passim*
    striking aspect of, 18, 64, *passim*,
        (see Words)
    of symbols, 227 ff
Müller, Max, 112
Musical aspect of language, 234

Nahuatl, 53 n
Navaho, 53 n
Norwegian, 81
Numbers, 226

Oceanic languages, 5
Old Norse, 96

Onomatopoeic, 110 ff

Participle, 214 ff
Parts of speech, 128 ff, 204 ff, 214 ff
Persian, 219
Phoneme, 25 n
Phonetic preferences, 7, 182, 190 ff,
    213, 235
Phoneto-semantic, 9, *passim*
    chain, 82, 88, 92, 105, 137, 161,
        166
    pair, 42
    word linking, 41 ff
Phoneto-semantics, science of, 1
Phoenician, 31 n
Poetic aspect of languages, 161, 234
Polish, 1
Portuguese, 20, 217
Predicate adjective, 213
Predication, 213 ff
Preposition
    of, 211 ff
    to, 218 ff
Prepositions, nature of, 210 ff, 219,
    221, 223
Pronouns, 205 ff, 210 ff
Pronunciation, latitude of, 122
"Provincialism", degree of, 191
Psychology of language, 225 ff (see
    Vocabulary building mechanism)

Relativity, 231
Romance languages, 1, 20
Root
    idea, 128
    nominal aspect of, 127 ff
    as unit sound, 217
    verbal aspect of, 82, 86, 101, 127,
        134
Rumanian, 20
Russian, 1, 99, 205, 218

Sandhi, 234

299